D0882657

HOPE IN TIME OF ABANDONMENT

By the Author

The Technological Society
Propaganda
The Political Illusion
A Critique of the New Commonplaces
The Presence of the Kingdom
The Theological Foundation of Law
Violence
To Will and to Do
The Meaning of the City
Prayer and Modern Man
The Judgment of Jonah
The Politics of God and the Politics of Man
False Presence of the Kingdom

Hope in Time
of Abandonment

By JACQUES ELLUL

Translated by C. Edward Hopkin

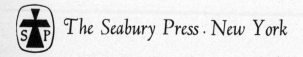 The Seabury Press . New York

First Published in France under the title *L'Espérance oubliée*
by Editions Gallimard, Paris
© Editions Gallimard, 1972

English Translation by C. Edward Hopkin
Copyright © 1973 by The Seabury Press, Incorporated
Library of Congress Catalog Card Number: 72–81025
ISBN: 0–8164–0247–7
775–473–C–5
Design by Paula Wiener
Printed in the United States of America

Preface

I am to speak of hope, but not as an affair of the intellect. For me it came by unforeseen paths, in the course of a severe trial in which everything was once again called into question. This involved not only my deepest personal attachments, and the significance of whatever I might undertake to do, but also that which constituted the very center of my person, or at least which I believe constitutes the center of my person. It involved this faith so unquestionable, but which I find to be so fragile. All was called into question, and I found myself once again before the unpredictable plan of God. That adds a different dimension to what I might otherwise have been tempted to say, but which in truth I would not have said.

I had written for quite some time on the subject of hope, as in an article of 1954 for the *Cahiers de Villemétrie*. In all this I stressed certain things which today are fully recognized, for example, the decisive importance of the promise, the approach of the Second Coming, the eschaton *which comes.* I further stressed the fact that it is *from the standpoint* of the fulfillment of the promise that the whole is to be understood.

This didn't cause much of a stir, which was normal. It was merely a case of being intellectually correct in a "good" (i.e., Barthian) theology, because it was all there in Barth. But I didn't know what I was saying. There is an intellectual formalism which, in the very act of communicating the word richest in meaning, empties it of its meaning. In our day one is tempted to called it "orthodoxy."

From an altogether different angle, I had for a number of years intended to write a book on "The Age of Abandonment." It seemed to me that our society in its sociological evolution, as well as the individual in this society in his psychological outlook, were types of what the Bible says happens when God turns his back and is silent. The Church, in her confused, grandiose, and childish actions, seemed to me proof that that was indeed the case.

When the time came to do it, it was more and more borne in upon me forcibly that I could not write about the abandonment of God, and that the word now given me, as well as the power dwelling within me, were those of hope. And yet—*Eppur si muove*—my observations and interpertation on the level of intellectual analysis remained correct.

Thus it was that, in a way which cannot be explained rationally but which is inescapable to the person living it, I was led to combine what I was living with what I was at the same time thinking. Thus "Hope in an Age of Abandonment" became a must for me.

So I shall be talking about hope, but it will not be in the theological or philosophical manner. I am familiar with the great work of Jürgen Moltmann. Far be it from me to emulate him by redoing a theology of hope, to which I would have nothing to add. I can even say that from the standpoint of my purpose his work was not particularly useful to me. I am also familiar with what Castelli and Paul Ricoeur have written on the subject, from the philosophical point of view, for the Philosophical Society of Rome, and also in the essay on "The Conflict of Interpretations." But again, I am not a philosopher and would not be the one to make use of them.

I have arrived at hope by an altogether different route. My purely sociological and historical intellectual approach had led me into a blind alley. There was nothing to say to a person of my society beyond a stoic exhortation to keep going in God's abandonment. I was up against a wall, against a finality, against the insoluble, against the inescapable. After that—nothing.

And after that—everything was given me, but by a different route. No intellectual step prompted this conviction, apart from that by which I took note of the concrete situation. I did not define this concrete situation, but it was fundamentally hopeless without my daring to say so. Such was, or so I was convinced, the basic question to which all the other questions could be referred—no hope, no meaning, no way out, no history.

That was how the person of this age was living. For me it all led to this observation, that here was a situation which quite obviously contained a question. There was the mute and unconscious interrogation on the part of all the people of this age.

But what could I do about it? Moreover I knew all too well, in true orthodoxy, that it is very wrong to look to the biblical revelation for an answer to the question one is asking or with which one is faced. I knew, in true orthodoxy, that it is God who questions us and who awaits a response from us, not the other way around. No consoling formula or solution was to be sought in the Bible. That was simply the way things were.[1] When the response is called for, one has to make up one's mind.

Yet, at the same time that all my work so far had been without hope (even though I managed to write correctly *about* hope), hope asserted itself. It did not do this as a logical consequence of biblical exegesis, nor of premises laid down beforehand. It asserted itself in terms of the point at which I had arrived, in terms of the end of the road to which I had come for myself and which I saw as the limit for the person of my society. I continued to live —at the same time, if there be a capacity for transcending limits which seem so objective, concrete and secular, it could only be the power of the intervention of God, who remained the Wholly Other at the same time that he was the God of Jesus Christ. Hope became near, living and all-embracing. No longer was it a theological formula. It became also the response (I do not say the solution) and the decision, at the same time that it was the gift freely given

---

[1] Moreover, it is quite surprising to observe that those same Christians who reject Christianity as a consolation for the afflicted, as a spiritual succor, as the completion of anguish, hope, and faith, vie with one another to find an answer to the material needs of man—housing, food, literacy—but really by political means. They reject the idea of God as a "stopgap" and clearly prefer the psychoanalyst to the confessor. Yet they readily accept any of the world's courts of appeal (political party, union) as the stopgap. They reject the concept of Christianity as an answer to the basic needs of man, while they go all out to find answers to his material needs. Thus they combine what has always been a gross, simplistic, and rudimentary materialism (the important thing is that man should be given food and should be satisfied at that level. It is out of the question to proclaim a word of truth to a hungry man, etc.)—they combine this with a naïve spirituality (Christianity must not correspond to any need, for otherwise one is not certain of serving God for nothing. One cannot be sure that the faith contains no motivating self-interest, in other words that it is "pure"). The two attitudes go together, and one is as infantile as the other.

(I do not say the all-purpose method of position papers and organizations).

Surely there was no solution to the problem which confronted our age. No organization could claim to dispel the confusion in which modern man is immersed, in which he is already lost. But there was a word which was the very one capable of being understood by this man, and which no hermeneutic could produce for us. The word is the only decisive, effective, conclusive and radical act which, through grace, has any chance of being pure. For the person without hope there was a word of hope, which changes nothing from the material point of view.

But it would seem that Christians are the last to get excited over the priority of material change, the last to imagine that nothing has been accomplished if one has not raised the standard of living or protested against the use of torture, the last to suppose that nothing has happened when all has been said, thus the last, through a bad historic conscience and through naïve materialism, to waste what has been given them on behalf of others. "I give you what I have," said Peter to the beggar (Acts 3: 6).

Yet this is just what today's Christians fail to give. They are afraid of fooling the beggar, of deceiving him, of incurring his animosity. So they recognize his demands, but since they have no answer they beat their breasts in desperation, saying that the world is right after all and wants nothing to do with what the Church has to give. Naturally, if she doesn't have to give what she is commissioned to give she has nothing to give.

But it is a matter of discernment. We must learn to hear what the question is which is really being asked by the person of this age. It is not being asked in the public square, nor in speeches and parades. It is not being asked by the actor facing his audience. It is being asked offstage, in the secret places of the heart. It shapes the architecture of the other questions. Unseen, it is gnawing and killing.

It's a matter of a gift, which one receives and transmits. The miracle is the discovery that the gift which has been given us answers precisely, exactly, and decisively to the question discerned.

It is also important for the Christian to be willing to bring himself to believe in miracles. Otherwise he can indeed do nothing but keep silent and engage in a frantic search for some pathways to the light which no longer exists.

After a lengthy meditation on the spineless age, which comes close to being our own, Castelli says, "Much has been written about hope, almost always in a hopeless manner." I am trying to do it, naïvely, for the purpose of emerging from the blind alley, knowing that there truly has been this gift granted to us.

J. E.

Contents

Contents · xiii

PART I

Symptoms and Impressions

THE FACTS which I shall recall here are the same which I have so frequently described and analyzed in my other works, but not from the angle from which they are now being considered. They have to do with signs which reveal the absence of any way out for the world in which we live, the absence of a prospect for the future. They have to do with impressions which a person can have here and now, which express that same reality.

Signs and impressions are never clear or spelled out for the generality of people. They show up in events, in innocent statements, in behavior. Yet there are degrees of awareness. Certain of these elements can in fact be perfectly clear, perceived, and known. Others can be matters of experience without being explicitly stated, while still others affect the innermost being of the individual without his knowing it, producing a trauma of the whole personality while remaining entirely in the unconscious.

There are those of which one complains and from which he truly suffers. There are his explicit protests and his fundamental despair. There are its visible grossness and its real inconsistency. There are the person's situation and his way of dealing with it consciously, from which he suffers unconsciously.

1

Losing the Way

THE CLOSED WORLD

We are living through the experience of a closed world. Never have there been so many openings, scientific breakthroughs by the most stupefying, lightning-like extensions of technology, the secularization of thought and of civilization, the opening of doors to "the cosmos"; yet never has man felt so closed in, so confined, so impotent. With the help of intermediaries he participates in the great human adventure. He watches television. He sees the first steps of "man-in-himself" on the moon. But he is not man-in-himself. He is the white-collar unit, this man in a gray suit whose life mechanically unwinds like the perforated roll on an old player-piano. Each turn of the roll is a year and, when deposited every December 31 on the preceding year, obliterates it. The notes played on the piano are the sum of his programmed deeds.

Of course, the mechanism has to turn, and since five hundred million people do just the programmed things expected of them, the mechanism does in fact turn. It turns very well indeed, in spite of stupid opposition. With the day organized and the year sliced into exact parts, one is assured of being able to take advantage of vacation times which will be a semblance of freedom. One knows that he will be given a certain raise in salary and that, within the framework of the overall programming, one will be able to make one's little plans in complete independence.

But it turns out that one's little plans correspond with those of others. Though each set of plans is entirely custom-made, one finds four million Frenchmen on the highways in automobiles, the individualized mode of transport, and on the same roads at the same time. Of course, each one wills it and has made a choice. Of course, too, there is a tremendous range of professions from which free men still to be born will be able to choose. More than ever, we are finding it possible to do what our ancestors could not do, benefit from foreign cultures and enjoy other astonishing advantages.

Yet this man feels caught in a snare, as though a lid had fallen over him at the very moment when the man-in-himself was breaking through the lid of the skies. He has felt closed in by an unyielding trap, just when everyone was catching the vision of a pleasant life for all.

It does no good to argue. The contest between the optimists and the pessimists has run its course. One can prove to the members of our modern societies that our ancestors never enjoyed this much means, freedom, happiness, well-being, available opportunities, long life, culture, pleasure, leisure, communication, and dialogue, but one will never convince the person in our modern society that he is living in a little paradise.

Also, he is beginning to realize that it is not the fault of the horrible bourgeois (having become one himself) and of the capitalistic system of exploitation (the one thing which has succeeded in supplying him with all these advantages). The communist ideology is dying out. The flashes of Maoism and leftism represent the final glow of a dying fire. We are seeing its last firebrands flare up in the midst of the embers left over from the explosion of a spurt of gas which is putting an end to the house.

There have been witnesses to this experience. Poets have accounted for the growth of the unrestricted in terms of the absurd. But it was not a matter of the absurd of the cosmos, of nature's being incommunicable to man. To the contrary, the latter had been entered, measured, and controlled, if not understood. Henceforth it was a matter of the absurd created by man in his society, by his own means. Kierkegaard had sensed it. Kafka expressed the agony of it. Surrealism had battered at its doors vainly searching for an outlet. Camus reduced it to a concept, but one testifying for the man in revolt.

When this had been said, and said again; when the sensitive witnesses of the world which was both open and closed, and which was the more closed the more man multiplied his means of opening it up and dominating it— when these witnesses had prophesied that which they already felt and which was breaking in like a tidal wave, then the philosophers came along.

Camus had shown them the way. But to conclude for the universal absurdity of life on the basis of an inability to deal with *these times* amounts in fact to walking out on the job, in spite of the high regard one may have for Camus. The absurd is an escape, a protective device. One attaches an intellectually satisfying label to the experience, to this situation. The label frees one from further consideration of the reality which it designates. One examines the label itself and deciphers its meaning. Then one lives indeed in the absurd, while scanning the unfathomable depths of infinite, very distant and very lofty spaces, to which one diverts a value. Camus was searching. What followed him was the protective device of a false search.

Sartrism has formulated the incoherence of this progress in terms of incoherence itself, just as structuralism has made an exhibit of structure precisely because structure had already dominated the scene. Structuralism is in no sense an intellectual advance, a better way of understanding. It is a reflection of the current human condition in this closed and organized society. That is why it seems to me a fallacious change for the specialists to go all out to introduce a method of ethnological and sociological analysis, together with the sort of philosophy or metaphysic which some of them would like to extract from it.

In point of fact, if Lévi-Strauss has put the finishing touches on his structural analysis that is because he already had a philosophy stemming from our western social milieu of 1950. His metaphysic was a reflection of the state of humanity robbed of itself by the blind, and yet voluntary, organization of structures. To be sure, he applied his method to the study of primitive societies, not our own society, but that was merely a matter of opportunity and facility. Every society lives with its structures. This obvious fact can be seen as compelling, absolute, radical and apparently explanatory of everything, not because the study and analysis were made of primitive societies, but because consciously or unconsciously one eye is kept on the effects of structures on our own.

It has been in terms of our own relentless structuring that structuralism was born. Its usefulness is as an explanation of our times, but it is too difficult and complex for that purpose. As a method it stops after the very first stage. It is explanatory of our times only as a metaphysic. From that point on, it is itself an unintentional part of the evidence.

The structures of our society are becoming more and more demanding and precise. The more they assert themselves the more man knows that he is without prospect for the future. It is not the atom bomb, the threat of world destruction, which ruins that prospect but the rigor of the system of organization. One can say, of course, that man is deceived and that the technological system is not as rigorous as he thinks. However, the important thing is that that is how he lives it. He is fundamentally convinced that a new kind of determinism has been established in society, an inescapable play of forces over which he has no control.

The person of this age is in the grip of just such an awareness, corresponding to two seemingly contradictory experiences. On the one hand, the system continues to develop. Structures are put together and go into operation. Whether the person knows this or not is of little consequence. He lives as though there is nothing he can do about it, as though nothing will ever change, as though he has no hope of arriving at the centers of decision. He bows and submits. He accuses the "they," and rebels without hope. It comes to the same thing in the end. He declares his need to participate, which is merely this experience turned upside-down. But he knows that even that will change nothing. His future is more precisely inscribed in the structures than it is in the stars. He is faced with an inevitable.

But over against that, and inversely, the news releases throw in his face a hundred disjointed and unpredictable happenings. Everything, it would seem, is changing at high speed. To stop and focus on it, so as to encompass and comprehend it, would be impossible. The scene is only what I am trying to see. Everything follows everything else for no reason. Incoherence seems to preside over this succession of events. The impression I get is that of a bewildering world which is mobile but inflexible. It is incomprehensible, touchy, disquieting as ghosts' veils, a broken world, full of holes and full of the irrational. There is nothing to be done about it. One is lost in it. Henceforth the future is unpredictable.

This twofold experience happens at one and the same time to the same person. He experiences the two parts together and cannot deal with them. Both bring him to the same resignation through the absence of a prospect for the future.

They also bring him to a new inconsistency, for we are in the strangest possible situation, in which man is living just the reverse of what, objectively, he should be living. In the most pacified and guaranteed society which has ever existed, man is living in uncertainty and growing fear. In the most scientific of societies, man is living in the irrational. In the most liberal of societies, man is living "repression," and even hyper-repression. In a society in which the means of communication are the most highly developed, man is living in a sort of phantasmagoria. In a society in which everything is done to establish relationships, man is living in solitude. . . . It would seem as though each advance nurtures its exact opposite in man's living experience.

Never has man possessed so many means for making history, and for making his own history, yet never has he felt so completely determined, so subjugated. Here he is, caught in an astonishing system of actions and reactions. The more he struggles to loosen what he considers his bonds, the more he tightens them. Technology is creating for him a marvelous world of capabilities and objects. He accepts the capabilities without even noticing, and then he begins to fear the objects, for his life has no meaning and he is afraid of being supplanted by things. The only possible meaning of all his activity is precisely the procuring of still more objects for himself, for that is the only value the system can have to offer him as compensation for his efforts. He buys continually and thus increases his agony at being overrun by objects.

Closed world, system, the absurd, anguish, not only is that what twentieth-century western man is living, but on top of that he asks to have this world shown him, proved to him, staged for him. He rushes to plays by Samuel Beckett and Edward Albee, which are neither violent nor controversial but simply a projection of what any person in this world experiences. It is a combination of anguish and the absurd. By such entertainment man feels himself confirmed. It effects a transition from the lived unconscious to the verbalized conscious, precisely through the use of disjointed, minimal, uncommunicating verbalization without content. It witnesses simply to each one's absence, to fate, to ultimate meaninglessness, to the impossibility of history.

EXPLOSION OF THE IRRATIONAL

That the irrational is breaking in on all sides today is taken by many as an omen that we are escaping from our closed world. The student is in revolt, but not in the same way in which the worker has rebelled on behalf of a more just, a better organized, and a more settled society, in which he can have a share. The student is in revolt against this organized and settled society itself, against this proliferation of things and of well-being, of skills and machines. When the black American rebels, the result is a raging torrent of lava which suddenly devastates an entire neighborhood, often a black neighborhood. The hippie rebels in glorification of flower power, of the hypnotic dream and the musical trance. Absent is any program or project.

People have often reproached the young for not having a project or a program. When students say No to a university, they have nothing new and definite to suggest, no overall plan of what a university ought to be. "What is it you want?" All they can reply is that "the whole thing go up in smoke." . . . "But that's no answer. What about the future . . . ?" At that point silence, because there is no future.

The same lack of a project, of a plan, of a program characterizes the black Americans. Their organizations are completely incoherent and they put forth declarations which are extremely self-contradictory. As far as the hippies are concerned, it is of their very essence not to have a project. One lives for today. One seizes the present moment and tries to make it as beautiful, as seductive, and as charming as possible. The "consequences" are rejected. They try out new modes of expression and a new kind of life experience. They renounce safety measures and provision for the future. They reject any action toward a fixed goal. They reject all "consequential" thinking.

That is all radical. They are trying to get at the root of evil. Convinced that all will be recaptured in the end, they promote only the Nothing. That at least, or so they think, can never be recaptured by our cumulative and englobing type of society. With this incoming wave, the protest against the war in Vietnam, against the misery of black Americans, against racism, against repression are mere pretexts and secondary rallying points. The essence of the movement is nothing. It consists in aspiring not to see beyond the present moment. It is the Great Rejection of everything that is recommended. Everything which is must be reduced to nothing, because whatever exists is repression and alienation.

What is to come out of this nothing? On this point the greatest uncertainty still reigns. For some there is, in spite of all, the call to an absolute spontaneity. When man shall no longer be in an iron collar, in a machine which is grinding him to bits, when he finds himself in a sort of desert of ruins, then, brought truly to himself, he will be able, as he has always done, to discover that which best corresponds to his inmost being, which has been distorted and tortured by organizations and systems. It is the spontaneity of the fundamental freedom of the individual.

Others, however, who also talk of spontaneity, want only to recognize the spontaneity of the member of the proletariat who has been alienated and treated as an "it," when his alienation shall finally have been broken. This is no longer a spontaneity of nature, but of status. It is no longer a spontaneity of the creative individual, but of a community, of a category, of a class which has come off unscathed, and out of which a sort of vital movement will produce the resources for rising again.

Still others refuse even to envisage the possibility of an afterward. They are no longer concerned with any future creative spontaneity. They exist in the present moment and have no will for anything else. They try to live the given second to the fullest, and this cancellation of every possible future implies that they give themselves over to the ultimate irrational. There is no more value. There are no longer any criteria for action. There is no longer any intelligent deliberation. There are flowers and love, which one takes and leaves. There is hunger one minute and surfeit

the next. There is desire finally set free, an ownership of
the world which exudes from every pore, a calm exaltation,
a sharing in musical ecstasy, a fusion of the senses, drugs,
and pop music. It is a resurgence of Orphism, an essential
stripping bare of the self. Any taking of action in connection with events is renounced in favor of communion and
a freedom from morals and restraint. There are ineffable
mysteries in which one participates without being able to
talk about them. In fact, as has been said, there is nothing.
Yet this nothing does not prove that this behavior is nonsense, because the important thing is the communion, the
liberation, the ecstasy.

This growth of the irrational, in whatever form, appears
as the true protest against the technological society. It
appears as the honor, if not as the salvation, of mankind.
By an odd turnaround, these desperate attempts, these
behavior types which seem to us so strange and outland-
ish, these rings and collars, these Hindu symbols and long
hair, these Molotov cocktails and conspiracies, these re-
fusals and insults, these hatreds and hallucinations, this
loveless free love and this confusion of crowds, with music
as the only evident pattern, all this novelty which the
young people are throwing in our faces, is again nothing
but the reflection, pure and simple, of the known situation.
They, too, are marked by the absence of a future.

Of course there will be a tomorrow. Time marches on.
This moment will be followed by another. But there is no
future, no building, no job, no logic, no ultimate unfolding
of life, no harmony, either present or to be sought after.
There is no possible continuity, no steadfastness or loyalty.
No experience has meaning for the future.

Nothing, moreover, counts as experience. There is no
lesson to be drawn for improving tomorrow's conduct,
tomorrow's tactics, tomorrow's living, because tomorrow is

nothing. There is no providing, no continuity. Later on will be a simple instant, like the one I am now living. I want nothing, because to want is, again, to bank on the future, to submit to an ambition, to depend on something which doesn't exist and never will. Then there is the Gospel precept: "Tomorrow will be anxious for itself. Let each day's own trouble be sufficient for the day" (Matt. 6:34).

But it isn't merely an individual matter, in which each one decides thus to bar the future in order to live only a present without a tomorrow. It's also a style, which lays claim to becoming general and global. It means to impose itself as well on institutions, organizations, and groups: the black neighborhood, the university. There are to be no more programs, examinations, studies to be pursued, positions to be won, no more carefully structured courses, with paragraph one and paragraph two. The whole is poured out in the moment of free dialogue and informal exchange. There, at the point of greatest poignancy and intensity, the personality is developed. By a confused and diffuse relationship, a sort of transfusion of learning takes place.

Future-sick, like all the people of this society, the young and the blacks throw themselves into activity which issues in nothing. But it has to be said on their behalf that, whereas the adult in this condition refuses to see it, is aware only of the profound disquiet within himself, represses it into his subconscious, is seriously upset by it but doesn't want to admit that he is not master of his future, multiplies provisions, models, organizations, regulations, projections, resulting strictures, planning and programming, suddenly along come the young to lay bare the situation as it really is. They have had the courage to accept it, to say it, to take it upon themselves with all its consequences, that is to say, to live without a future, and so to organize the one moment.

There's no hope. Very well, then, let's make up our minds. Since all is absurd, let's fix it so that I can live this today to its fullest, cut loose from the future which is the very thing that makes today's endeavor absurd. For all practical purposes I relegate to the absurd, to the darkness crawling with monsters, the future which no longer concerns me. I have no more desire to be an empire-builder nor a world-builder. The passion which motivates me does not spring from any conviction nor truth. If there is no truth because there is no future, then nothing is worthwhile except to live passionately the thing that I'm doing this instant, whatever it might be. I have no reason to be concerned with its underlying causes, which psychoanalysis and sociology have taught me go so very deep. Nor do I need to bother about its consequences, because history is a tale of disenchantment on that score. The thing is to live absolutely and solely in the present, "caught between the empire of disenchantment and the kingdom of illusion," which I want no part of.

The only difference between the adults without a future and the young people without a project is that the former are at pains to conceal from themselves what they are living, while the latter display it brazenly and make it a rule of life. When the young forcefully affirm the irrational, the more so when they live it and operate in the communal manner, when they reject morality as something without foundation and dead, a source of hypocrisy, when they reject reason as stiff, cold, inept, and in fact senseless, when they take the plunge into the wellsprings of life and claim to open up the secrets of a marvelous new world, then what they are really doing is unmasking the actual situation of every person in this society. They are revealing this irrational which I tried to emphasize above: the contradiction between that which exists objectively and the way man lives it, experiences it, and feels it, this man who, the more he is satiated the more he complains of a lack, the more he is reassured the more he is afraid, etc.

These are basically irrational behavior patterns. In order to ward off his insecurity, this man dives with his head down into every religion and belief. He accepts every myth. But he doesn't want it said openly. He wants to maintain his dignity as a fully evolved man of the twentieth century. If he goes to a fortune-teller and anxiously studies a horoscope, he will do it in secret.

This irrational has not been laid bare by youth intentionally, but their own irrational attitude is itself a laying bare of the inner conflict. They are, in point of fact, the children of the adults which we are. They have revealed to us the cause of our inmost condition. Bearers of the future because they are young, they announce that they are without a future because their fathers have lived without a future. The young, for their part, glory in it. They cancel continuity and immerse themselves in the present.

SAD YOUTH

But take a good look at them, these young people, "their foreheads circled with flowers," these students who break loose, who want to plow up the world so virtues can sprout some day from the ruins. They are miserable. Let's not talk about a crisis of youth. That's too easily said. For the adult, the crisis means that the child isn't like his parent. Yet we have shown that they are the exact, visible reflection of what we are. They are forcing us to see what we refuse to admit, so why should we talk about a crisis of youth? There is no crisis. There are misery and youth. Misery—yet never have they been so happy, with splendid options, scholarships, trips, facilities for work, a lowering of the level of examinations . . . what more do you want? Now we are busy securing job openings for them, an easy transition from student life to working life, and even wages to replace scholarships during their student days.

That's just it. They are exactly what we are. They are living the opposite to what the material conditions of their lives make available to them. They feel that they have no future. Rather, that burned-out tomorrow is spoiling what is given them today. They're living and they're not living. They look with terror on the world which is held out to them. They do not dare enter it. They never feel strong enough nor well enough prepared. Their haughtiness and insolence sharpen in proportion as they feel, live, conceal, and vainly suppress their frailty.

The true crisis of youth is to be seen in the growing maladjustment of the young, described by the expression "wave of the maladjusted" and characterized by their bizarre dress, drugs, their running away, and their excessive "involvement." We are no longer in the era of conscious, intentional commitment to a party supportive of values, and dedicated to building a better world and developing a better human being. Now they know that nothing ends in nothing, that their involvement makes no more sense than all the rest of it, and that an action without meaning cannot bestow meaning on anything. They know, or think they know—which amounts to the same thing. Like their elders, they are caught in the network of deadly illusion.

Here they are, young, yet unable to laugh without cynicism, in Orphic ecstasy, yet unable to give way to childlike happiness. Having exhausted everything, they are themselves exhausted. They are a generation wearied and turned off by what their fathers have seen too much of.

They are in the grip of the absence of history in a world which is nothing but history. They are old ahead of their time, their features hollowed by extreme experiences and by bitter and harsh disillusionment. Exasperated over nothing, they are the new adolescence which, on top of the legitimate tragedies of their age and the inevitable conceit of youth, still pile the tragedies and conceit of a world they can't stand, and which they know only by hearsay and by its exorbitant demands upon them.

So they run away. In their dream, their odd dress, their being shut up within their own circle, their use of drugs, their revolutionary activities, their taking to the road and their dissipation—they are running away. But this is never the stern, purposeful and purely individualistic experience of Rimbaud, Monfried, Nizan. It's a devil-may-care free-flow of a mass, of a plasma. By their behavior they express the internal contradictions of the society in which they have not been able to have a part, and which they reject. They are running away, yet seek only to belong. They insult the adult from whom they expect nothing but genuineness. In their ferocious individualism, they are completely gregarious. They want absolute life, yet adopt suicidal behavior. They are excessively pampered, yet they live out all their experiences in the style of accusation and desertion. These inconsistencies are summed up in just one single formula: they are without hope. That's exactly what it all comes to.

The absence of hope is the key which makes it possible to subsume under a single aspect the moods and behavior of modern man in general, and of the adolescent who is this same man carried to the flash point, to the explosive and visionary stage. We see a final expression of this in the multiplication of suicides . . . suicides by fire on the part of too many young people. "Their determination to die is born of the will to set against the sovereignty of evil, in a society incurably sick, the sovereignty of that purity of life which chooses nothingness, since there seems to be no other path to harmony and love. It is a protest of conscience against a civilization which flouts the values of the spirit. Hence it is an idealistic act of faith, and a giving up of any hope of serving those values by an act of life. Hence, also, it is an assent to man's failure in history. . . ." So writes P. H. Simon, and perhaps he is right.

But, above all, it is the act of a person carrying too much of a load, whose acknowledged fear and impression is that of being rejected by everyone. How is it possible for the young, with their sensitivity and their absolutizing of every experience, to resist the crushing weight of the tragic news releases, in the midst of which the adult only survives thanks to his thick-skinned indifference, thanks also to the experience of a past which has turned out to have a future, thanks to the mistaking of this future for a history and to absorption in one's work? This is the armor of nothingness. The adolescent doesn't have it. He cannot conceal from himself the absence of hope in the world. He is dying as a result.

THE REVERSAL

The timeworn wisdom of men has held out against the experience of the vanity of their efforts. If we add up the account of the great historic ventures of the twentieth century, how can any hope be left, or any reason for acting? The glories of colonization (which had other motives besides the economic interests of a class and capitalism's need for new markets, the only motives mentioned by the childish and shoddy explanations offered by today's pseudo-Marxists) have terminated in the horror we all know. We in France caught the first shudder of it with the Viollette Report on Indochina and with Gide's *Voyage to the Congo*. From that point on, everything evolved inevitably to bring about the Malgache massacres and the Algerian tortures.

The struggle for law and civilization ended in the marshlands of peoples' republics and sharpened nationalisms. The revolution of 1917 gave birth to the bloodiest of dictatorships, to the emergence of the most chilling monsters, uncovered at last for all to see. The revolution of 1933, carried out in the name of honor, manhood, and the equality of the common people, buried itself in the concentration camps.

The struggle for freedom has multiplied dictators and transformed regimes which had been democratic into centralized and authoritarian regimes. Liberation has paved the way for careerists and has put us back into the worst ruts. Anticolonialism has opened the floodgates of tribal conflict and has led to the exploitation of Africans by Africans, to neocolonialism, to military dictatorships, to hateful nationalism.

Who could ever add up the balance sheet of all our setbacks, all our hopes which have been not only disappointed but flouted, all our generous ideas which have resulted, precisely and without exception, in the reverse of what we had hoped for? What person in our day would have the courage to say with Lanoux's "Canayen," when twenty years later he saw in Normandy the results of such great sacrifices: "If it had to be done again, all right, I'd begin it again . . ."? I know of very few who would say that.

For us, everything has turned into a sham and a lie. Behind each experience we discern the wry face of death and derision. If there are some today who see hope in China, that's because they don't really know what's happening there. We're in the same situation with respect to China that we were in with respect to Hitlerism in 1933 or Stalinism in 1950. The fact is that only those who *want* to delude themselves can see some truth in it. All the wars, all the revolutions, all the great undertakings of history have brought forth monsters. The more glorious and all-embracing they were, the more absolute were their monsters.

We are witnessing a strange phenomenon, which could without exaggeration be called "imposture." It involves the transmutation of the original intention into its opposite. This is not the same thing as the classic *disparity* between dream and reality, a gap between purpose and result, a divergence between the action as contemplated and its realization. All that is simply part of our ancestral experience. But today it is no longer a question of disparity, of a gap, of a divergence. It is a question of the diametric opposite. When a movement is carried out on behalf of freedom, it produces the worst slavery. If it is on behalf of justice, it gives rise to countless and endless injustices. I don't know of a single one which has accomplished, even in the slightest degree, what it set out to accomplish.

One cannot counter with generalities. It is not a "wickedness" on the part of man, a sign of the presence of capitalism or of imperialism. We are in a singular age, of which this fundamental imposture is one characteristic. What action remains possible thereafter?—what meaning? Is not Emile Michel Cioran right when, in his *Précis de Décomposition* (Gallimard, 1949), he applies Pascal's reference (horrors!) to the misfortunes brought about by those who go out of their room?

This is not the place to describe the phenomenon in

detail, nor to attempt to explain it. I shall try only to say what the person in this society lives and feels. This experience of radical perversion, of reversal, of imposture, has been common for half a century. When the youth of today are distrustful to the point of no return, they are saying the same thing as the veterans of 1914 who cried scandal at what "those in control" were making out of their sacrifices and their victory. The most bitter rebels of our youth were the Croix de Feu of 1934. They are justified in rejecting all return to the old ways, yet every step they take makes them wrong. The disgraceful Wolinsky becomes a servant of the consumer society. The youth revolt is a "top priority" business operation for editors, moving-picture producers, and advertisers. The hippie movement taps a considerable trade, and the "pop" ensembles are organized by the moving picture and broadcasting industries. In their protest against a return to the old system the young people see this clearly, and they are sometimes panicked by it. Each with his own originality, his own point of view, and his own drives is immediately used and drawn in. In the last analysis, the same holds true whether one is thinking of economics, politics, or social affairs generally.

This is an actual reversal. The protest against advertising is used *in* advertising. The flight into the nonpolitical is turned to the advantage of some political position. The challenge thrown at a "Napoleonic" university produces a university still more under the control of the state, still more centralized, more given to expediency and more mechanized. A mere protest against the old ways is not enough to avoid being recaptured by the old ways. The reason is that the protest presupposes Machiavellian motives on the part of some person or persons who are willfully restoring the old ways, whereas the situation would appear, rather, to be the product of structures which function automatically, without any contemptible input on the part of individuals, or even of conscious groups. Nor do these structures any longer correspond to the older analyses of the classical, or of the Marxist, sociologies, nor to the revolutionary stereotypes derived from Marxism. The reality is something different. Our society escapes the previously known categories.

The experience which the ordinary person can have of this is one of frustration and an absence of sense. Each one lives, more or less consciously, with a "what's the use" written in his heart, so he rushes into some activity (or retreats into inactivity), driving an automobile, buying new things, losing himself in his work, erecting barricades and throwing Molotov cocktails, or withdrawing into his technical specialty. He knows that those things at least correspond to themselves. But the moment he emerges from these short-term certainties he is let down by the fine-spun analyses which get nowhere, and by the endless palaver which manages only to cheapen the effort toward a world conscience.[1]

THE PERVERSION OF VALUES

It is not merely a matter of the product's being the reverse of what was intended. It is, at the same time, a matter of

---

[1] What could be more ridiculous than the debates of the Parti Socialiste Unitaire, or the discussions of the leftists among themselves, or of the Union Nationale des Etudiants de France. And to think that one still, in good conscience, pokes fun at the Byzantine theologians who (or so it would seem) argued over the sex of the angels. The political, theoretical, and strategic "analyses" of these groups are far more removed from reality, anachronistic, otherworldly, and meaningless than anything that the worst theologians have ever been able to write! A few decades from now one will be puzzled that people in their right minds could have argued in the manner of mixing false problems with true feelings.

the general perversion of what might be called values. I shall not enter here into the debate whether values exist or not, whether they have a certain truth or metaphysical being in and of themselves, or whether they are purely sociological. I observe merely that everybody refers to them and talks about them. One speaks of truth, of liberty, or of justice without knowing for certain exactly what these are, without being able to give a precise definition of them or to say what one means by them. One cannot avoid making use of them. One of the earmarks of this society without hope, of this age of abandonment is that in every walk of life people find themselves characterizing situations by their opposite values.

At the simplest level, it has become quite customary to speak of an erotic film or play as being "pure." Surely this does not come from any desire to proclaim the contrary to what would have been said a century ago, or to serve notice of one's own emancipation. The formula has become so hackneyed and commonplace that it has to be taken seriously. To show masturbation or human copulation on the screen is very pure. The same goes for prostitution and incest. To transform Grimm's *Fairy Tales*, by a pseudo-Freudian magic, into a pornographic show is very pure. Nothing can be more pure than nudity, physical love, and the caresses of the *Kama-Sutra*. We are wallowing in complete purity.

Is this a case of antimoralism? of a rejection of sin? of anti-Christianity? of self-justification? of proclaiming one's newfound liberty? of conceited exhibitionism? The very fact of being able to interpret on these two levels makes one think. If it were really a case of antimoralism, or of a rejection of sin, there would be no need whatsoever to affirm this purity. One would quite simply abandon that category. But here we are introducing precisely the old values in order to justify what we are doing, reversing in the process the meaning of the value. In this way one adopts a supposedly independent stance, yet without ceasing to obey the same scale of moral values.

Now this phenomenon is general. The concept of revolution is another case in point. Each movement claims to be bringing about a revolution, and the most antirevolutionary politics is characterized as revolutionary. The party in power, or the dominant party, or even the State itself, represent the revolution. I have studied this phenomenon elsewhere and shall not go into it again, but the fact needs to be stressed that once it is the State which is carrying out the revolution, and those opposed to the State are the ones who are called "counter-revolutionaries," it becomes easy to understand that the ordinary person is confused and does not quite know where he is.

We can take each value and make the same observation. Freedom is guaranteed by the most dictatorial of governments, and also by the strictest regulation. Rousseau's thesis, that it is in obeying the law that man is free, has been stressed to the point of the ridiculous. When Rousseau put forth this aphorism to distinguish the person who obeys an objective, universal, and predetermined rule from the person who is subject to the caprice of a tyrant, the saying was quite understandable. But today it is accepted as self-evident that a motorist is only free in proportion as the rules are made as tight, restrictive, and finicky as possible. And that is only one example. All areas of life are subjected to the same thing. Now this regulation is precisely the former tyrant's caprice, having nothing to do with law as the expression of the public will.

But the tyrant today is abstract and possessed of a hundred thousand heads with changeable wills which are inconsistent yet logical. Each regime today refers to freedom as a matter of course. Each dictator, whether political or administrative, assures us that everything is being done on behalf of liberty, at the same time that all intellectual organizations cry scandal whenever "restrictions" on liberty make their appearance. Regimes which repress their adversaries by imprisonment and violence are solemnly condemned, as though one were unaware of this as a universal characteristic of the present age—hypocrisy of intellectuals with dirty hands.

The same observation can be made with respect to justice. It has become an exact translation for injustice. Justice today no longer has anything to do with distributive and remunerative justice, with "the art of the equitable and the good," with "*suum cuique*—to each his own. . . ." Justice now consists in transferring the power of the person who possesses it to the person who does not, so that the latter can wield it over his former master with the same violence, the same injustice, the same insolence, and the same savagery. It consists in taking what the rich man has in order to give it to others, who are to become rich with the same arrogance and the same selfish delight.[2] Such is justice in our day, and the victim of the injustice (not the same as yesterday's victim—but still one cannot be too sure. The poor man of today in Cuba, China, etc., *is* the same as yesterday's poor man, with the former rich thrown in for good measure)—this victim of injustice fails to see what has been gained in terms of justice apart from the political proclamation which, as a matter of fact, counts for a great deal.

---

[2] I know that the reader will reject this, on the ground that in social revolutions one takes from the rich in order to give to the entire populace. But that is completely idealistic and incorrect. In theory, the people have received the goods confiscated from the exploiting class, but a governing class is created which lives in luxury and accumulates the money. This is true not only in the Soviet Union but also in Cuba and Algeria.

Now in this perversion of values Hitler and Stalin played important roles. Not that they originated it, but they greatly contributed to it. They, so to speak, crystallized the tendency. Time and time again we heard one or the other offering proof that his regime was assuring true freedom at last (in contrast to the loathsome, false and deceitful freedom of liberalism). Each offered genuine justice (in contrast to the absurd and stingy bourgeois justice), true equality (in contrast to stupid, traditional democracy). We were at least departing from the beaten paths, but now we know what these claims amounted to in fact.

Now this was not a plain, ordinary lie, a gross duplicity, an absurd hypocrisy. People in their day really believed in this freedom, justice, and equality. It was explained that those concepts, to be sure, were no longer to be understood in the same sense as before. One performed intellectual gymnastics to demonstrate what the *real* freedom of Nazism or of communism was, as opposed to the purely formal freedom of the preceding era. *This* regime *was truly* the regime of equality, of peace, etc., just as are China or Cuba for true believers today.

It was the same with respect to democracy. When the communist dictatorships were set up in 1946 they were called "people's democracies," and one was faced with a manifest abuse of language. Deep research was immediately undertaken to see in what sense these were indeed democracies, in view of the fact that they had been baptized as such. This produced a different concept of democracy, so that today no one any longer swallows hard when speaking of the German Democratic Republic, etc. What went unnoticed was the fact that this was no mere alteration of the content of the term. It was a total *reversal* of the value. One was calling "democracy" something which was strictly a dictatorship, and not even a dictatorship of the proletariat.

Thus each value has become its own opposite. I am not saying that it is the opposite of what had been customarily understood. It is not just a question of formal habit. Even though language is a convention, that does not make it purely and simply alterable, so that I can say "cat" when I mean "bread." Words like "justice," "freedom," "truth," "democracy," have an emotional content, a power. I am not claiming that they have a meaning which is eternal and fixed for all time. But surely they have a meaning subject to variation within a reasonable range. I cannot say that to torture someone is to respect his person, and yet that is just what is being said today.

The new and noteworthy feature is the following: it is normal for a group or a society to change its central value in the course of history. Once it was order. At another time freedom becomes the value to which priority is given. Then happiness is the center around which all action revolves. It is likewise normal, in the case of a given value, for its content to undergo a change. When one speaks of justice in China under the Han dynasty, one is not thinking of exactly the same thing as the justice of the prophets of Israel, which in turn is not the same thing as *dikē* (that which is right). Justice in Aristotle is not the same as justice in Augustine. Still, there are points of similarity and even of identity. All the variations are at least commensurate with one another. What is new in our day, and perhaps for the first time in history, is the use of a word designating the former value as a means of identifying its exact opposite. The reversal is complete.

What is new is that a person should be able to say, without being wrong, "This Chief of State is talking about justice, which means that he is about to perpetrate the most total injustice." Nor is this limited to a specific regime. The same thing is true in the United States, in Spain, in Greece, in China, in Czechoslovakia, in Algeria, in Cuba, etc. This is new, and unfortunately it is true.

Now this reversal of values, of which the individual is becoming aware with more or less clarity, has a deep and serious effect on contemporary man. He can no longer believe in such words, which have become mere sounds. Again, if that were all they amounted to, the matter wouldn't be so serious. But these are words which have expressed man's hope. They have been the source of his motivation. They are not indifferent sounds turned upside down. They constitute a powerful poison of the soul, of the entire being. They destroy man. For, whether one likes it or not, he still has within himself the thirst for justice, for truth, and for equality. To quench his thirst, he is being given the acid of injustice, of deceit, and of exploitation.

Thus the person of this age no longer has a fixed, sane, and reliable point of reference whereby to direct his activity and his life, whereby to arrive at some judgment of what he himself is doing and what is being done around him. He no longer has a clear and certain criterion for distinguishing the good from the bad. All that is being offered him is a compass gone berserk and misplaced lights in a fog.

Such is the true import of this reversal of values, and that goes for us all. All, without exception, are victims of it, of this bread of deceit and of mirages which vanish with each new approach. Now the person who can no longer put any credence in values, who no longer has a fixed landmark for knowing where he is, this person can no longer entertain a hope. The whole thing has been a continual lie. Progress has been from a mistake to a lie, from misery to an illusion, so that he is foundering in a skepticism that is lacking in stature and clarity of vision. He is succumbing to spiritual misery with the emaciated emptiness of the eyes of death.

DEATH OF THE WORD[3]

This reversal of values also corresponds to another phenomenon, of which it is, from some points of view, only one more expression. It could be called, in a pinch, the language crisis.

For the past fifteen years or so, there has been a great to-do about language. Countless scientific studies have brought its analysis to a fine point. Language is placed at the center of man, of science, of society. It becomes the master key to all thought. Yet at the same time, these very subtle studies lead unfailingly to an almost total formalism. This vital language, in the final analysis, is a mere form. Its content has no meaning.

This is indeed noteworthy. It shows that, in point of fact, these analyses belong to a particular epoch, that of the distintegration of language, of which they are both the witness and the agent. It is indeed true that words no longer mean anything, or more exactly, that one can use them to designate anything else whatsoever.

That such disintegration is taking place is evidenced by countless facts: political speeches with devious content, surrealist poetry, dadaism, and the plays of Beckett. A completely incoherent language can draw crowds to listen

[3] At this juncture I wish to state my admiration for the profound meditation of André Neher, *L'Exil de la Parole* (Editions du Seuil, 1970), which came to my attention too late, after this work had been completed. I find many points of agreement with him.

for hours to pointless discourse (a reflection, to be sure, on the human condition). Queneau's exercises in style and the travesties of vocabulary of Zazie are good examples, and precisely so because the public is enthusiastic about them. One must, at all costs, escape from the prison of words.

But propaganda had already prepared the way, well in advance of the work. For decades we have been glutted with words without a referent, or at least with no referent apart from the action in which they had managed to involve us. Moreover, the job is not yet finished. One need only observe how the leftist propaganda, completely devoid of sense, is able to attract the young, causing them to accept as obvious something which is entirely nonexistent.

In the same category, we have on frequent occasions called attention to the proliferation of words. The less a thing exists the more the void has to be covered up by grandiloquence. The excitement of May and June 1968 is characterized as a revolution. Che Guevara is a new Jesus Christ. Every young author is a genius. To set foot on the moon is a decisive step in the history of mankind. The policeman who does his job is a stormtrooper. A student demonstration becomes an international enterprise of subversion. We could go on for pages. We are living in a world of glorified words, in a desert of glorifying formulas. It is merely a symptom of the language crisis.

But at this point there is a question which cannot be avoided. This disintegration of language, is it felt by the ordinary person? We have repeatedly stressed the experience of the individual, the fact that he "lived" a certain reality in a certain way. We have treated this actual experience as the decisive factor. That is a valid procedure when tracing the path of the loss of hope. Now, with regard to language, it would not appear that the individual feels this crisis.

To be sure, he is filled with skepticism. All agree that the speeches of a politician are valueless, and that his promises are of no importance. The slogan "Deeds rather than words" has unanimous approval. No longer does it occur to anyone to offer a solemn oath as a guarantee, or to put any faith in the oath of another. The oath has been completely devalued and no longer carries any weight. This is undoubtedly part of the general "desacralization."

Yet its significance is important. It is precisely the fact that the word is entirely dissociated from the person. It is no longer the person in action, the person fully involved in his word. It is, to the contrary, a means of disguising the person, of concealing the self. The word is no longer a commitment and a disclosure of oneself. With reference to oneself it is pure sound, a sound I can utter without putting myself into it and which, by that very fact, is *always* a useful instrument for deceiving my hearer. That is the real significance of today's universal devaluation of the oath.

So the ordinary person is not actually conscious of the crisis of the word, yet at the same time he is well acquainted with it. He expresses it indirectly. He finds his place in a world in which one's word is merely words, merely the language of disidentification. To be sure, the person continues to use this language, but on the utilitarian level. Of course there is no crisis in the sense that I can ask the butcher for meat and he understands what I mean. The system does work for those common, everyday communications, and it is that which gives the impression that the language is surviving. But it has to be kept within the commonplace. Beyond that point one notices both that the language is increasingly inadequate and also that the propaganda of devaluation and the buffoonery with which it is ridiculed are signs of its being put to death.

The creation of a universal, abstract language, completely detached from the commonplace and the limited, detached also from that other universal which is humanity, with its load of feeling, of the irrational, of blood, tears and joy, the creation of a language which would be a pure play of signs, of references, of structures, of variations and differences, a play of words in accordance with the rules of Nōh, the stringing out of sentences as functions of algebraic calculations—all that can only take place in a milieu in which language has already been stripped of its significance.

It is futile for Lefebvre to appeal to a metalanguage. If one can dissect the language and perform an autopsy on it, as is being done today, that is possible only by treating it as a corpse. It means that it already is a corpse. What we are now being invited to do is to look at language in retrospect. One does not fabricate a metalanguage and a system of harmonized meanings at will and on order! The language study now being undertaken rests, as far as the intellectuals are concerned, on the profound conviction either that communication is impossible or indeed that there is nothing to communicate. Language is itself the last object, and it is the intellectuals who, in their way, are bearing witness to today's reality.

Though the man in the street doesn't know this and has no conscious experience of it, he nevertheless feels its effects and is made uncomfortable by it. Here again we have the loss of fixed and reliable points of reference. Words are no longer words. Swamped by the written and spoken deluge, he does indeed feel the lowered value of this superabundance and is depending more and more on pictures.

Now it must not be forgotten that a picture is solely the expression of an external world. The picture is a report of what happens around a person. The latter, intrigued by the picture, no longer expresses himself and no longer expects others to express themselves. The only remaining possibility is to make contact with the external world, and this moreover answers only to the requirements of calculated efficiency and utility.

If today we can celebrate the triumph of the visual over the auditory, and can confine our communication to the superficial, outward world as characterized by pictures, that does not mean that the person does not feel something painfully within himself which he is unable to analyze. Make no mistake, the dependence on pictures, the priority given to the sketch, the diagram, the plan, the drawing, the illustration is nothing but an inept defense against the inability to communicate. For the language crisis not only means solitude. Almost more than that, it means the absence of duration. Meaningful discourse is registered in a continuity. A picture, on the other hand, is a flash which makes possible an instantaneous, all-embracing view of inseparable impressions.

A complete language which is agreed upon beforehand and is the means by which man expresses himself and makes contact with others is a kind of act of faith in continuity. Its rules must be dependable and must be accepted by the other person in the same way in which I accept them. The word must not be distorted in the meantime, and must be received by the other person in the way in which I said it. It must make lasting sense. The thing signified has to be established, and I have to be assured within myself both of its continuance (as a thing signified, it must still be there tomorrow with the same characteristics) and of its particularity.

Unless the metalanguage remains untouchable, no communication is possible. Language is man laying his hand on time. The language crisis projects man into a world of inconstant forms which he can never depend upon. It is the deep-seated impression that nothing any longer is to be counted on beyond the present instant.

However, it is almost impossible to be sure which is the determining factor. Is it the language crisis which brings about man's loss of mastery over the future? Or is it, rather, the accelerated change in the outward appearance of the modern world which causes language to lose its substance? In either case, man finds himself bereft of one of the instrumentalities which he was receiving and developing to assure his future.

At this point we need to bring out, very briefly, an accompanying fact: the crisis of law. One of the meanings, one of the values of law, one of its basic reasons for existence, is to assure the future. It is the virtue of law to stabilize situations in an age which produces change in everything. Man has to be able to count on a certain continuance of agreements, rules and modes of conduct, without which the common life would be impossible. Law is the indispensable fixating factor, so that when the current crisis of law is coupled with the language crisis the profound instability of the times stands revealed.

Here again, of course, the individual does not take into account the gravity of the stituation. He no longer attaches any great importance to law because its crisis isn't killing him. Yet what an outcry is raised when rules are continually changed, when the judicial world becomes "a jungle"! Underneath this outcry there lies a more deepseated uneasiness, which is precisely that of not being able to count on anything enduring. Hence man is left with a basic insecurity in his social world. Nothing is foreseeable because nothing is clearly determined. At every moment he is faced with a void, a darkness, into which he is supposed to take a step, to put out a hand. Wonder of wonders, it works. There still are some forms and guarantees, but always in the past tense. Never are they assured in their continuity, their process, their procedure.

From this comes modern man's feeling of the extreme fragility of his society, of a hidden overall crisis, of catastrophe lurking in the shadows, ready to be let loose by any one of his acts. It is a mentality of magic and superstition which develops in direct ratio to the crises of language and law, as a sort of shield. One has to manage as best he can with the future unknown. Since the means we once had at our disposal are gone, let's carry out whatever rites are necessary to propitiate the powers of darkness.

ILLUSION

The triumph of the image, in an age when everything has become spectacle—I shall not go back over that characterization—corresponds also to the fact that man is living in an illusory world, illusory because made up of images transmitted by the communications media. His world is no longer that of his daily experience, of his lived mediocrity, of his known personality, of his repeated relationships. It has become an enormous decor, put there by the thousands of news items which are almost completely useless for his life, but which are striking, arousing, threatening, glorifying, and edifying in their radical insignificance. They give him the feeling of living an experience which is worth the trouble, in contrast to the rest of his experience which is colorless and too plainly unimportant. It is an odd perversion which leads the person of this age to bestow importance and sense on that which does not concern him at all, but which he reads in the newspaper or sees on television, and yet to reject the importance and sense of that which is in fact his own experience twenty-four hours of every day.

However, this changeover is not hard to understand. On one side we have all the luster and accumulated prestige of the most magnificent technology combined with the most resplendent and terrifying reports, and on the other side the gray world of ordinary loves, always slightly bungled, of uninteresting work for "curtailed wages," of foreign companions and the woman who does the cleaning. It is better to live in illusory magic, and from that vantage point to judge the banal and the boring. The latter stand out in all the greater contrast as one rejects the daily round without going in search of its humble values and its humanity.

But then that is to give oneself over to the illusory, to illusion actually, which one takes to be the real. I am not at all saying that the person thinks television is more real than the factory. That is not how the changeover comes about. But we have in politics, for example, the inability to distinguish the factual from what is pure imagination, or in economics the refusal to take practical possibilities into account in favor of dreams. In the same way, revolution can take on an aspect of brilliant clairvoyance, at the same time that it is anemic, and utopias are continually reborn.

To live in the poetic illusion presented to us by the spectacular environment of the modern world is to do away with the need for making history. The demand is always for everything right away. The revolutionary dream saves one from the daily conquest, just as the dream of absolute leisure eliminates the struggle to give meaning to today. Illusion is necessarily metaphysical. The ordinary person, since he is now placed by the communications media in an imaginary universe, lives in a world of metaphysics. That is why he is so easily moved and yet so inaccessible at the same time. He is going nowhere. A believer in progress, because progress as such is what it is all about, he is becoming less and less capable of personal discipline and development.

He is only at ease in a climate of the absolute, of all or nothing, of eternity. But that excludes hope. He skips over the real. He skips the mediation of time in order to land full-blown in the ideal, ultimate society where everything is taken care of. He dreams, but he no longer hopes. So when, through some misfortune, the dream ends, the illusion vanishes, and the ideal is seen to be unattainable, nothing remains but death.

2

Symptoms of Sterility

I have tried to present some aspects of "life as lived." What are the deep impressions of man in this twentieth-century society? Why is it that, always and by a variety of paths, one finally comes out powerless to hope? But there are outward signs as well.

THE AGE OF MAGICIANS

Here, then, is this man for whom the future is once again a hazardous mystery to which there is no key. He falls back on the magician, on the political prophet, on the miracle-working wise man, on the one who unveils the future and offers assurances. He transforms the physician or the scientist into a sorcerer. He looks for some Promethean or some Mephistophelian intervention which will provide the final breakthrough and the security of a sure future. The success of *Planète* (a science fiction monthly), and publications of that type, of horoscopes, of fortune-tellers, of sects, the growth of the irrational in politics and the increase in intellectual incoherence—all these are sure signs of the absence of hope. Efforts to plumb the world's and my own future are completely drained dry in a "thus it was written." The attempt to lay hold of the unseen powers, to appease them, to seduce them and use them is a magician's springtime and the prelude to a summer of drought and sterility. Nothing can render a person more sterile and ineffectual than this return to magic.

Let it not be said that this is merely incidental behavior, surface or peripheral sentiment, or that it is confined to "popular" (uncultivated!) circles. Quite the contrary. It is this recourse to magic which is central, and it is the rational conduct and the professional restraint which are peripheral and superficial. It is in his attempt to recreate the sacred, and in his looking for a miracle, that modern man is fully identified.

This comes equally to light among the most sophisticated intellectuals. The whole team of the periodical *Tel Quel*, for example, is specifically characterized by its Magianism. Spellbinding art, pop music, Michel Butor or Alain Robbe-Grillet, the Underground, all these represent in reality a search for, or a step toward, the magical and the undecipherable.

Now if "at the beginning of things" magic could have been the agent of action, of mastery over the world, and of the affirmation of the individual over against the group, in our day it is a regression. For this is not a "new magic," but the old one. Faced with a formidable technological system and with relentless structures, man takes refuge in the ancestral activities of magic and the occult, of night-time and dreams. He is afraid of what he has done and thinks to find a remedy in a return to the original springs, but what was a spring three hundred thousand years ago is now a mirage of water which leads one astray into ever greater sterility. Today nothing is more reactionary than the Living Theater, the Underground cinema, pop music, and Scandinavian eroticism. These are, to be sure, understandable reactions, but they are debilitating and falsifying at the very height of the hardest struggle man has ever faced.

The magician is, above all else, the one who is able to disclose the future and eventually to change it. Nowadays we no longer have haruspices. Our century, which to be sure still uses tarot cards and coffee grounds, would no longer be happy, on the whole, with what is openly called superstition. To all appearances it has become scientific, and it brags about being rational. Fortune-telling is practiced only in secrecy and shame. Even today's fortune-tellers have taken a rational turn. Never has the future been so scutinized, but now we do it in the scientific manner. Forecasts, projections, possibilities, prospects—these enterprises abound, and of course they bear the stamp of a certain rigor and rationality. Statistics and samplings are multiplied.

Some of the methods are quite consistent, but it has to be noted at the same time that the imagination plays an ever increasing role in such endeavors. The procedures, as a matter of fact, are more and more rational, but the object on which they are brought to bear is not. That is to say, it was soon noted that it is impossible truly to predict, for the reason that such a prediction would imply a selection from among certain privileged facts and hypotheses. So a choice had to be made between two procedures. One would either be content with the construction of models, abstract structures having little to do with concrete reality except to represent it conceptually. These models can then be made to operate in such a way that one can foresee their evolution. But this is an abstraction of the real, comparable to the images the magicians might have used to represent the universe.

The second procedure is that of simulations and scenarios. If abstraction was the decisive factor in the first, the imagination is decisive in the second. It involves the invention of a series of coincidences, so that *if* such-and-such happens, the logical sequence can be seen. Thus one starts out with imaginary factors (not entirely, to be sure) and one treats these scientifically. Ultimately, if one managed to simulate all the imaginable concrete situations, each time adding this or that factor and making the corresponding changes in the other factors, one would have embraced the whole of the real. In these operations the frontier with science fiction is impossible to distinguish. Let's say that, in general, these are science fiction novels which are not too unreasonable, which do not relate to startling and inaccessible discoveries and do not have to do with too distant a future.

However, when one takes this path it is hard to identify the frontier with divination as well. We are carried back toward the intellectual operation (for those who consulted the gods also possessed a great intellectual culture and a prodigious capacity for observation) of disclosing the future, with the same anxiety, the same panic as of abandoned children, the same uncertainty, the same inability to master whatever it might be. This seems all the harder to accept because we have the impression of mastering facts through technology, while remaining unequipped for building the future.

The throwback toward the irrational, the absurd modes of behavior, dependence on the imaginary—these are acts of man without hope who is trying to unwind a *rational* thread which he is holding by one end, and which is to pierce the darkness of the future without any discontinuity. Or again, they are the acts of someone trying to capture a slippery and multifarious future in order to make it solid and ascertainable.

It is at that very point that man finds himself more ill-equipped than ever. He has now become aware that he cannot construct the future his way, and on the other hand, he no longer believes in any outside forces or person, the gods or God, who act upon this future and to whom he might appeal to intervene in order to change it or develop it.

Man is unable to make his history, and he knows that now there is no other person who is making it either, only blind mechanisms, obscure powers, inexplicable interactions. It is an undiscernible, inscrutable future into which he is advancing step by step into the night, just as in the heroic ages, only this time he is doing it in crowds, en masse, by the billions, and by an accelerated process which leaves him no time for respite, no time for scrutinizing this absence. In this situation without hope, how could he fail to have recourse to the magician?

THE AGE OF SCORN

Following André Malraux, our age was frequently characterized as an age of scorn. It is undoubtedly true that man has never so been given to scorn, consciously or unconsciously, the scorn of his fellow man. We have seen it burst forth in the manner in which man has been treated for two centuries. It is a strange thing to see this growth of scorn in the democratic situation. The true aristocrat (not the fallen nor the dispossessed aristocrat) is a person without scorn for his inferiors. In a slaveholding society the aristocrat does not scorn his slaves. I know that today, among our little toughs and our welfare workers, this attitude is characterized by the worst of all words, "paternalism." They prefer scorn. They can have their fill. It is an expression of the inferior destroying the superior. In fact, it is not enough to destroy a material superiority. One has to annihilate the spiritual and intellectual superiority as well, the superiority of character and of virtue. The only way to accomplish this is by scorn, and also by derision, of which we shall be speaking later on. But historically scorn came first.

It is true that the aristocrat, losing his own identity and won over by the bourgeois mentality, was also capable of scorn as a way of destroying lowly folk through his vanity and egocentrism. More often, however, he went all out to be cruel, totalitarian, and excessively demanding. It was when the sovereignty of his power was threatened that he reacted with scorn. This reaction was spreading in the seventeenth and eighteenth centuries, but it became especially evident among the last of the powerful aristocrats of the nineteenth century. By that time they were themselves the objects of scorn.

What we have here is basically the attitude of a person who is not content to conquer and dominate. He must also destroy the other person inwardly, must treat him as a thing, destroy him spiritually, repudiate him. To kill him means nothing. There is no satisfaction to be had from his death unless he has first been vilified.

The nobility in time of combat always placed a high value on the opponent. They respected and honored him in accordance with the old tradition whereby one honored the dead or the vanquished enemy, and treated him all the better the more valiantly he had defended himself. There was no place for scorn. This absence of scorn, however, could be combined with great harshness. The Spaniards calmly burned their adversaries. They didn't scorn them. As conquerors of America they killed, pillaged, and burned right and left, yet had no hesitation about joining forces with the natives and integrating with them completely.

After the conquest, colonization was based on scorn, on the repudiation of the natives as human beings, on the repudiation of their culture, their religion, and their traditions. It was ridicule and self-destruction imposed from without—[the advertising slogan] *"Y a bon banania"* and the Vietnamese girl. What a strange situation. It would seem that the more our manners are refined materially the more scorn there is. We no longer whip the blacks, but we despise them all the more. We no longer burn our adversaries, but we crush them inwardly.

What a subtle age this is, which has transferred violence to the spiritual realm, taking on humanitarian manners while adding to our scorn of human beings. But it was not yet realized that scorn is contagious, and that it grows by the same process by which violence grows. Violence alone can answer violence, by a mutual, low-gear generation. Only hate can answer scorn, and the hate becomes scorn the moment the victim is no longer weak and is able to resist his former oppressor. Machiavelli gave good advice when he warned never to allow a person whom one has offended to remain alive.

To the scorn of the colonizer, the colonized responded with a hidden, camouflaged, and often unconscious hatred. Once liberated, his response flared into a withering scorn. The softening of manners was only for a time. Democratic and liberal benevolence, even though

counterbalanced by scorn, survived thanks only to contrivance, effort, tension, and willpower. Today physical
savagery has come back and has swooped in on our society once again, yet without any loss of the prompting
to scorn. The two are now added together. It is the supreme absurdity of our time endlessly to set forth declarations of the rights of man when what prevails in fact is
the scorn of men.

It does no good to recall Hitler and the concentration
camps. What was new about that was not the fact of the
camps themselves (there were concentration camps during the Boer War, for example), nor the fact of the sequestering of a significant portion of the population, nor the
fact of scorn, of the determination to destroy the other
person inwardly. The new element was, rather, the open
proclamation. There had been scorn for the colonized, but
it was not said out loud. The opposite was affirmed. The
Nazi effrontery was to say with satisfaction and rigor what
others had already carried out.

Now it is essential to understand, especially in these
matters, that (contrary to what is generally said) to do
something without saying so, or to set forth a statement
which is the reverse of one's actions, is not merely hypocritical. It is also to disapprove of oneself. If that can seem
like an attempt at self-justification, at an appeasing of
one's conscience, from another point of view the statement
thus set forth is necessarily a limiting factor in the acts
undertaken. When, as opposed to this, one comes to the
point of equating word and deed, the door is open to every
insanity and unbridled activity. To declare doctrinally or
prophetically, to affirm as valid, to proclaim in discourse
whatever one is doing is to guarantee the proliferation
of the action. It is to go the preceding situation one better,
to reach the outer limit of horror.

A faith proclaimed in accordance with a faith lived increases faith tenfold, and the converse is true of scorn. To treat a man with scorn while claiming to honor him is absurd and hypocritical, but it does set a limit to the concrete possibilities of scorn. That is why, even though I find them low and ridiculous, I am not ready to abandon the declarations of the rights of man. They are a barrier, however fragile, against the universalization of scorn. I believe in the decisive, and even in the ultimate, importance of the word. The glaring novelty of Nazism was to proclaim with pride, emphasis, and satisfaction the scorn of man, the scorn of categories, classes and races. But the whole man and every man are included whenever a human group, however limited, is made the object of scorn. So the result was the removal of all restraint. The diabolic devices for the moral and spiritual annihilation of the person are well known, devices to destroy his honor, his dignity, his decency, and finally his person.

We have never gotten away from scorn since. Scorn was just as serious in the Stalinist camps. There was the scorn of the bourgeois class in the Marxist-existentialist development after 1945. There is the white man's scorn answering the black man's scorn. How can we forget the atrocious mutual scorn of the war in Algeria, with its tortures and degrading mutilations? [4]

But also to treat man as property, whether as "the most precious capital" (Stalin) or as an object of one's own satisfaction and desire (the rage among the intellectuals of sadism) is merely an expression of this scorn. These intel-

[4] In this world of scorn, Colonel Trinquier's statement on the film *La Bataille d'Alger* brought a glimmer of hope as an expression of honor. Similar, but how rare, is the witness borne by Remy, in his preface to G. Fraschka's book, *L'Honneur n'a pas de Frontières* (1970), in which the author seeks to show the honor of the great German fighters of 1940–45. Remy renders homage, in fact, to those who were his enemies.

lectuals of the left since Georges Bataille are the fervent, if unintentional, adepts of Hitler. We have never stopped. We are beset by scorn. Without meaning to, we express ourselves in this manner, even in the churches.

We have to try to understand the meaning of this inhuman insanity. To scorn is to condemn the other person to complete and final sterility, to expect nothing more from him and to put him in such circumstances that he will never again have anything to give. It is to negate him in his possibilities, in his gifts, in the development of his experience. To scorn him is to rip his fingernails out by the roots so that they will never grow back again. The person who is physically maimed, or overwhelmed by mourning or hunger, can regain his strength, can live again as a person as long as he retains his honor and dignity, but to destroy the honor and dignity of a person is to cancel his future, to condemn him to sterility forever. In other words, to scorn is to put an end to the other person's hope and to one's hope for the other person, to hope for nothing more from him and also to stop his having any hope for himself.

And what is the penalty for scorn? It is that having killed the hope of another, one can only lose hope oneself. He who scorns is he who no longer entertains any hope for himself and who forbids it to himself. In that case, the only thing left is spiritual nihilism. That, in fact, is what we have lived through.

At this point we must guard against a misunderstanding. I am not making any ethical appraisal of scorn. I am not trying to say that scorn is wicked. It also has its tragic grandeur. I am not trying to find out whether man merits the scorn which others display, or not. I am not condemning the attitude of scorn in the name of humanism. I am not singling out any value of the person which ought to be preserved. To be sure, I, too, have my ideas on the subject, but that is not my purpose here.

I wish only to state that we are living in the age of scorn, and that no matter from what angle one looks at it, no matter how one analyzes it, scorn implies, requires as a presupposition and entails as a consequence in a way that is inevitable, the suppression of all hope.

THE AGE OF SUSPICION

The other capability of this age is that of suspicion. It is different from scorn, but no less overpowering. Nothing is any longer itself. We have learned to look behind and beyond for the nameless, the elusive, the wriggly depths, the hidden forces, the secrets. Such is the supreme lucidity to which we are condemned. It is a strange evolution whereby, beginning with the thinking of a few, suspicion has spread through all the intellectuals, and from there is taking hold of everyone.

Suspicion was born on three different levels, in accordance with three different points of view, in consequence of independent procedures, and in fields of thought which are unrelated to one another. This is true to such an extent that the initial authors could even be opposed to one another and considered mutually irreconcilable. I am referring to Marx, Nietzsche, and Freud. In short, it could be said that suspicion is their one point in common.

For Marx it was a question of discerning modes of social behavior which underlie public statements, doctrines, political or economic attitudes, secret motives, hidden interests, purposeful decisions. He put forward the theory of the false conscience, of self-justification, of ideology, according to which man is always in bad faith. Man neces-

sarily acts on the basis of an interpretation of the world
and of society and its behavior that does not and cannot
in any way correspond to reality. He has shown, in addition, that each person obeys the interplay of economic
forces and of collective interests.

Finally, he relocated the individual in a group, in the
class which he necessarily represents, from which he can
never detach himself and on which he depends for his
symbols, images, choices, and conduct. As an individual,
the person may be full of virtue, of good qualities, etc.,
but that in no way changes his essential self, which is
defined by the class to which he belongs and which he
represents in all his conflicts, whether he likes it or not.
Thus, behind the outward attitudes there is a reality
which fails to correspond, and which even is quite incapable of corresponding to those attitudes, because no
one is able to present his own self as the total incarnation
of his class. Hence, in order to know the person who
speaks and acts, one has not to know his person but the
class to which he belongs. This class is his hidden reality.

Nietzsche pursued the distinction between the person
and the reality which it conceals in a totally different
way. He relentlessly tracked down the false appearances,
the moral fabrications and ideologies, the social relationships based on misunderstanding, and the entire diminution of man brought about in the process of his economic
development, labor relations, the new morality, the social
virtues. There again, it was a matter of looking behind
the front which man presents in order to see the swarming
interior with its profound and frightening truth.

Everyone knows the paths along which Freud has led
us, starting with the sick person teaching us, on the evidence of the sick person, what it is that constitutes the
depths of the conscious, willing, and artificially con-

structed being—the unconscious drives, the composition of this base on which every person builds his personality, the ocean of the irrational and of the involuntary in which we are all submerged. The person is such a minor outcropping of the powers dwelling within that we have learned not to trust it any longer.

School of suspicion—that, in fact, is what it all comes back to. We have learned no longer to place our confidence in anything, no longer to have faith in anyone, no longer to believe in a person's word, nor in a sentiment, no longer to accept the lasting quality of a relationship, no longer to believe that it could be authentic or truly representative of the person. We have learned that every good feeling merely expresses some self-satisfaction or some hypocrisy, that all virtue is a lie, that all morality is false, that all devotion is vain or a sham, that all speech hides the truth. We have learned that only the lie is true, that only the murder of one's father is consistent with one's being, that incest with one's mother is the greatest desire, that we are never disinterested, that we are incurably insane for money, whether we have it or not, for our social class, for our childhood.

Furthermore, the foregoing all departs from the domain of ethics. Until that time Christianity had indeed taught that man is "bad," "a sinner," but it taught grace and pardon at the same time. It was from the standpoint of grace that man was able to know the depths within himself, and it was with the aid of grace that he discovered sin as a reality, a serious reality, no doubt, but one which had been left behind. On the other hand, this was an ethical judgment open to dispute. It was not inevitable (what was indisputable for the believer was the judgment of God, not the evil within himself).

So these same facts which Christianity has emphasized (the tendency to incest, the thirst for power, hate for one's neighbor, etc.) are now described scientifically, encircled, defined objectively, and explained in an unimpeachable manner. The great change consists in the transformation of the base principle itself. These facts now become inevitable in and of themselves. They no longer are the evil in man. They are the very being of man. Moreover, we can no longer speak of evil in this connection. It is not a matter of ethics. It is simply a reality.

The tragedy is that these difficult concepts, these profound analyses and rigorous scientific observations have crossed over into the public domain. Men of letters and moving-picture producers carry a heavy responsibility, because the average man has picked up a monstrous and bewildering view of himself, of other people, and of his society. It has all passed into the public domain, distorted by oversimplifications, by the failure to distinguish between morality and science and by the premature conclusions which that implies.

Man has been faced with his own nothingness, his own specters and ghosts. He has been given over to pseudo-scientific fantasies, to vampires endlessly reborn from their consumption of all the virtues and of every good vainly attempted. He has been dragged by a stroke of fate into an inescapable tragedy, into the negation of himself. How go on living under these conditions, since no matter by which end one takes hold of life it is a falsification? At both the social and the inward level, in my social relationships, in my contacts with others, with the wife I love, with myself, I have learned that everything is falsified.[5]

[5] Do we not experience this extremely simple reaction, that of not believing? It is an act of defiance (often justified, of course) toward the newspaper or television. It is an act of defiance toward every word addressed to me. I *begin* by doubting, by rejecting, by suspecting, and it is the same with all my current human relationships. Now it needs to be emphasized that this instinctive defiance has nothing to do with the critical intellect.

I cannot now avoid the questions, "What is hiding behind this? What am I hiding from myself? What are they hiding from me?" They force me to ponder chasms which are literally bottomless. For, the moment something presents itself to me as an explanation, the same question arises, exactly the same: "What is there which is still hiding behind this something?" It is a descent from sphere to sphere into a hell deeper than Dante's because it is not called hell, and no one dares acknowledge it as such. It is not external to myself. I have no guide to explain it all to me, and to identify the real state of affairs. Everything needs deciphering. Everything has to be brought out into the open. The merciful and kindly shadows which were letting us sleep and live are rejected.

There no longer is any sleep for modern man. Whenever he manages to drop the slab back over the tomb of the monsters in order to devote himself to "something constructive" he cannot help knowing that they are still there, wide awake and determining his fate. The era of a quiet conscience is closed. The era of a chance to hope is gone, for there is no hope where suspicion is king. Every time a possibility, a breakthrough, or a meaning takes shape, immediately the question bursts in upon us, "From what social class, from what complex, from what ideology, from what myth, from what interest does this hope spring, since it is nothing but the falsification of a situation one has refused to face?"

Such is the state into which the three geniuses, humanity's great malefactors, have thrown us. They represent the opposite of mercy and love. I venture that, in spite of their science, it could be said that they are the opposite of enlightenment as well. They are charmers who have bewitched the soul and the intelligence of mankind by focusing our attention on problems which are fundamental but without any possible answer, by directing research down dead-end paths, by confronting the conscience with charms which are as scientific as they are illusory, by causing us to descend into depths from which we can never climb back, drawn on as we are with each new discovery by an even greater darkness, which we think ourselves duty-bound to throw light on in its turn. There is in their work a very large proportion of mystery, the mystery of seduction.

It is worthy of note, as a matter of fact, how easily we can use the word "after" when speaking of a great philosopher or a great economist or a great sociologist. We come *after* Barth, and still we can do something different from what he did. One can be *after* Durkheim or Weber and come up with a different sociology. In contrast to this, the Marx-Nietzsche-Freud trio fastens us to a wall like a pinned butterfly. It is no longer possible to say "after." Whoever comes after appears right away as a falsifier or a traitor. That's what Bernstein was for Marx and Jung for Freud. They have simply hypnotized us. They have staked out the field of the intellectually possible, and have opened what seems to us the only right path. It is in fact a hypnosis. They have drawn the chalked circle around the hen, which the latter is *incapable* of crossing. Together we are caught in a trap which is intellectual, spiritual, and social, a trap with no way out, a trap which forbids all hope, and which freezes us in an industrious, scintillating sterility.

If we are to recover any hope we shall have to go through a veritable disenchantment on the intellectual, spiritual, and social levels. We shall have to exit from the magic cave to find the sunlight once again and the authenticity of virtue. With regard to this trio, we would have to perform the same operation which Kierkegaard performed on the Hegelian myth, for let us remember that it was Kierkegaard, and not Marx, who was able to rise above Hegel and relocate man. Marx has only managed to shut man up still more within the Hegelian domain, and he has added economic determinism to state determinism, sometimes called liberty.

What Kierkegaard did, we should be able to do again. But he was able to do it only with strict reference to the revelation in Jesus Christ, that is to say, in committing the reality of the intellectual operation he was undertaking to the freedom of action of one more powerful than himself. All depends on that. But our enchantment consists precisely in the determination "for the sake of honesty and responsibility" to depend henceforth on our own powers alone, and to reject the transcendence and the radical power of the Wholly Other.

Certain it is that, trapped as we are, we are not about to unbait the hook, to undo the net. That is *no longer* within our own power and competence. But this "no longer" is simply the sign of the end of all hope.

THE AGE OF DERISION

Scorn and suspicion were born together and have grown up side by side. Derision is their natural sequel. Derision has been part of our psychological panorama for perhaps the past twenty years. How can we avoid mocking that which suspicion has shown always to be a lie, a hypocrisy, an appeasing of conscience, a justification, when one was talking and living such things as honor, virtue, the good and the beautiful, love? Since all that was pure fiction, it was necessary to uncover the reality. But this uncovering by rigorous, scientific procedures was not within everyone's reach, and it affected only a few.

However, Lenin had already discovered the system of uncovering, of "revelation," which uses crude but spectacular arguments to show the "deeper motives," the "reality" underlying the opposition. Karl Kautsky, according to this, is capitalism's valet, an ally of the bourgeoisie. The concept was developed of the "traitor-in-fact," which soon opened the door to still further simplification, and to the use of damaging insult which is so powerful as propaganda. Bukharin becomes the insidious vermin, the toad, drooling over the communist victory. Tukhachevski becomes a spy in the pay of Hitler. They not only were attacked on the political, intellectual, and theoretical fronts. They were insulted, reviled, degraded, and made the objects of derision.

This road leads necessarily from Marx's suspicion to Lenin's disclosure to Stalin's derision. The moment the category of the false conscience is generally accepted, the way to make this falseness of conscience explode in front of everybody's eyes is derision. As soon as Sartre applied the filthy-hands-and-flies procedure, the derision of everything thus attacked was achieved. In the face of attested truth or demonstrated virtue, derision is the one weapon sufficiently strong, popular, and easy of application for vilifying the adversary and for robbing him of the very thing he took to be his judgment, the thing which implied either agreement or dialogue. Derision admits of no dialogue, no encounter. All it allows is a pointing of the finger, before the jeering god of mobs, at the person who protests his innocence, and who disappears shamed, with no chance to make a reply.

Derision involves falsification. The person thus vilified is loaded with the whole of the ridicule and contempt felt by public opinion. He *is* all that in himself. He is tagged as such. He is the very incarnation of it. From that point on, all proof is superfluous. If one were to try to find out what is true and what is false among the accusations, there would be no more derision. There is no necessity for investigation and proof. The tagged person suddenly finds himself absurdly and falsely charged with a whole collection of stupidities, treacheries, and corruption. It isn't true of him? Never mind. It becomes true as soon as the machinery of derision is set in motion.

One of the high-water marks of our age has been the "Cultural Revolution," one of the great weapons of which was derision, "derision by denunciation" by the famous Dazibao, or "derision by insult," when the opposition, the denounced, old men and professors, were dragged through the streets wearing the clothes of disgrace, topped by a dunce cap and covered with spit and filth. This death by derision takes us a step beyond our start with scorn. Under the wise and good paternalism of the great Mao, the work of derision continues without letup, just as the work of scorn unfolded under the poetic, appealing, and exalted verbal outpourings of Hitler. The People's Republic of China is the exact oriental counterpart of Nazi Germany.

But derision doesn't come necessarily as a result of a governmental decision, nor does it take place exclusively in the political realm. Our entire society is sinking gradually into this corruption. We can take the aged as an example. It is true that in our society we are beginning to show some care for the aged. Decent and pleasant homes for the aged have been established which are no longer asylums. Retirement income is provided, and a new science of gerontology is being developed. Yet, at the same time, the press and television are broadcasting the ideology of youth, glorifying only the young, in accordance with the sociological trend, the progress myth, looking to the future, and so forth. A special trade is created for the

young, and it is not good for an adult to go into one of
those shops. If he does, he immediately becomes the butt
of icy sarcasm. Young people monopolize the sidewalks
and make the elderly step down.

There is an uneasiness among the young, which I have
written about on frequent occasions, and they compensate
for their uneasiness by the scorn which they bear toward
their elders. It has been said rightly that the elderly detest
the young, but that the latter give it back to them in good
measure. Now the communications media echo this situation and oversimplify it. That leads to the scoffing, the
humiliating acts and remarks, and to the general derision
of the aged by the young. As though the natural arrogance
of youth were not enough in itself, as though the misery
and the physical decline of old age were not enough in
themselves, we have to add this on top of it all. We are
living in an atmosphere created in part by the communications media.

Art, too, has blown the trumpet of derision, but we
have to distinguish the art of the exposure of falsification
from the art which broadcasts it and the art which, scor-
pionlike, kills itself by becoming the object of its own
derision. An example of the first is Fellini's extraordinary
film *La Dolce Vita,* which exposes the falseness of our
time. It is not a denunciation of the "vices" of our society,
but of the reign of imposture. It brings out the falseness
of the culture, of the intellect, of art (Steiner's), the falsification of miracle and piety, of filial and paternal love, of
freedom (in the concluding orgy), the falsification of the
nobility and of nature (the recorded sounds of nature, the
departure in the small hours of the morning after the
orgy). Everything in our modern world is made false,
reviled, and exposed. In the end, we conclude that nothing any longer has meaning (the useless flowers and the

solitude of the monster which is man). It probably is one of the most gripping films on the topic of our descent into negation by the path of derision.

More often, however, instead of pointing it out, blowing it up, and putting a finger on the infamy, one feeds on it, takes delight in it, and manages to enlist art in that direction. The last films of Bunuel are examples of this, as in the theater of derision, made up of nearly all the new political theater, whose sole weapon is ridicule of the opposition, together with exultation as a language of derision, like the slogans at the Sorbonne in which the procedure consists of turning a sentence around to give it a different meaning. There is the sculpture of derision, like the works exhibited at the Second Biennial of Paris (1970). There even are toys of derision. Ugly toys have been contrived, toys base in form and content to be given to children, so that they, too, can feed on the vulgar, the hideous, the repugnant, the slimy, the slovenly, the unsettling, the shapeless. The ugly and stupid toy is our society's last word, attesting its cheap but persistent effort to make derision an accepted ingredient in our common behavior.

If we still cannot discern this at the human level, we at least see the effects of it in art. There derision is producing sterility. Whenever the intellectual arrives at a certain degree of conscientious self-criticism, whenever he reaches a certain depth of intellectual suspicion, whenever he gets into the relentless layer-on-layer of bottomless introspection, into a vague analysis, into an ever more exacting microscopic examination of the self, of one's thoughts, language, art, and state, he necessarily is led not to write any more, not to speak any more, no longer to give expression to anything. Suspicion of oneself and of one's thinking leads to derision (the sole remaining weapon in the struggle against the bombast to which we are always prone), and derision leads to silence.

The same is also true of a too conclusive political criticism which thinks to be fundamental. If it be true that everything is necessarily the ideology of a false conscience, that there is an embracing determinism from which no one can escape, that whatever one might say, or do, or express, necessarily redounds to the benefit of the ruling class, then one should no longer do or say anything.

Deepening suspicion leads to the skepticism and cynicism so brilliantly expressed by E. M. Cioran. Yet it is difficult to understand how his radical cynicism, and the derision which he heaps on everything, allows him to continue to write and to express himself. Absolute silence is the only thing consistent with his position. The final barb of intellectual analysis leads to the derision of that very activity itself, and to not producing anything more, just as does the final barb of artistic research.

The situationists came to that conclusion in their very first notebooks. Since the criticism of a society must be total, the only work of art that an artist of the situationist school could produce would, in the end, be an absence of a work of art. But artists a few degrees further down the scale understood that art is a base deception, that a work of art is a scandal, that a theatrical performance is the expression of something "ready-made," of a separation of the actor from the public, etc.—and so, in order to come out of it, one must heap derision on the work of art, on the theatrical performance (which is to be done by means of the happening, the Living Theater, silence in the theater, or by an attempt to merge actor and spectator). In sculpture, a subway map labeled will serve the purpose, or a town plan, or the sculpture might consist of a pile of cigarette butts. All this demonstrates the link between derision and the basic stupidity which takes itself for the final penetration of introspective thinking. Thus derision brings about the sterilization of the other person, together with one's own sterility.

We are in the presence of a quite remarkable society, in which man, by making it a point of honor to crush everything with derision, brings about his own radical sterilization in contrast to his fecundity in matters of technology. Technology is not ridiculous. It is not made the object of derision. Far from being sterile, it is prodigiously fertile. Lo and behold, as a counterpart to this proliferation, this self-begetting, this reproduction by partition which characterizes the technical object, man masochistically depreciates himself before what has become his God. He cannot compete with technology in power, precision, finesse, and intelligence, so he founders in self-accusation. The system of derision is really an essential aspect of a society in which technology becomes God.

Modern man's relationship with it is comparable to that of certain of Dostoevski's heroes with God. It is a relationship of endless self-accusation and debasement. Since he can no longer compete with his machines, man devalues himself and goes into derisive prostration. He sterilizes himself in the very domain which was supposed to be his own, that of love (eroticism is a derision of love), that of artistic creation (the rejection of the beautiful, and of the finished, whole and meaningful work), that of Christian faith (the masochism of Christians endlessly heaping derision on themselves is a particular instance of a general trend). Man is sterilizing himself because the true creator, the true source of fertility and productivity is technology. Man, endowed by technology with an excess of power which enables him to surpass himself, denies and rejects himself. By derision he accentuates his weakness, so as not to risk a disastrous and humiliating competition with the too perfect harmony of his means.

We have made the rounds of the various paths which are bringing man to sterility. This sterilization of man (I do not say of his productivity and technical inventiveness) is the major sign of the absence of hope. People are going forth into a derisive world surrounded by others who are debased, reduced to objects, their hearts hardened. Some have surrendered to the forces of corruption and imperious opposition. Others have adopted a stoicism which asserts simply that in this human disaster the thing to do is to keep one's chin up and act as though none of this had happened. In either case it amounts to a renunciation of the possibility of a new civilization, of a society in which man might be, or might still become, man.

THE IMPOSTURE

Now the thing that stands out in this situation is precisely modern man's rejection of any real breakthrough. In our day, man refuses to be consoled in a true sense. He is plunging headlong into the artificial paradise of drugs, ideologies, passions, and involvements. He is rejecting any real acts of conscience in favor of fictitious ones. What we have here is a two-part drive on the part of "the modern being."

One aspect of this "modern being," one of the elements in this conflict of forces, is the passion for false explanations, and the rapid, immediate adoption of the fictitious conscience. Modern man is proud of his lucidity, for he knows that he belongs to an elucidating world. Yet, at the same time, he cannot stand the sight of his actual condition, so he accepts explanatory schemes which seem to provide a clue without really doing so. He clings to a vague existentialism while rejecting the truly existential. He accepts without question a simplistic materialism, the class struggle, and the group conflicts in the production world. He beats his breast over colonialism, imperialism, racism, world hunger, and the underdeveloped countries, for the very reason that none of these things really commits him to anything, since each is fictitious explication,[6] and none of his own real world is involved.

He accepts all the accusations, provided they bypass his real guilt. He wants indeed to belong to the generality of "we are all assassins," but not to the logic of the technological system. In order to avoid the thing which really calls him in question, he adopts just the explanation which calls him in question fictitiously. That lets him off. He displays a guilty conscience, and that proves that he does not belong to the horrible bourgeois world. He accepts the accusation borne mutually by all the members of the same group. He confesses to being guilty, all the while carefully covering up his actual responsibility. In that way he acquires a clear conscience at the bargain price of a fictitiously guilty conscience.[7] The Sartre operation has had such success only because it answers precisely to the profound wish of modern man to play this game. Sartre is a typical example of false accusation, of the fictitiously guilty conscience, of the ideology derived from a guilty conscience. Thus Western man adopts the

[6] Here we must, of course, avoid a misinterpretation. That hundreds of millions of people are going hungry, that there are exploitation and racism, etc., are undeniable facts which I do not dispute! Where the fault lies is in the explanatory ideology developed out of these facts, or about them. That is where falsification and self-justification prevail.

[7] In applying this analysis, I myself belong to the age of suspicion.

thing which lets him live in the world of accusation without being accused in the depths of his own person.

This latter is the second drive of the "modern being." Here is man who feels threatened, who feels even more that he is being called in question (actually, not just ideologically) to a degree to which man has never felt this throughout his history. He feels the agony of perils which he refuses to name, and he does not want, in this case, to receive the consolation, the word of deliverance. Unconsciously he prefers to remain in his agony. He wants to live in frantic distress. The one satisfaction he has is a work of art, or a door-closing statement which deprives everything of its meaning.

Man wants no word of salvation, nor any true consolation (he accepts all the fictitious consolations, the escapes, the appeasements and amusements), perhaps because the true consolation would make him face up to the fundamental questions of his presence in the world and of his real responsibility, questions which he continually seeks to avoid. He drowns himself in a dreary and disguised despair. He dwells within his anguish, and his most cherished secret is that of his own disavowal.

THE DISAVOWAL

For man today lives only by a continual disavowal of himself. The suicidal behavior and derision we have noted, the turning of man into an object, and the alienation now so well known, find their end and their summit in the disavowal of man by man. I am not, of course, raising a metaphysical question. I do not mean that there is an absolute type of man, an inviolable human nature. Yet it does seem to me that one can infer from the overall movement of history a certain trend with respect to man. It is as though there had been some project pursued through the millennia which was gradually revealing its outlines and was coming to fulfillment. Man was tending to affirm himself as an individual in the midst of groups and communities. He was affirming himself as subject in a world of objects. He was manifesting himself in terms of conscience and did not seem disposed to yield his dominant position to anyone.

All these prospects for his development are now called in question. By various paths man has created substitutes for himself which progressively are depriving him of his role (and it is the development of technical procedures to the point of central control). He rejects the subject-object distinction as a mistaken view of the world (yet this amounts to accepting and justifying the turning of man into a thing). He tends toward the fusion of diverse communities and abandons the particularity of the individual (and this tendency is the same whether one is thinking of communism, or the hippie communities, or the communion created by drugs). He no longer retains his pride as man and he takes on a self-negating humility which does not augur well.

When man builds up these tendencies to the point of seeing himself, with Michel Foucault, as an accident soon to be erased, or with Cioran becomes convinced of the nullity of everything, including all that has gone into his greatness as man, he is far from continuing the pious Christian tradition of witness to the virtue of renunciation and humility based on the nothingness of man before God. Neither is he following the Buddhist teaching on illusion. The fact is quite otherwise. His attitude contains no serene and transcendent view of the human condition. It is, to the contrary, a frightful grimace, a bitter, empoisoned irony, a pseudo-science which pontificates and prophesies the end of man.

Doubtless the thinking of a mere few is not of great importance, but this thinking has not come about by chance. It is in fact the expression of a common movement, as proved by the sudden success of Foucault's book. Man seeks his own negation in derision, in scorn, in a disavowal of everything that had been his history and his virtue up to now. This attempt is no longer spontaneous and accidental. It is formulated, intentional, and directional.

Once again we meet up with the astonishing inconsistency between the brilliant unfolding of man's technological powers and the whittling down of man himself to the point of self-negation, as though some fate were making him efface himself in the presence of his work, or better yet, were causing him to disappear in it. What sense can it possibly make to prove all our high achievements if we end up like Calvino's knight who doesn't exist. To pile technological exploit on technological exploit, to string out statistics, to extend the lifespan, to increase consumer goods, to organize participations, to instigate revolutions, to speed up communications indefinitely, to raise the standard of living—what good is all that if the person who is supposed to benefit from it disavows and rejects himself just when he was about to reach the very thing for which it was all being done, and which constitutes its purpose and meaning? At the very moment of completing the great project, the hero, disgusted with himself, gives up and abandons an almost finished world to commit suicide.

In tedium, he not only turns against himself, but he goes all out at the same time to destroy everything fragile, everything which fails to put up a stubborn resistance:

guileless sentiments, the "natural" virtues, simple joys, the ecological balance, the family and love, childhood (destroyed through being pampered) and adolescence (corrupted by glorification), modesty and probity, word and meaning, God and nature. Our hero, cynical and desperate, devotes his energies to killing everything which was beginning to die. He sees nothing ahead but a fall, so he wants to drag down with him everything which could have been, or which could have had value. As a result of having built a world of power, man has eroded himself. He sees himself without remainder and without worth. We are now in the final stage of this decomposition.

Of course we can wonder whether this is not just a passing crisis in our history, like the one, for example, which the Roman Empire went through, or like the crises which the Chinese Empire experienced at least three times. Is not history about to get a fresh start? And in magnifying our own crisis aren't we giving way to subjectivism? to the well-known error of perspective which gives greater importance to the close at hand than to the distant, to what is current in our own day than to what belongs to the past?

To that I must reply on two counts. First of all, I think our crisis is much greater than all the others, for if, like the others, it is a crisis of civilization, in contrast to all the other epochs our civilization is global. Hence the crisis is worldwide. We can look to the ends of the earth and still ask the question, "Whence comes our help?" There are no more big blond barbarians to submerge the Roman Empire, nor Mongols nor Manchu to do the same for the Middle Empire, to bring in new blood and a zest for life, with meaning included, a renewal of virtue, an obvious language, an importance and a price placed on human life.

There are no more barbarians. The peoples of the third world are committed to exactly the same path as we, and in ten years, or fifty, will give in to the same disavowal of themselves, to the great disillusionment, to the surrender of the self. The communists are content to finish what capitalism started. Nothing really decisive is forthcoming which gives any hope of renewing man's drained-out powers. Nothing decisive is happening, merely events, combinations, institutions, structures, revolutions, organization, plans. Man once again is waiting for *something to happen,* the something which will make him live again. He has no more resource within himself. Decadence? It goes much deeper than that. Let's call it atony, a rejection of life, like the mental anorexia which afflicts certain babies.

But suppose I am wrong, and that the crisis is merely regional and temporary. It still affects the entire Western world, and this Western world has disseminated a world-wide civilization with which all peoples everywhere are increasingly aligned. If the crisis of Western man is confirmed, it is truly a world of ruins which we are bequeathing to other peoples.

I am well aware of the objection that this crisis of the West has been predicted and heralded for a long time. Spengler wrote his *Decline of the West* a half century ago. Berdyaev wrote his *New Middle Ages,* so you see. . . . This type of argument always amazes me with its lack of historical depth. It is true that democracy's dilemma as described by de Tocqueville in 1830 did not show up in the events of 1840, but everything he foretold has progressively come to pass in the nearly a century and a half since. The same is true of his analysis of the conflict between the state and the body politic. Only now are we seeing this universalized. With regard to *The Decline of the*

West, we have marched, step by step, down the road mapped out by Spengler. A prediction made a long time ago is not proved false for not having come to pass immediately. The fulfillment takes place on the scale of history, and we are witnesses to a much deeper crisis than had been foretold.

To be sure, we can carry on for a while! This generation may have its apparent successes—further journeys into space, and philosophies which are more and more exciting as they grow more and more destructive. The Roman Empire took two centuries to collapse. Perhaps we can do that well for the whole of humanity. But at the heart of our flashes of brilliance the central fact will remain, the self-loathing and the absence of hope associated with it.

Could it be, then, that we are in the preparatory stage of the mutation predicted by Teilhard? Isn't this merely a crisis of transition? We know that Teilhard assembled the clues to our society (communism, technology, universalization, etc.) in order to prove that we are entering a new era, that of universal fusion, which would give access to the omega point. I have no intention of getting into a general discussion of Teilhard's thought. I observe only that his thinking is closely conditioned by the fact of technology, and that Charbonneau was right in calling him the prophet of the technological society. His thought is a system for justifying the status quo.

But what I would like especially to emphasize is that it seems strange to me that a reversal of the permanent direction of known history would be the fulfillment of that history. All history has progressed in the direction of individuation. Now, suddenly, it is seen to turn in the direction of synthesis and of the disappearance of the individual. Of course, this is conceivable metaphysically (I refuse to speak of theology where Jesus Christ is transformed into an objective point and into a catalytic agent), but the thesis seems to me impossible to maintain historically and to have no chance of being true.

No, the crisis is a crisis. There is no dialectic which can comfort us. We know absolutely nothing about what this crisis may lead to. It ill behooves us to play the prophet. I simply observe that the absence of hope puts in its appearance no matter what the end. We do know that the living thing does not continue to live unless it possesses a firmly rooted will to live. He in whom the will to live fails is sure to die, and it is the same for peoples as for individuals, for civilizations as for nations. We also know that one can only keep on wanting to live if there is a hope, an expression more complete and more full than merely the project on the one hand and its meaning on the other. It must be an expression which embraces both. When we see hope die, death itself is present.

After man's disavowal of himself, the only possible consequence really is silence. It is futile for the philosopher to assure us that we can find leverage in nonbeing (Carré, *le point d'appui sur le néant*, 1956). In vain Cioran gives as a reason for living the fact that man who is free to kill himself does not do so. We have reached precisely that point at which man, stripped of himself through an excess of conscience associated with the excess of his powers, will no longer find cause why he should not exercise the sovereign power of suicide, whether it be physical or spiritual, collective or individual suicide. The latter is already in process of being carried out and universalized.

We have explored the paths by which the end of hope has come—not all of them, to be sure, only certain of the well-known ones. We have seen the way in which man lives out his selfhood in this society, and that it is profoundly negative. We have enumerated the clues. But this end of hope, which confronts us with the most important question that could be put to us, toward which all the principal traits of our society converge, which all our current philosophies expound, which explains so many of our group movements, this end of hope has nothing to do with despair.

Despair is aware of itself. It cries out. It is tragic and romantic. It gives rise to acts of heroism and to "beautiful song." It drives man into action. It incites to rebellion, and challenges the person to be more truly himself.

The end of hope, on the other hand, is discrete and silent. It is an open vein in a warm bath, draining out all the blood, bringing sleep without pain and without reaction. It gives rise to nothing. It is scarcely aware of itself. One has to assemble countless indications, as we have tried to do, in order to have some idea of what is happening. There is nothing tragic about it. One succumbs to it simply because there is no reason not to do so. One stops resisting the death impulse with will, energy, sexual appetite, and the love of life. One fades away because, where there no longer is any hope neither is there any form or being. But this is at such a deep level that there is nothing at first glance to indicate what is taking place.

Hope, in its death throes, does not cry out for help because, with nothing to hope for, to what or to whom would such a cry be addressed? It doesn't declare itself, doesn't tell about itself, doesn't advertise itself. It merely leaves a void, and by this void we learn of its former existence. This void is at the heart of all that we are and want to undertake. There no longer is any reason for the undertaking. That is all that this void can say if, inert and silent, it is still an observer. A hope terminated has left its trace, but no longer can any road open up.

PART II

The Age of
Abandonment

I HAVE BEEN led to put my deepest conviction in writing, a conviction which has come to me after so much research into our society, after so much effort to discern the action of God in our age. But still I write it with trembling, and I can only proceed in fear. It is my belief that we have entered upon the age of abandonment, that God has turned away from us and is leaving us to our fate.

I am sure, of course, that he has not turned away from all, or rather, that he is perhaps present in the life of an individual. Perhaps it is he who still speaks in the heart of a person. But it is from our history, our societies, our cultures, our science, and our politics that God is absent. He is keeping quiet, and has shut himself up in his silence and in his night.

I know very well all the reasonable reactions and the contrary proofs which such a proposition arouses, some of them sociological, others of them theological: "Why should it be so? If God is love, how could he abandon those to whom he has given everything? If God has humbled himself, why would he take his spite out, in a sense, by pulling back and shutting himself up in his distance? Only a pessimistic view of our civilization could lead to this conclusion. It is because 'you' want your own privacy, you want to keep quiet, you want to shake the dust of this society from your own feet, that you attribute your feelings to God and conclude that he has withdrawn. What egocentrism! What anthropomorphism! Since Jesus Christ, there can no longer be an abandonment on God's part. Jesus is Emmanuel, God with us, forever. There is no more break with him. Jesus is the Saviour. His salvation is offered forever, without interruption. Jesus is the Lord. He is that, and by that fact he cannot abandon this earth into which he came to die and to rise again. He is that, and he does not hold his Lordship in suspension. The world cannot be abandoned by God since Jesus Christ. Finally, what a simplistic view it is of a God who speaks one minute and keeps quiet the next, who comes and goes. It's a bit childish."

I know. I've thought over all those arguments and objections to this conviction which was born in me. I've taken another serious look at everything which would let me continue to affirm objectively that God is always present. I have criticized my sociological analyses. But nothing has been able to convince me. With all their appearance of wisdom and soundness, these objections are futile. In spite of all these reasons, I affirm today that God has indeed turned away, and that his word as such is no longer being spoken. Perhaps it isn't forever, but only for today. I even think I will say that it surely is not forever. Yet it is our situation, and if that is the way it is, it is not the fault of a general wickedness. It is not the growing number of injustices which is at stake. It is something else. It is not the unbelievers who are keeping God away. It is, on the one hand, a matter of structures. On the other hand, it is the responsibility of Christians and of the Church, who do not know how to be what God expects of them.

3

The Diagnostic Error
about Man

Our theologians commit a considerable number of diagnostic errors concerning the present age and concerning
man because they have not accepted the fact of this abandonment. The first error, involving all theology since Bultmann and Bonhoeffer, concerns man. It's the well-known
interpretation of modern man according to which modern
man has become scientific and rational, and has come of
age. I shall not go back over the critique of what has to
be called a monumental misconception, completely out of
touch with reality, a scientific ignorance of the actual
nature of our society and of man, and a watertight dogmatism unrelated to fact.

If modern man is not amenable to faith, if the preaching of the message of faith is completely foreign to him,
that is not because he is scientific. It is not because he has
left the mentality of myth behind him. It is not because he
rejects a message which makes him childish. These rea-

sons all derive from the theologians themselves. They have their own problems with belief, and they project them, en bloc, onto what they call "modern man."

It is true that the person of this age is impervious to the preaching of the Gospel, but no change in the mode of presentation, no demythologizing, no translation into other "signs and symbols" will have any effect. *If* modern man had in fact given up the domain of belief in favor of the domain of reason, *if* he had left behind the mentality of myth, then yes. Such a renovation could make sense. Unfortunately, since the diagnosis is fundamentally false, the therapeutic procedure is necessarily false as well. This double error is part of the context of the abandonment in which we find ourselves.

Modern man is impervious to the preaching of the Gospel. That is connected with a number of sociological causes which I shall not recapitulate here. I shall emphasize one factor only. Man is said to have acquired a critical intellect, and for that reason he can no longer accept the simplistic message of the Bible as it had been proclaimed two thousand years ago, or even a hundred years ago. That is indeed one aspect of the diagnostic error, for we have in no way progressed to the stage of the critical intellect. Western man is still as naïve, as much a dupe, as ready to believe all the yarns as ever. Never has man gone along, to such a degree, with every propaganda. Never has he applied so little rational criticism to what is fed him by the mass media.

But if he has no critical intellect of any kind, he nevertheless is full of suspicion, as we noted above. On the one hand, he takes up with all the latest fashions in politics and modernity. Yet on the other hand, he suspects everything of being a lie and a delusion. He feeds on the group errors, but is everlastingly suspicious of the word of anyone who approaches him individually. He is wrong about where the suspicion belongs, and that is why I cannot talk about the critical intellect in this connection. He goes along with all the worldwide enterprises, but thinks he's clever in being suspicious of the lone person in front of him.

In this situation he feels that the person is out to take him over, so he looks for the underlying motives of his actions. If he comes up with motives in which he himself shares (making money, for example) he is content and will go along. But if he discovers no motives on his own level he begins by being suspicious, begins to suspect, and so refuses what is proposed. For him, quite clearly, "everything is a lie," and he says as much about the speeches of politicians, the newspapers, radio, and television. It's all a lie, yet he goes along because he is caught up in a collective, global movement. It's all a lie, he thinks, but that judgment finds no concrete application, because when a lot of people are all going the same way, that way becomes the truth. On the other hand, suspicion is decisive for the unusual, solitary word. Everything of that sort is a lie, and I must trust none of it. This attitude of suspicion, an attitude of the person which is the opposite of love, has nothing to do with the critical intellect. This attitude is one of the fundamental reasons for the rejection of the Gospel.

The other factor is the refusal to be consoled. Let us consider that fact, already examined above, under the aspect of the hearing of the Gospel. Modern man wants to live in a time of power and disasters. Only great catastrophes interest him and move him. He becomes a hero, a whole man, when he is submerged in atrocities, when he shares in the tragedies of the times. There has to be torture. People have to be dying of hunger, or crushed by dictatorships, or exhausted by forced labor. This is the world in which man wants to be. It can never be too horrible. He laps up the news of crimes, accidents, floods, and volcanic eruptions, which is strictly identical with the news of wars, bombardments, tortures, and revolutions. That's just what he needs (there is a great demagoguery and a slight sado-masochism among Christians, who add their little horn to the grand jazz which proclaims the total and absolute misery of man in our age, talking endlessly about torture in Brazil or Greece, about apartheid and the necessity for revolutionary violence). Man has to have just that, and certainly not the opposite, certainly not consolation and joy.

Then he wants to rebel himself, to accuse, to condemn and to add to the misfortune. Or he may run away by means of amusements, eroticism, greed, and wasteful spending; but those are simply complementary forms of this willed disaster. Eros and Thanatos, on the one hand; wasteful spending (which is a destruction of goods) and torture, on the other.

The thing which would tend to prove this in the religious sphere is a look at what is still happening and succeeding. It is a known fact that the "sects" are catching on in popular circles, but what is their proclamation? Perdition, the judgment of God, hell and damnation. If our theologians had a modicum of good sense in their so-called analysis of modern man's psychology, they should at least have asked themselves the question, Why the extraordinary success of Jehovah's Witnesses, and especially with the working man? Had they asked that question, they might at least have noticed that what is "happening" is precisely the thing which is the most mythical, the most antiscientific, the most crassly ecstatic, the most apocalyptic. It is the will to tragedy and disaster projected onto the religious sphere.

Modern man is filled with suspicion, and he wants not

to be consoled. We have tried, above, to show that this is
the most deadly poison to hope. If man rejects the Gospel,
it's not a question of faith. It is a question of hope.

FAITH OR HOPE

We have here the central question for preaching, for
evangelization, and perhaps for the entire Christian life
today. We persist in centering all on faith, on believing
or not believing. Now, for the present, the accent has
shifted. It is placed on hope, on living with or without
hope. Modern man is said to be no longer capable of faith,
no longer suited to belief. It is said that our modern world
does away with faith, and that it is no longer possible to
believe what used to be believed in the creedal statements
of a former age—but what a mistake!

Never have people believed as much, everything and
nothing. The modern world is above all else a religious
world. It is loaded with religions—communism, Maoism,
nationalism, revolution—all are purely and specifically
religious attitudes. The modern world is not really secularized, in spite of all the absurd ballyhoo based on a whole
series of misconceptions, and on an extremely superficial
analysis. This is essentially a world of the sacred. The
political enemy is "damned." Wars are ideological wars,
that is to say, wars of religion. Social movements are
sacred. Revolution is an act of God. Technology belongs
to the domain of the sacred, and science even more so.

The most that can be said is that man has completely
desacralized the natural environment, but he has transferred all the sacred to the cultural and the social. One
need only observe the entranced state of those who talk
revolution, or the complete irrationality of discourses on

politics, irrespective of the specific question under discussion. The modern world is overflowing with myths. It is constantly producing myth, but they are no longer *the same* myths as before, and they no longer come by the same process. This contradicts the superficial view that man, attached to ancestral forms of myth, is being demythologized. We are caught up in the development myths (and those of underdevelopment), in the myths of self-management and growth, as well as in the myths of fascism and imperialism. World and man are crammed with faith, with religion, with belief, with mythology.

If the debate were on the question of the transmission of the Christian faith, the obstacle confronting us would not be that of reason and science, but rather, the multiplicity of "faiths." [1] In any case, it is quite inaccurate to ask, "How witness to the faith in a rationalized, secularized world?" To keep insisting on that is a waste of time. It is a display of blindness on the part of the Church and of theology, and it is a second proof of the abandonment in which we find ourselves. The question could very well be, "How witness to the Christian faith in the midst of all these beliefs and these new myths?" I do not look upon that question as totally useless.

In other words, I think that the warfare of faith should continue, in fact, to be waged against the idols and the false gods. I believe that Christ the Lord has to be proclaimed anew in the face of all the lords of this world, and that the struggle is as radical today as in the days of the primitive church. But with regard to helping man and finding an answer to his anguish, his longing, his misfortune (in which, to be sure, he takes delight), it is not the

---

[1] This summary indication of the question will be taken up and demonstrated in a forthcoming volume on secular religions.

proclamation of the faith which is decisive, but the proclamation of hope.

If this seems to contradict what I was saying above about man's taste for disaster and his determination to shut himself up in it, consider the following. When the central message of the Church was the preaching of salvation, that proclamation answered indeed to the suffering of man, who did not want to be lost, but at the same time it ran counter to his attachment to all the consequences of sin. He is an inconsistent animal, this man, who delights in eroticism and murder, yet at the same time cannot live with the burden of death within him. The same situation holds true today. Man feeds on tragedy. He wants only a dark horizon, lit with the flames of great conflagrations, yet at the same time he is eating his heart out in anguish and dying for lack of hope. He cannot stand that there should be no history, but he can only conceive of history in terms of wars, pestilence, and famine.

That is where we now have to proclaim, bear witness to, and live hope, and perhaps become martyrs for it in the process of proclaiming the radical exclusiveness of the hope that is in Christ. Yet we still persist in pushing the message of *faith*, which no longer belongs to our times. How can I say a thing which can seem so scandalous to a Christian? I can say it because, as I have already observed, I believe that the proclamation of the Gospel is a response to man's real unhappiness, to his desperate search. Where man is not looking for anything, he cannot hear the Gospel. Where he is quite content, he has no need of a Gospel. "Those who are well have no need of a physician, but those who are sick"; "Woe to you that are rich, for you have received your consolation" (Luke 5:31; 6:24). That is the crucial message of the Beatitudes.

Now faith relates to truth. We were saying above that modern man has at his disposal a multitude of beliefs.

What is more, he scarcely bothers any more about truth, because, though very poor, he is a multimillionaire in the quantity of truth. He has going for him the truth of science and medicine, and that's all he needs. He has his fill of truths. What can the truth of the Gospel possibly have to add? That this is the very problem that generations of theologians have worked on is proved not only by the Gospel of John, which is a response to a generation disturbed precisely by the question of truth, but also by the continual discussion about intellect and faith, then by the later debate between science and faith. But that is not today's question.

Still, I'm aware of the objection: "These truths are not in the same category with revealed truth." Quite so, nevertheless they occupy the entire field of the conscience and of the intellect. There is really no room left for revealed truth. All we can say to these soakers-up of "scientific truth" is just what Jesus said to the rich. Hence that problem has a place in the battle of faith, in the struggle against the spiritual lie, to which we alluded above. The message that needs to be carried to this powerful man in the midst of his riches and his know-how is not the message of peace, mercy, and love. Never do we find in Scripture a one-sided approach on the part of God and Jesus Christ. The condemning God of the prophets is always and immediately the God who raises up, comforts, pities, strengthens, and promises. Jesus, who came bringing salvation by giving his life, is the same who also condemns the Pharisees, the Sadducees, the doctors of the law, and the rich. One approach does not go without the other.

If I could apply this to the word of the Church and of Christians today, I would say that in the domain of faith it can only be a matter of the prophetic word, of struggle and radicalism. It can never be a proposal to substitute the faith in Christ for what people today believe and know.

To the contrary, I take my stand here in the area of people's misery, weakness, bewilderment, false conscience, and schizophrenia. For that reason, it is the message of hope, also prophetic in another sense, which needs to be central.

But is there not another way? For nearly a half century the Church has tried the "message of love," and of course I know what every reader will think when he recalls the text, "But the greatest of these is love" (I Cor. 13:13). Under the present conditions, is not that what today's preaching should be, above everything else? As a matter of fact, I think the chance for its being the center of witness and preaching has gone by. So much foolishness has been said about this love. A lot of other things have been made out of it, so that every possible misconception is now abroad. When, today, people suppose that there is no conflict between sexual love, eroticism, and Christian love, and that we should simply combine them and restore to eroticism its "Christian value," when it is stated that violence against injustice, and revolution are valid expressions of love in our times, when the technological enterprise is likened to the love of Christ, these are aberrations, each one of which could be legitimate in a pacifying and assuaging discussion of love, and are always justified by the most honorable sentiments and intentions. They show, however, that either in her work or in her preaching the Church has completely missed her opportunity and that the proclamation of love has now fizzled out.

Only the deep need of man today drives me to say that the center of the Christian message now is hope. Furthermore, this is not an "exchange of values" which I am proposing! It is not because preaching about faith no longer answers any problems and no longer sinks in, nor because the preaching of love has failed and I am falling back on the third choice, on the line of retreat. I am not reaching for a consolation prize, nor making a desperate attempt to recover something which might possibly work. Certainly not. If I were convinced that before God, within the command of God, it were necessary to continue preaching conversion and revealed truth, no prior failure, no battle to be fought, would make me hesitate.

I am led to opt for hope by quite another route. If it is true that the world in which we live is a world of abandonment, if it is true that God is silent and that we are alone, then, as I shall try to demonstrate later, it is under these circumstances and at this moment that the preaching, the proclamation, the declaration, and the living of hope is urgent. It must be prior and central.[2]

---

[2] For once, I cannot agree with Neher when he puts hope and salvation in opposition to each other. He says, as I do, that hope belongs only to abandonment, when there is nothing to be hoped for. But he obviously has not grasped the meaning of salvation in Jesus Christ, which is neither a reward, nor a happy ending, nor a guarantee. When he insists that there is hope whenever one experiences a Good Friday not to be followed by an Easter, that is true. But for the dying Jesus there was no guarantee of Easter, and for every Christian abandoned in his night, the call to hope is both the certainty of salvation and the placing of it in the hands of a God who today is silent. The certainty of salvation and the resurrection gives no proprietary right, no installation, no naturalization. All remains grace. The antithesis, "either hope or salvation" (it is basic that the choice be made and that the thinking favor hope rather than salvation), leads Neher to some unfortunate conclusions: that everything now depends on man and his action, his freedom, his decisions; God is hiding in a fog, such that no one knows any more whether or not there is anything to be done. The end of Neher's work is disappointing, in this dissolution of the biblical God in favor of the maturity of technological man. It is what is bound to happen when everything is focused on hope as a work of man *in opposition to* salvation as a work of God on man's behalf. Moreover, Neher is comparing two magnitudes which are in no way commensurate. Hope is a human act in response to God (or does it originate in man?). Salvation is a work of God, which derives from his own prior initiative and his grace. To be consistent, one should oppose hope and *faith* to salvation, but I think Neher would have a hard time eliminating the faith of the Old Testament and in showing that it is opposed to hope!

TWO DIALECTICS

I am aware that this affirmation can provoke amazement, and the question: Why do you have to choose? Why make it a matter of alternatives? The Gospel message clearly is made up of "faith, hope, love." Why break up what obviously is one? If the Church has preached a lot about faith, do you have to substitute one message for another? Isn't it better simply to add? Perhaps it is true that the faith question has been too central, but surely you could now underline hope.

Let us be clear. Certainly, from the theological point of view, there should be no separation, no choice of alternatives. It is all there in the one whole. Theology has to take into account the content of revelation in the most complete, correct, and up-to-date manner possible. It is the source, the resource, and the controlling factor in all preaching. But theology does not speak to the person. The person's theological knowledge does not bring him to the point of Christian action, of changing whatever it might be in his life, of turning toward another light. What he knows theologically helps him to understand it after he has lived it, to restate it after he has experienced it, to check his steps after he has walked, nothing more than that.

Put it this way. What is decisive, deciding and existential is the proclamation, and this proclamation which strives to reach the heart and change a life, which has as its purpose to bring about a conversion, cannot focus on the totality and complexity of everything in the Bible. It cannot be a demonstration or a summation. It involves a choice, a course to be set, a stand to be taken. It presupposes a particular point of view. It is *a* word, unique, and not a jumble of words, not a chain of propositions. Luther chose salvation by faith, just as the primitive church chose the Lordship of Christ. What I am saying is that hope is the center of today's proclamation.

For centuries the Church has focused on the preaching of the faith, on the will to be converted to the content of her faith. That is no longer possible, both because man on the outside is no longer listening, and also because within the Church we are experiencing what I think is an insoluble confusion over what precisely is the content of the faith. It is no longer a debate between orthodox and heretic, as it used to be. It now touches the very heart of the problem. Whereas it used to be that heretics still affirmed a set of truths, what is now in doubt is the very possibility of a creed. If it is left to the Church, there no longer is anyone in the Church who can put a creed together, even a heretical one. If we shrink back in agony as soon as it becomes a question of getting down to brass tacks about the content of the faith, if we do not dare say, "This is the limit beyond which we can no longer speak of the Christian faith" for fear of becoming a Torquemada, if we then take the dangerous path of going back to the ancient creeds out of a false prudence, we find that, however trustworthy and admirable, the creeds can no longer be the core of preaching today. Immediately we have to recognize that we can no longer address ourselves to the proclamation of the faith, because it is plain for all to see that, as a Church, we no longer know what the content of the faith is, even if we still know what we believe as individuals.

In contrast to this, I know and am convinced that the Church still has her hope, which she continues to live by, and that she knows vaguely in whom that hope resides. It may merely be that she does not know how to express it and fails to realize that that is the center of her word today.

Since this hope, understood as a human reality, corresponds very well to what our society implies, let us go one step further. After having said that hope is exactly what modern man needs in his anguish, we then said that hope is the crucial lack in our Western society. We noted, in the third place, that it is the genuinely vital and unifying force in the Church today. That brings us to the conclusion that the characteristics of hope match the requirements of a message for this society.

But let us be careful about one thing. I do not mean that the Church should let her message be a mere tracing of society's possibilities and demands. She does not have to wait for some "prior consent" on the part of the social group, in terms of which she would construct her preaching. It is nevertheless true that the external conditions of communication have to be taken into account before the preaching can take place. Luther's preaching was, in spite of everything, in terms of the humanist rediscoveries. It was in their terms, and yet in tension with them and in conflict with them. There was the conflict of proclaimed truth, and yet agreement with respect to the rediscovery of the Greek and Hebrew texts, etc.

I think that, at the present time, no word can be heard unless it is responsive to two fundamental propensities of our "epistemological base." I am not referring to its being existential. Anything can be that. Nor am I referring to its being scientific. We have seen the foolishness of that pretension. The two propensities to which I refer are the dynamic element and the factual element. Modern man, launched in what he believes is progress, in what seems to him to be a very rapid development, can never accept a message which has the appearance of being in any degree static. Modern man is also turned toward the factual, the concrete. He has little faith in ideas, submerged though he is in ideologies. He is a materialist by fact, not by doctrine. He is attached to a real, which seems to him the only reality to be identified with truth. He has to have tangibles to hang on to. Now hope seems to me to answer precisely to that need.

The Christian faith, in the first place, with its definitions, its dependence on a given something which has been revealed once for all, looks hopelessly static to modern man. It is a "wearever sole for the person who is not going anywhere," as Michaux said. It relates to a past, to a beyond and to an eternity, all of which are motionless. Hope, to the contrary, is headed toward a future. Either it is dynamic or it does not exist. If it exists, it cannot be other than power in action. That is the only form in which it can *appear* and can be lived (and that is indeed why there was hardly any place for it in the institutional Church and in established Christianity!).

In the second place, the dialectic of faith is an intellectual one. It is impossible to prevent theological dialectic today from becoming ultimately an expression of the Hegelian dialectic. We shall try to show that the movement of hope is also dialectic, but that, in contrast to the dialectic of faith, it is inescapably a dialectic of the concrete. The reason is that hope cannot be systematized. It implies action in the tangible as a condition of its very existence. It presupposes a positive, genuine change, in proportion as the dialectic unfolds. Otherwise there is no hope. The fact of the matter is that Marx's thinking found such response among the proletariat because it was a bearer of hope, and Marx's dialectic is a dialectic of hope precisely because it relates to the tangible and the concrete. Thus the proclamation of hope seems to me today to correspond both to what is needed and to what is possible.

However, if I've succeeded in demonstrating that there is where the effective center of the Church's preaching lies today, that must not be interpreted as though hope should be separated from faith and the latter reduced to nothing. What we are talking about is proclamation and the center of attention for the Church and for Christians. We now know that hope does not follow automatically. We noted above that it is not a normal, direct, and expected consequence of faith, any more than is freedom, or purity, or self-discipline. One has to work at it. Of course, there is no hope where faith in Christ is dead, but a living faith can also be without hope, as we constantly observe among Christians today. Such a thing should not be? But neither should there be a Christian who is loveless, or a robber. It is just a fact.

What I mean, quite simply, is that the central question for man (and for the Christian) today is not whether to believe or not, but whether to hope or not. If someone says to me that a person obviously cannot hope in something he does not believe in, I reply that it is a matter of the dominant factor. In other words, for centuries hope has been defined in terms of faith (and rightly so). To believe in the Lord Jesus implied hoping for his return, the resurrection, etc. It is this relationship which now has to be turned around.[3]

---

[3] Hence I am distressed at this point to oppose emphatically M. Leuba (and St. Thomas Aquinas, whom he quotes). He writes: "It is not because he hopes that the Christian believes. It is only because he believes that he *can* hope"—*non enim potest spes habere de aeterna beatitudine nisi credatur possibile: quia impossibile non cadit sub spe* (*Summa Theol.* II, 2, quaest. 4, abt. T, ad 2). I think there is confusion here between the thing hoped for and hope. This view is certainly correct from the standpoint of the objectivity of theoretical theology, but not from the standpoint of the living relationship between the person and his Lord. Hope plainly has a power other than believing in the possibility of the Parousia. Therefore I do not say that the Parousia would add something to the truth already revealed (which is Leuba's argument in *Herméneutique et Eschatologie,* p. 116), but rather, that hope has a different dimension of experience from faith.

The question is not one of denying the faith and saying that it is of no importance. Rather, it is no longer the dominant factor. Today it is hope which is called upon to arouse, incite, and induce faith; and to define it, that is to say, to give it content. Now, in the Christian life of today, we are called upon to believe what we hope. We must awaken people to hope, for only there can faith take root.

THE SILENCE OF GOD

Man today has no hope, and we seem to be faced with the same problem with hope as with faith. If man does not believe, how can faith be born? If man does not hope, what can one say to him which will arouse hope within him? We need to ponder this absence of hope.

Material conditions alone do not explain it, though of course they have a bearing. We attempted, in the first chapter, to relate this death of hope to a certain number of phenomena in the modern world, but they are not causes (and perhaps we need not search for causes in the older sense of the term, in causalist doctrine). They are not even explanations. It is a matter of an interrelationship among certain basic facts of the age, for in the last analysis, if man in our time has lost hope, it is because God is silent (but once again, of course, we must not take that for a cause or an explanation!).

The silence of God means the absence of history. Nothing could be more vainly presumptuous, more ridiculously sad, more profoundly unimpressive, more crucially impertinent, than to say that "man makes his history." Man heaps up nonsense and absurd action. He strings pearls, in other words events, without order or standard. Man reveals himself in his inconsistencies and in his conformities. With his blind and exuberant activism he certainly constructs nothing, especially not history. He creates successive empires and conquers the moon. He kills, then dies. Caught in a Brownian movement, he agitates furiously. He attributes great importance to what he's about to do and to live, only to discover later on that it was worthless.

Think of the monuments to the dead of 1914, or of the 1944 purge. What is the significance of all that? Exactly nothing. Yet, at the time, one thought one was acting for what was right and true, for freedom and history. Nor is it the capitalist regime which "causes history to jump the track." One would have to be childish, superficial, and blind to believe that. It goes just a bit deeper! Only a completely abstract philosopher could believe in a progressive incarnation of The Idea, in liberation through transition to a classless society, and that such a thing *is* history. One would have steadfastly to turn his back on the content of lives, of societies, of activities, of events, of politics, on their content and on their reality, to believe that it makes any sense, and that history is made in this way by a piling up of human results.

As long as there is no fixed reference point outside this flow, outside this sequence, there is no history. As long as there is no intervention of a factor which is radically other, there can never be anything but combinations of like with like, lacking any possibility of the attribution or the discovery of meaning. Imagine a perfect system of navigation with maps, sextant and compass, but no magnetic pole. Imagine algebra with no signs, only a succession of letters and numbers. No equation would be possible, no deduction, no solution, no precision. The same is true for the events and the works and the actions with which man pretends, like *Miles Gloriosus* or Matamoros, to be making history. Left to itself, such a history is "a tale told by an idiot." It takes the coming of another intelligence, another wisdom, to keep folly and idiocy from being dominating mistresses.

However, the other which comes must really be *other*, if we are not to keep returning endlessly to the same circus. Here is where the Word of God becomes creative of history. Out of these same events, out of these same actions, it extracts a history endowed with orientation and meaning. To be sure, it is still the history of people. It is not a holy, or a different, or an independent history. But because it comes to light in this or that manner, it reveals at the same time that nothing which was done had been done in vain, that what lacks sense has a hidden sense nevertheless.

But have I not put forward two contradictory propositions? On the one hand, it is due to the Word of God that there is a history. On the other hand, it is the Word of God which reveals that this history has a meaning. So, according to the second statement, there is a history which exists by itself, and man merely lacks the key. If the Word of God is what provides this key, it cannot at the same time be the creator of the history, since the latter existed beforehand. However, there really is no contradiction, because history *is* the hidden meaning of events. There only is history where there is an awareness which discerns it and lives it.

That is why, to take the classic metaphor, when a glacier moves, forms, has its beginning and end, distorts, cracks open, splits off, and fills in again, there is no history. Man's string of feverish activities, the glorification of his epics of war, the creative accumulation of his work—all that is not history if there is no living consciousness of it as history. But such a consciousness cannot exist unless it is able, at the same time, to receive the instruments to be read and the point to be aimed at. Buddhism is entirely consistent here: no God, no history, only illusion, totally vain and meaningless activity, from which it is proper to disengage.

Marx, on the other hand, is grossly mistaken when he claims to enclose man in his dialectic which includes meaning. That only holds true to the extent to which Marx had been imbued with the Christian sense of history, and was filled with the Word of God to the marrow of his bones. He had renounced it, yet he knew its prophets so well. His system had an appearance of validity in a society which was still living by the faith of Christ. That is all gone now, and the thinking of Marx is destined to disappear with the death of God. I say, his *thinking*. Its drive will continue, with its tactics and battles, but having lost its justification, foundation, and validity, it now becomes a sum of idiotic acts which founder in the opposite of what they were designed to achieve.

Only the Word of God throws light, for the consciousness of man, on what he is in process of experiencing, and so enables him to perceive that there is in fact a history. The Word at that moment is the creator of history. When God is silent, absolute darkness reigns. We can agitate all we want, but no future opens before us, for the simple reason that in a truly dark night there is no front or back or right or left. The spatial orientation no longer relates to the temporal. I take a step without knowing exactly whether, in this *after*, I have really gone *ahead*. I may very well have stepped back, and the time sequence only misleads me all the more.

God is silent. The consciousness of history is extinguished. History is canceled. Tremendous efforts, ingenious ideas, cries of desperation get nowhere. The age of abandonment is an age of futility. From now on, man knows only one thing: whatever isn't written in the stars or revealed by a fortune-teller is futile. What is the use? He is ready once again to submit to fate, because "that" seems to be consistent.

God's silence is evidenced also by the language crisis. Here we find the same problem as with history. We see that man fidgets, reflects, talks, philosophizes, and constructs all around the word "language," as he does around the word "history," precisely because there is no discerned history or common language. Discourse on history replaces awareness of history. The scientific analysis of language replaces communication.

One analyzes in great detail and with increasing depth the system of signs, for the reason that they no longer mean anything, and man is going all out to restore value to a dead instrument. All he can do is substitute a system for sense. But after he has completely elucidated the sign, that which signifies, the thing signified, the phonemes, the morphemes, the language, the speech, the word, the codes, the metalanguage and the referentials, after he has demonstrated the possibilities and dismantled the system, nothing is any better transmitted by the language than before. No communication is established.

Man wants only to know whether his language carried true information to the other person. If it was an authentic communication, that was because it came from an ultimate referential, from a metalanguage which was something genuinely beyond, and which was the Word of God. God speaks, and man becomes capable of speech. Without the initial dialogue, without this prior confrontation, this evocation, this provocation, the meanings put together by man remain confusion, a poor go-between, because they have no deep support, and have become mere conventions.

The conventionalist theory of language is certainly true when language is cut off from its nourishing root, and from the sense which comes to it from an initiative not included in the language itself. If there is no nourishing earth, the most beautiful tree can only wither away. One can perform an exact analysis of its structure, its organization, its different parts, the working of each component —one can examine the function of the chlorophyll and the relation between the sap and the fiber, but all that is dead if it is not nourished by the presence of the compost from which the roots extract what the tree needs. The same is true of language. It is not its structure which allows it to be what it is meant to be. The study of the structure only shows how it works. It can never make it function so as to become the means of communication and, at its best, the bearer of truth.

To cut language off from the possibility of lying and truth telling is to prohibit all communication. But before the lie and the truth can become possibilities, there must obviously be a reference to something other than the language system. There must also be a reference to something other than the person who is speaking. To freeze the language into codes and structures is precisely to suppose that there is not any something else which could intervene. To seek to base speech within itself and on itself is to ratify the solitude which comes when God is silent. By the same token, it is to accept the fact that henceforth man is to talk indefinitely in order to say nothing.

Of course I don't mean by that, that human language is fated to talk only about God and to be a preaching instrument! That would be absurd. Neither do I mean that speech is based on a word of God discerned and recognized as such. What I am saying is that the most ordinary speech, the most everyday, political, scientific, poetic, amorous, and imaginative speech, only contains something, only conveys something, only creates and communicates, to the extent to which it rests on a deeper reality, on a more basic relationship among persons, thanks to which factors it is able to fulfill those functions.

That reality, that relationship, is the Word of God addressed to man. All human languages derive their potential from the degree to which man is summoned by God, to the extent to which the Word of God reverberates, whether man knows it or not. It is in this dialogue, conscious or unconscious, in this summons, whether open or concealed, in this relationship, individual or collective, in this communication, direct or mediated, that man's speech acquires meaning. All else is superstructure.

Sometimes God speaks and man challenges that speech. "Why do you not *understand what I say?*" asked Jesus of the Jews. "It is because you *cannot* bear to hear my *word*. You are of your father the devil" (John 8:43–44). The passage is wonderfully enlightening. The Jews claim to have Abraham for their father, and hence to have no need for a word from outside. They are thoroughgoing structuralists! They have set up a system which is closed, self-explanatory, and self-sufficient. Their mechanism of communication operates within this network. For, to be sure, Jesus is not here attacking the Jews alone, nor as Jews, but the attitude they represent.

They have forged their language on the basis of the fatherhood of Abraham. They think to say something, while excluding anything which might intervene from another source, and so they really are not saying anything. They bring forth an abundant prolixity. When the

Word of God comes to announce truth and freedom, they do not accept it because they have grounded their speech within itself. That is why they cannot even understand the language which is the bearer of the Word of God, the language of Jesus. You do not even understand what I say (the most direct and simple things) because you *cannot* hear my word. That hearing is rendered impossible by the existence of a language put together as a sufficient entity and closed in on itself.

This language of yours witnesses to an altogether different reality, and the reason is that you have the devil for your father—not the wicked one, certainly, but the *diabolos*, the divider. To believe in his descent from Abraham, that is to say, to believe in an interhuman system of communication which is self-sufficient and coherently structured, is really to be an agent of noncommunication, a witness to the division among men and to the impossibility of mutual understanding. When the relation with the Word of God is cut off, then communication among people becomes misconstruction and misunderstanding. When man rejects this Word of God, when he cuts the communication, then God, in turn, is silent, and the language crisis becomes evidence of the abandonment.

But a final question then arises. If God is silent, what are we to do? If we call ourselves Christian, what is there left for us to say? Is there not a chance that we will be preaching what we know in advance is not the Word of God (if God is silent) but, at the most, an invalid word about God? Does not preaching die on our lips when we become aware that we are in an age of abandonment? Are we not speaking solely because we are possessed with the hope that perhaps this human word may become Word of God?—that, whenever he sees fit, the Holy Spirit can transform the most hackneyed prayer, the most fruitless testimony, into an explosive manifestation of power and truth? Are we not mute and sterile if we are convinced ahead of time that there is no further Word of God in our time? And doesn't that contradict what I was saying above, that the present mission of the Church is to preach hope?

If that is what we think, it is because we have not yet perceived what hope really is. It is true that if we are in the age of abandonment, then our preaching on all other aspects of the revelation is empty, obsolete, and outworn. In an age when God is silent, no other possibility remains but the proclamation of freedom and the proclamation of hope. But to understand that, we must push further ahead into the world of abandonment, and must know, before the God-in-hiding, what our inauthenticity is today.

4

The Diagnostic Error
about God

THE DEATH OF GOD

God is dead.[4] Such is the diagnosis. False. Yet it is based
on true symptoms wrongly interpreted. God is supposedly
dead because man *cannot* any longer believe in him, or
just plain does not *believe* in him any longer. The vocable

---

[4] The death of God is often linked with the silence of God, but a number
of distinctions are called for here. In the first place, we obviously must
not confuse the problem of the silence of God, which is existential and
historical, with the metaphysical concept of silence answering to the
question about God, a silence required by God's transcendence. From
this latter point of view, the disappearance of the God problem would
represent the highest form of religiousness. "Would not the place of manifestation of the absolute be the absolute of silence?" This was one of
the ideals of Buddha, and it is taken up again by modern Christian
theologians. But it can be said that this concept, this explanation, has
nothing to do with abandonment. It is a metaphysical question, having
to do with a God in general, with nature, or the essence of God, which
can scarcely excite us. It can hardly plunge man into anguish and

"God" is completely empty and refers to nothing, because language is reduced to its structure. We must, of course, distinguish between different viewpoints. On the one hand, there are those for whom it is a matter of mental imagery. On the other hand, there are those for whom it is a question of fact.

For the former, modern man can no longer believe in God, because he has become rational and scientific. He has lost the mentality of myth, which alone can conceive of faith in a God such as the God of the Bible. Looking at it from the opposite direction, "When God, through demythologizing, loses cultural contact with the faithful, he is bound, little by little, to disappear from the religious consciousness of his worshipers. A God who can no longer

---

tragedy. That silent God has never spoken, has never acted, has never come near to man, has never been made flesh. Therefore one can engage in this discussion with serenity—but it is not the God of Jesus Christ, and hence it scarcely concerns us.

However, it is the God of Jesus Christ whom Gerhard Ebeling, following Dietrich Bonhoeffer, is talking about when he says (*Widerstand und Ergebung,* 1955), "In coming of age, we are led to recognize the truth of our situation before God. God makes us know that we must live as men who have come to the point of getting along in a life without God. The God who is with us is the God who leaves us (Mark 13:34). The God who lets us live without the working-hypothesis God is the God before whom we must constantly stand, to live without God, before and with God." We must challenge a whole set of confusions in this interpretation. On the one hand, man comes of age (we are not here denying that fact). He comes of age by his knowledge, his intelligence, his technology, and that is what brings him to getting along without God. But that is now expressed as a decision by God—"*God* makes us know that we must live, etc." This conquest by man, this action by man, now becomes the result of a decision by God. How interesting, in view of the fact that the whole passage, and the entire thought as well, actually gives the initiative to man. Besides, the concept is a purely intellectual one, that of the "hypothesis of God." Science lets us do without him. And finally, this interpretation, which contradicts, among other things, the

be called upon is still within the reach of the mystic but, for the ordinary mortal, demythologization sooner or later means the death of God." That is the best one can say. God is nothing, a fabrication of the mythical religious consciousness. He disappears totally with the myths to which he gave expression.

For others (Gabriel Vahanian), we find that modern man no longer believes in the Christian God. Now, to the extent to which this God of Jesus Christ has chosen man as his "condition," in which condition he reveals himself and does not exist except in revealing himself, in which condition he is love and does not exist except in being loved—when these possibilities of relationship disappear it can be said that the God revealed in Jesus Christ no longer exists. Such is the frequent, current diagnosis.

But it should be noted that these theologies are directly dependent on the sociological context, of which they are both the direct and the indirect expression. So true is this that, to the degree in which they exhibit a society where

---

entire Old Testament, necessarily leans in the direction of saying to us that the prior revelation is in error, or else it was conceded by God because man in those days was far inferior to man today, which is open to dispute, to say the least. In other words, we are not dealing with a decision on the part of God, who in the mystery of what he is becomes silent and turns away. What we have here is a positive interpretation of the situation which is consoling and edifying. What luck! Now we can do what we want, because God has recognized that we are grown up.

But there is yet another, equally fundamental criticism of this doctrine, namely, that again the mania of the theologians has explained the *why* of God's decision. Formerly, one would calmly have explained that God turns away *because* we are sinners and bad. But this interpretation has been rejected. Today we are optimists. God has abandoned us *because we have grown up*. It is simply forgotten that one would think it theologically absurd to assign motives, causes, and reasons to a decision of God's! It is not very responsible. It ends in beautiful formulas, but it fails to account for modern man's situation and for revelation.

technological absurdity reigns, they can be said to be theologies of the absurd, even absurd theologies, which they are in fact.[5] They cannot truly present themselves as theologies, for, by the fact of their relation to the society, they really constitute an ideology. Since they take their rationale, their criteria of judgment, their root, and their model from a sociological observation (namely, that man's mentality has changed as a result of technological progress), and no longer take a fact of revelation as their base, they have no validity as theology.

They, rather, are ideologies in the full meaning of the word, since they give expression to, justify and legitimate the "constitution" of modern man. It is this constitution which, in the eyes of their creators, lays down the law about what can be said in theology. But this embraced determinism has no value other than to integrate the discourse into the world's sociocultural context. The discourse does not relate at all to God because, by prior assumption, no discourse dictated by a psychological structure or by a sociological context has to do with God as such. It relates, in fact, to a social entity, with a view to validating it and helping it arrive at a statement about itself, which is exactly the role of ideology. The conclusion drawn by these authors from their estimate of the constitution of modern man is that it is the normal constitution. Hence, that is the way it had always been, and consequently God himself has always been an ideology. But this judgment of normalcy is never proved. In any event, we get a better view of the role and the place of these ideologies of the death of God, and how it can never be other than a case of a theology of the absurd.

Nevertheless, these "theologies" also contain a profound

---

[5] When they present themselves as theologies, a mistake which Vahanian does not make.

truth, for it is indeed a fact that man can kill God. It is indeed a fact that, in one way or another, man (in being current) can destroy God in his becoming current, since God, out of love, has made himself the one who puts himself not only on man's level but also at man's disposition. God has given himself over. Man can actually treat Almighty God, creator of heaven and earth, as he has already treated the Son, for it was the totality of God who was in the Son. God the Father is not sheltered from the insults and outrages to which Christ was subjected (all the prophets say that). He does not take shelter from the death received in his Christ. But it is not the sociological notion which disappears with the presupposition that sociological notions are all that there are. It is the living God who makes himself such that man can become capable of killing God. Man's unbelief, in effect, brings it about that God does not exist, because he who is love wills only to exist in, by, and for the love of another.

But it is easy to slip, as follows: in Jesus, God chooses the only path of his humiliation and abasement. He chooses impotence. He binds himself and paralyzes himself, in such a way that there can be nothing more, and nothing other, than an impotent God, "pinned." "And if he chooses impotence, that is in order to give man freedom, the power of choice, the power of worldly aggrandizement." [6] "The being of Christ, who epitomizes the meaning of the presence of God in the world, and who sums himself up in the suffering of the defeat of God considered as omnipotent, signifies his impotence in this way." By this nice bit of sleight-of-hand we are back with the porcelain God of the classic theologians. Once liquidated, the

---

[6] The Catholic theologian I. Mancini, in his *Analyse du language théologique* (1969).

Jesus-Christ-God business is stored away in a corner of the attic. It is understood once for all that he is powerless (a good thing for him, because that is the way he wanted it!). Hence, he no longer has to get involved in our business. All he has to do is leave us alone.

This is a new ruse to justify the titanic political and technological undertaking of man, to whom everything henceforth is permissible. The theologian steps in here to justify Mikhail Bakunin, when he said, "If God loves man as the Christians say he does, all he has to do to let man go free is to kill himself." In this sensible interpretation, to be sure, the entire Old Testament and the Apocalypse are left to one side. Also left to one side is the revelation on the subject of the power of man, in the cases of Cain, Tubal Cain, Enoch, Babel, etc. What we have here is a simplifying monism which, in its turn, also excludes hope.

For in truth there is nothing to be hoped for from this institutionalized impotence. There is nothing to look forward to from this fallen monarch, bound and ridiculed, who is left without resource and without any power of decision. If we have a hope, it refers us to ourselves, to ourselves as this hyperactive and totally hopeless man. In the lack of awareness on the part of the philosophers and theologians, this new crucifixion of Christ necessarily evokes once again, "they know not what they do." With their excellent sentiments and their good will to liberate man, they are ignorant of the harm they are doing to man, and of the fact that, by their folly, they are drowning and stifling him all the more, to the point of ultimate desperation. In this theology, God disappears in his impotence so that man can give free rein to his own power. As always, it is the problem of the balance of power.

However, if that is the case, it is nevertheless by God's

sovereign decision. God does not play a passive role in this business. He does not just let himself be eliminated. He is an active sovereign, the one who has made the decision, who has taken the risk and the gamble on the subject of his relations with man. "No one takes [my life] from me, but I lay it down of my own accord" (John 10:18). Condemned and dying, Jesus is still sovereign.

It is the same with God. If he has chosen (and he alone made the choice) the path of self-emptying, the risk is all his, but the choice is a sovereign choice. If he chose love as his sole expression, to all practical purposes he effaces himself whenever there is no love to receive his own, whenever no word of love goes out to meet him. We are completely outside the realm of changing psycho-sociological representations. If God, who has chosen to be totally and uniquely love, is no longer loved, if his love is rejected, then indeed nothing of God is any longer perceptible to us. At that moment God, in fact, is no longer anything.

But it is for us that he is no longer anything. Strictly speaking, we can say nothing about the God incognito, about the God who could have been able, who would have been able, who was able not to reveal himself except in this manner, all the while remaining completely autonomous. Concerning this autonomy of God, concerning this hidden face of God, we can say nothing, even whether there is such a thing. It is all the more true, to be sure, that we cannot say he is dead!

Still, there is one more step we can take. We were saying that God no longer is anything. As a matter of fact, it would be better to say that, on behalf of the practicing unbeliever, the systematic atheist, the doctrinal or the practicing materialist, the antitheist, God (who, as the Old Testament shows, could in his sovereignty crush this nonexistent gainsayer), makes himself nothing in order always to remain at man's level. But when God makes himself nothing, it is still for the sake of unbelieving man. He remains sovereign in so doing. In that case we have to be on our guard, for God is both the weak adversary who accepts the combat without putting up a fight and also the one who is capable at any time of revealing himself as possessed of infinite power. This nothing, which he has agreed to be, can become the kind of consuming nothingness which engulfs and kills whoever has provoked him.

It is not impossible that we are witnessing phenomena of this kind in the psychological realm, and that Nietzsche's fate awaits us all. We must take care, however, not to interpret that as a judgment pronounced by God, as a condemnation or a revenge. The allusion is merely to the fact that God doesn't cease to be the Almighty when he submits to being nothing. This nothing becomes a crushing power in which man loses himself never to find his way again. The human challenge thrown at God can never be the sort of objective, scientific, very knowledgeable, and very infantile contact represented by our modern theologians of the death of God (Vahanian excepted, of course, for he is precisely not a theologian of the death of God!).

There is also another aspect of this investigation, namely, that which has to do with the name, or the word, "God." Current language studies make it possible to say that, in the end, one is not saying anything when he pronounces the word "God." Words either are mere artificial labels or they only take on meaning from the system in which they are used, and there are still other scientific analyses. The matter seems settled. Linguistics obliges us to eliminate the word "God," because it has no content other than mental habits of the past. All right, but then I would like to call attention to two aspects of this word in the Old Testament.

For one thing, it is not a word, but a name, as Bonhoeffer observed. It is common knowledge that whenever God reveals his name it is in a way which either is untranslatable or unpronounceable. It might mean, "I am who I am," "I am he who is," "I am who I will be," "I will do what I will do" (Harvey Cox's translation), "I am going to come as he who is about to come" (Kerenyi's translation), or "I am there" (Buber's translation), etc. Or it can be unpronounceable as YHWH.

For another thing, there is the famous prohibition, also known to everyone, against pronouncing the name of God "in vain." The traditional interpretations of these passages concerning the name of God are diverse. Some consider it a special case of the general category of taboo. It would be an application of the "sacred of respect." Thus, when one speaks of God, it is not a matter of saying something (which would have content), but only of pronouncing a name. The emission of the corresponding sound either is impossible or forbidden. "This is strictly the language taboo. A certain word must not pass the lips. It is eliminated from the repertoire of the language, dropped from usage, treated as something which should no longer exist. The paradox of such a taboo is that the name still has to exist as a thing forbidden." (Benveniste)

There is another theory to explain the phenomenon, as follows: among many "primitive" peoples, and the ancient Hebrews in particular, the name (*dabar*) has a power. This is only a special case of the attribution of power to the Word. The *dabar* is never a sound, but rather an active intervention. When the *dabar* designates a person, it implies the whole person. The name of a being is that being, or rather, it is the specific property and the historic destiny of that being. This is so well known that there is no need to develop it here. The consequence is that whoever knows the secret name of God has at his disposition God himself, who is no exception to this general rule about the name. Anyone able to pronounce this name could act upon God and could irrevocably constrain God to act (this is magic, and the Kabala, in fact, made use of the power of words). Hence God refuses to release his name, or else he releases an unpronounceable name, in order to avoid giving himself over. Those are the two most current explanations of the phenomenon, and they are tied together.

They do not seem to me to be fully explanatory, or rather they are quite true and correct, to be sure, on their own level of explanation. But they fail to account for that little phrase in the text of Exodus 20 translated by "in vain." "To misuse it," is the translation in the Jerusalem Bible. The Vulgate has, *"in vanum et frustra"* (Hebrew, *lechaem*). Perhaps the bulk of the Old Testament passages on the subject of God would, taken together, permit us to go further and deeper. It seems to me that in all of God's replies to those who ask his name there is a great condescension as well as a kind of impossibility. He is not only a God who wants to hide, who conceals himself behind a name or a formula, who refuses to give himself over, or, as Neher puts it, who plays a game. He is also a God whom nothing can express, as in the vision of Elijah. What finally expresses God is neither the thunder nor the lightning nor the wind. It is the *qol demama daqqa*, "the fading murmur of silence" (Chouraqui's translation), or "the subtle voice of silence" (Neher's translation) (I Kings 19:12). This is God's reserve, a presence grasped only in absence, a revelation perceptible only incognito. Perhaps, in view of this, we should let the context of the entire Old Testament relating to God's action and the mode of his presence throw light on "the unpronounceable name" and on the prohibition against pronouncing it in vain.

Thus it becomes obvious that the name is in fact an empty, arbitrary sound, having no reference to any meaning (there's no acceptable etymology for YHWH). Precisely because it is empty and arbitrary, it cannot designate what is definitely "replete with content and not arbitrary," namely, he who is revealed in the history of the chosen people. But conversely, just as no formula can be adequate, no formula can be *definitely* replete with content and not arbitrary (since human speech is composed of mutual references, writings, and arbitrary decisions), just so, only the definitely empty and arbitrary sound can point to God. If God is he who appoints the history of Israel, then no constructed, legitimate, and meaningful speech can take him into account. Thus we can say that, biblically speaking, the word "God" can really only be theoretical, conventional and without content, for the reason that it lacks any possible referent.

Therefore no conclusion is to be drawn from the emptiness of the *word* "God," except precisely that it cannot be anything other than empty if God is God. But the *name* is the expression of the decision of *God* who reveals it. It is replete with meaning only by this decision. That is what explains the prohibition against pronouncing it in vain. This is not a reflection of God's fear of being possessed. It is, rather, a prohibition against pronouncing it other than as an empty word which points to a full absolute. It does so as a word which is necessarily false when we reduce it to the status of word, for every attempt to assure ourselves of God is false. We must precisely not give a meaning, nor a content, nor a value as such, to this word. But, conversely, neither should we conclude from the emptiness of this word the emptiness of the name, and the nonexistence of that to which it is supposed to point.[7]

In other words, by this last hypothesis it is the theologians of the death of God who pronounce this word in vain, in the void, by likening the emptiness of the word to the emptiness of God. Thus the Hebrew formula is a true reply both to the theology of the death of God and to linguistic analysis. It supplies a prior answer to this type of rejection and challenge of God (which is quite natural and spontaneous to the human heart).

I am aware of the objection that in reasoning thus I am still making use of the cultural assumption that God exists, and of a concept of God taken from the surrounding culture. The reply is too easy! Those who argue otherwise, and set up the whole theology of the death of God, make use of the no less cultural supposition that God does not exist, and of a refutation of God taken likewise from the surrounding culture[8] (not of a scientific and secular kind, but antitheistic and religious, with gods who do not disclose themselves as gods within the traditional metaphysical concepts). I fail to see by what criterion this second surrounding culture is supposed to be superior to the preceding one, and why the cultural definition of the nonexistence of God should be superior to the cultural definition of the existence of God.

[7] This is reinforced by the fact that, according to the interpretation of the Talmud, the Hebrew language has no common name, no generic word, no thematic word for God. It has only proper names. Thus there is no notion of God, no word in Hebrew for saying "God." There is only a proper name for the purpose of calling upon or invoking, never for the purpose of dissertation. There is not a something which I could talk about by designating it. There is he who delivers to me a name pronounceable only in dialogue and with a view to mutual commitment.

[8] Only Vahanian has seen the problem and stated it correctly.

For my part, I am merely trying to read the Old Testament texts over and beyond cultural definitions. They tell me a number of things which clearly do not derive from any known culture, and especially not from the Middle Eastern cultures surrounding Israel. There is an irreducible kernel there. Moreover, those who strive above all else for the elimination of God know this very well. Their chief enemy is this Old Testament. It has to be reduced to dust, dismembered and emptied of all content, so that they can finally discard the *membra disjecta* in oblivion. It is the constant temptation of rationalistic skepticism.

THE ABSENCE OF GOD

With that said, we now come face to face with the heart of the problem. The theology of the death of God springs from a crisis of faith, which is itself registered in the socio-scientific trend, and from a language crisis. But those crises are either uninteresting or secondary for modern man, for, as I have tried to show, the fundamental crisis is that of hope. If from the crisis of faith one could deduce the death of God, the death of hope brings us to an altogether different reality: that of the silence of God. Man does not lose hope because God no longer exists. The theologians have claimed to the contrary that God's nonexistence corresponds to man's exaltation, to the opening up of immense possibilities which had been blocked by he who was called the Vampire of man, or the Great Corpse. Thus the death of God should engender hope in man. Yet here is man without hope, man who is alive without living.

If the factual reality of modern man is this death of hope, the problem for theology is not the death of God but the silence of God. It is no longer: God is dead because man no longer believes in him; but rather: man is without hope because God is silent. Such is the basic spiritual reality of this age. God is turned away. God is absent. God is silent.

But immediately we have to distinguish this situation of "crisis" from that which Tillich, for example, understands when he speaks of God as absent. For him there is still a positive value:

What is the cause of His absence? We may answer—our resistance, our indifference, our lack of seriousness, our honest or dishonest questioning, our genuine or cynical doubt. All these answers have some truth, but they are not final. The final answer to the question as to who makes God absent is God himself!

It is the work of the Spirit that removes God from our sight, not only for some men, but sometimes for many in a particular period. We live in an era in which the God we know is the absent God. But in knowing God as the absent God, we *know* of Him; we feel His absence as the empty space that is left by something or someone that once belonged to us and has now vanished from our view. God is always infinitely near and infinitely far. We are fully aware of Him only if we experience both of these aspects. But sometimes, when our awareness of Him has become shallow, habitual—not warm and not cold —when He has become too familiar to be exciting, too near to be felt in His infinite distance, then He becomes the absent God. The Spirit has not ceased to be present. The Spiritual Presence can never end. But the Spirit of God hides God from our sight. No resistance against the Spirit, no indifference, no doubt can drive the Spirit away. But the Spirit that always remains present to us can hide itself, and this means that it can hide God. Then the Spirit shows us nothing except the absent God, and the empty space within us which is *His* space. The Spirit has shown to our time and to innumerable people in our time the absent God and the empty space that cries in us to be filled by Him. And then the absent one may return and take the space that belongs to Him, and the Spiritual Presence may break again into our consciousness, awakening us to recognize what we are, shaking and transforming us. This may happen like the coming of a storm, the storm of the Spirit, stirring up the stagnant air of our spiritual life. The storm will then recede; a new stagnancy may take place; and the awareness of the present God may be replaced by the awareness of the empty space within us. Life in the Spirit is ebb and flow—and this means—whether we experience the present or the absent God, it is the work of the Spirit.[9]

This beautiful page of Tillich's confronts us with the fact, and yet it is marked with the serenity which results from God's presence. He speaks of this absence as though it were in reality a presence, as though it were part of a "normal" movement, as though the going and coming of God were almost in the same category with the appearance and disappearance of the sun. When he says that the absence of God is still evidence of the presence of the Spirit, I say, Yes, of course, from the theological point of view, but I'm afraid that this is too facile a consolation, enabling us to make light of the situation and to feel that, after all, "We shouldn't take it too seriously."

In that case we are missing the depth of this spiritual reality of the absence and the silence of God, and we are incapable of responding to the question which God is putting to us by the very fact of his decision to be absent. Were we to say, "He is silent because . . . ," or "He is silent as the sovereign who decides arbitrarily what he wants," in both instances we miss the meaning, the truth and the depth of this turning away. We become incapable of understanding that there is a point, a purpose on God's part, to which we can be sensitive only if we are shocked back into the ultimate severity of the situation.

[9] Tillich, *The Eternal Now* (New York: Scribners, 1963), pp. 87–89.

It is certainly good to know, as a matter of dogma, that the Spirit is always there, and that it is he who hides God from us. It is good to know that this is a sign that God still loves us. But the resulting tranquility, the attitude of "Let us wait till it is over," is the very opposite of what God is urging us to hear and understand. We have here an explanation which, when transposed into movement and spread out through time, is in the same category with the dialectical definition of God as hidden and revealed at the same time. He is hidden in revealing himself and is revealed in his hiding.

That is true, profoundly true, but too assured, too "taken for granted," too certain of the tomorrows. The Aztecs were horribly afraid that the setting sun would not rise the next day, so they sacrificed victims each evening to call back the God who was disappearing. We know now that there is a natural cyclical movement. But the sun is not God. In the silence and absence of God we are truly orphans. We are forced to acknowledge that God might really withdraw without having any reason to return to us. That is why this silence of God, when it is really taken seriously, brings with it the loss of natural hope. What hold might we have on this God who turns his back? How can he hear our prayers, falling silent as he does? How can we get God back? His absence has no "because." How might we give his return an "in-order-to"?

If God is not a theological concept, if he is not enclosed in definitions, if he is not a metaphysical stopgap, if he is not the Great Clockmaker, immutable and impassive, if he is not an Abstraction, always identical to itself, but is he who enters into history with and for man, is he who constantly reshapes his action, and even his being, according to the work and the passion of man, is he who is the Living One, and the only truly Living One, then this silence, this absence are acts of God's decision, but they are impossible to accept, to tolerate, and to live.

THE IMPOSSIBLE POSSIBILITY

The Old Testament makes clear the radical fear which the Jews had of this eventuality. "Turn not away," such is the supreme and ultimate prayer. One can stand everything from God except that he should turn his back. God's wrath, the thundering of the prophets, the threat of condemnation—those are still God speaking. Even in his most exacting strictness, even in his terrible greatness, he is still the God who chose, loved, and bore Israel. He is still the God of the promise, who is faithful and will not go back on his promise. Behind the wrath of God the Jew sees the promise of salvation. Behind the terrifying face, he sees the countenance of love. Through the words of condemnation, he hears those of the promise. God is not the one who rejects and condemns. No matter how harsh his decision, it always remains within the framework of his love.

Thus, as long as the relationship with God exists, all is retrieved. But if God turns away, all is lost. How live, if the Living One is no longer there? How remind God of his promise if he is absent? What meaning can life have if there is neither Origin nor Other? Throughout the entire length of the Old Testament this cry resounds: "Turn not away"; "Cast me not away from thy presence." It is a terrifying moment. It is not a consoling testimonial of the presence of God, nor a necessary phase of the dialectical movement. In Psalm 74 we read:

O God, why dost thou cast us off for ever?
Why does thy anger smoke against the sheep of thy pasture?
Remember thy congregation, which thou hast gotten of old,

which thou hast redeemed to be the tribe of thy heritage!
Remember Mount Zion, where thou hast dwelt.
Direct thy steps to the perpetual ruins;
The enemy has destroyed everything in the sanctuary!
Thy foes have roared in the midst of thy holy place;
they set up their own signs for signs. . . .
We do not see our signs;
there no longer is any prophet,
and there is none among us who knows how long.
How long, O God, is the foe to scoff?
Is the enemy to revile thy name for ever?
Why dost thou hold back thy hand? . . .
Arise, O God, plead thy cause;
remember how the impious scoff at thee all the day!

The important thing, the tragic thing, is not that the enemy is present and conquering. It is not the political or the economic misfortune of the people. It is, rather, that these catastrophes cannot even be attributed to God's wrath. They are attributed to his abandonment. God has turned away. There is no longer a word of God, no longer a prophet. There are no more "*signs* of God." The enemy has set up *his own signs*, and that specifically is abandonment. There is no tragedy other than this substitution of the sign of man for the sign of God. This is the scoffing of the foe, properly so called, that God should be silent. It is also the reign of folly and the cause of dismay (Ps. 30: 8), of chaos (Ps. 104:29) and of death (Ps. 143:7). The entire Old Testament reverberates with this fear: God might turn away.[10]

---

[10] Here I take the liberty of disagreeing with Neher (*L'exil de la parole*) when he interprets this attitude as having to do only with the "hidden face,". and as a psychological reaction of panic. I think we have to distinguish between the hidden face of God who reveals himself, which is a theological problem, from the abandonment by God who is silent, in a way which seems final, and which strikes, not at psychological man, but at existential man. All is lost if . . .

Israel has actually had this experience. It has lived through the silence of God, as at the end of the period of the Judges. On the one hand, we are told that the Word of the Lord was rare in those days (I Sam. 3:1), and on the other hand, we are told that man acted according to his own will, in complete independence, without regard to the will of God (Judg. 21:25). The two facts are certainly connected. "Every man did what was right in his own eyes," because he scorned the Word of God, and because there was no word from God. God was silent because man scorned his Word, and was no longer capable of drawing any lesson from it. Man, convinced of the superiority of his own intellect, of his will, and of his ability to succeed by himself in whatever there was to be done, had of course no need of divine counsel, nor of any critical facing up.

But we know the outcome. It did not end in tragedy (although there was tragedy for the unfortunate Eli), nor in unparalleled wickedness. It ended in conformity. Man, determined to carry out his own will because he thinks it good, reduces God to silence, and then finds only one outlet, namely, to be like everyone else. We are familiar with the process. When man is not made hopeless by God's silence, it is because he has destroyed his awareness, to the point of wanting nothing better than to be identical instead of identifiable.

Thus the Old Testament gives us the two aspects: Israel's loss of hope in view of God's silence, as long as it remains aware, followed by the acceptance of that silence as "good riddance," which amounts to the draining away of Israel's unique character (today we shall say: of the person's unique character). Then, apart from the biblical texts, we also know Israel's tragic history throughout the whole of the period preceding Christ. The canon of Scripture was closed three hundred years before Jesus, and

Israel recognized that there was no longer a word of God which could be accepted as such for all the people. Israel is about to have a glorious, complex, and difficult political history. It gets lost in political meandering. It lives by treaties, conquests, the new royalty . . . and God is silent. Israel tries to recover a word of God, tries to make the so-called apocryphal books into a continuation of the revelation. But conflict and uncertainty surrounding Tobit, Maccabees, and Ecclesiasticus already make it obvious that these are in no sense a clear, striking, challenging word, to which Israel could give recognition as the Word of her God. God remained silent, while Israel attempted, in imitation of the great models, to elevate her word to the level of the Word of God, and to take the events of her own history as a continuation of the action of God. But it was soon evident that these were only empty pretenses, false appearances.

God was present, to be sure, for the piety of many. In the religious feelings of the Essenes and similar sects, there *perhaps* had been no absence of God. But for the people involved in a history which was manifestly without hope, and with no way out, God was silent. God was silent for nearly three hundred years, in spite of the fact that Israel was struggling through the events of history, was attempting to renew the thread of tradition and to fill the gap by sacrifices, prayers, fastings, commitments, works, theologies, activisms, and pieties. We know this, but it is especially important not to forget Israel's experience. The people of God are an example in this *also*, that they, too, have experienced the silence of God, and have crossed that new desert.

Jesus still comes to us to confirm the possibility which could be the deciding factor, the possibility of man's decision. Let us recall all the parables on the subject: the

king who goes away, leaving his servants to shift for themselves in the administration of the kingdom; the master of
the house who goes away and leaves his steward to run
the household, or to direct the personnel; the man who
goes on a journey and distributes money to his servants,
which they are to put to profitable use in business or in
the market; the man who planted a vineyard and went
away, leaving it to be cultivated by tenants; the bridegroom who is absent, and no one knows when he will
return.

We are tempted to say that these are mere imagery, but
it is not so simple. We are tempted to say that they mean
"only" that God is in heaven, and that he leaves everything
on earth to our care. But such an interpretation goes
counter to everything the Old Testament says about the
Covenant, about the work of God in history: God has not
withdrawn once for all into heaven, shutting himself up in
silence and leaving man to shift for himself. We have seen
that for Israel this was a situation of tragedy par excellence.[11]

We are tempted to say that these parables mean the
departure from earth of Jesus, who is no longer present
with us in the flesh, and that this "merely" characterizes
the intervening time while we await his return. The truth
is that most of them are not about the Son, but about the
absence of the Father.

Finally, we are tempted to say that these are eschatological parables for the purpose of putting us on our guard
while awaiting the return. That is certainly true, but it
seems to me essential to distinguish between the silence
of God and the distance existing between God and man,
a distance canceled in Jesus Christ, and which we are told

---

[11] This is the chief error in Harvey Cox's type of triumphalism. He thinks
man benefits from God's withdrawing to leave room for him.

will be canceled for all mankind at the time of the return and of the new creation. Contrary to these parables we have the certification that, despite the distance, God is present. "I am with you . . . ," "I will send you my Spirit. . . ."

It seems to me that these parables are also (though not exclusively) there to tell us that this presence, promised and attested, can be withdrawn; that, after Jesus, as was the case with Israel, there can come a time when nothing more of God is visible or audible, when there is no longer any experience except that of the absence, or the turning away. This is not merely a description of the permanent "between-the-times" situation, with the static setup of a presence of the absent one. I think it is also a warning of the possibility that there may no longer be anything to be lived or spiritually perceived.

This finds its confirmation and its culmination in Jesus' cry, "My God, my God, why hast thou forsaken me?" (Mark 15:34). It attests that there had been a constant presence of the Father with the Son, and an openness of the Son toward the Father. Then, it is erased. God is dead in Jesus. I shall not revive, in the wake of so many others, a meditation on this crucial cry. I shall not open up a theological discussion on the foundation for the drama which is here evoked. I confine myself to the connection between this cry and the possibility of the absence of God.

In the first place, we must surely put to one side the current interpretation, according to which Jesus is registering his defeat, especially that he had been living an illusion, that heaven was empty, that there was no Father, no God. The very structure of the sentence, which has been faithfully reported, shows without further investigation that the cry has nothing whatever to do with this romantic explanation. The latter is easy to accept only on the basis of an antitheistic assumption, of an exclusively humanistic notion of Jesus, and of an anti-Christianity. But that rests on a failure to understand this prayer.

On the other hand, it also seems to me that this abandonment is not circumstantial, that is, related only to *that* moment, *that* episode, *that* person. A very orthodox theology, and a very true one from one point of view, will say in effect that there, at that instant and for that man, God had deserted. Jesus was actually abandoned, but he is the only one in all human history for whom that is true. The abandonment, which is the turning away of God so dreaded by the devout in Israel, which is the judgment of God—that abandonment has been accomplished once for all in Jesus Christ. This is doubtless true. It is still more true that only Jesus could know and measure what the absence of God really means. For him alone it was the absolute tragedy. God's silence is only seriously felt by the person who lives, or tries to live, by the Word of God. The greater the nearness, the greater the love, the faith, and the knowledge of God, the more terrible are the absence and the silence.

For the unbeliever, God's silence is not felt as something serious. To the contrary, it is a return to what he considers normal. Still, he feels it to some extent without being aware of the terrible consequences and without being able to understand his own situation, for the reason that it is the product of an event in which he does not believe. In Jesus Christ, on the other hand, the awareness of being abandoned, the meaning of it, and the ultimate tragedy which it represents, were actually pushed to the limit.

Yet it cannot be said that because Jesus was abandoned there can never again be an abandonment, nor a silence, nor an absence of God. That seems to me quite theoretical.

It could doubtless be true for an eternal theology, a *theologia perennis*. However, in our earthly lives we are still called individually, as a Church, and collectively to cross spiritual deserts, periods of life or epochs of history in which God abandons man to his folly and nothingness. Hence the cry of Jesus seems to me to bear conclusive and unimpeachable witness to the ultimate *possibility* of this abandonment. If this word on the cross were not there, the theologians could say in all good conscience to those who are experiencing the silence of God that they are the victims of a psychological illusion, since no one can be abandoned by a God who is both almighty and loving, both provident and incarnate.

But there is this cry. Jesus was not psychologically deluded. God abandoned God. He abandoned himself. He went down into the abyss out of which he had brought the creation. There was a break between Father and Son, and what is more, a splitting apart of God within God— the possible impossibility. From that time on we know the possibility of God's silence toward us. To say that, since Christ was himself abandoned in that way, no one is similarly abandoned, is quite true. To say that, because God so loved mankind, he abandoned himself, canceled himself out for man, and therefore no one can any longer get away from that love, is also true. But we must understand the limits of these spiritual and theological truths.

This truth means that no one is abandoned as Jesus was abandoned, that is to say, in the ultimate, total, and limitless manner, in the completely inaccessible depth. It means that there never will be any question of a final silence, a final abandonment. The history of mankind (or of a man) never ends on the great pause of an absence of God. God's silence is embraced within a history already recapitulated in Christ. Like the abandonment, it can only be temporary and penultimate. It means, finally, that all who are abandoned, who feel left out, who experience total aridity of the Spirit, who pray Psalms 10, 13, and 22 . . . these all *are* in Jesus Christ. They are in the inseparable communion. They are in the indelible word. They are in the absement which is the preface to glory. They are in these experiences of Christ himself at the moment of his cry.

Thus it seems to me that we ought not understand this word in the sense that, from Christ's abandonment onward, no man can ever be abandoned by God, but rather, in the sense that this cry attests that it is possible for God to turn away from man. Nevertheless, in this very turning away, the person who is abandoned *is* in God, because God abandoned himself. But that essential truth does not do away with the spiritual experience of the void and the absence when God is silent. That could be the desert which we now have to cross.

THE TODAY OF THE SILENCE

God is silent. I think that at this present time, in this period of history, such is our experience and our actual situation. We can repeat the "Why?" There will be no more answer than Jesus received on the cross. Only the Spirit of God probes the Spirit of God. We are unable to discern the why, for there is no cause, either proximate or remote, first or second, final or efficient, for any decision of God's. The decision is its own cause. All we can say is that in this situation, in relation to some decision of man's, God is silent. He has effaced himself.

At this point we should make a necessary distinction. We have seen that in the Old Testament the fact that God is silent or turns away is felt as a supreme punishment. Can we then say that *now* this silence of God is a punishment of man? Here, surely, is where the theological formula can come into play, according to which the punishment has been visited entirely on Jesus Christ. Yet, on the other hand, this silence and absence will surely be experienced as punishment *by the faithful person,* who longs after the living Word, after the testimonial of the presence, here and now, of his God. If he really has the love for the Father which is expected of him, he cannot live in this void except as in the worst of all condemnations.

But it is precisely not a matter of condemnation. If *now* God is silent, it is not because he rejects but because he is rejected. We have known the terrifying God, the Almighty, the God of heavenly hosts and of dominions (and of course he is that still!), who condemns and who avenges his sanctity and honor, this God of floods and of wars of extermination. But the lesson of the flood is precisely that this God, the very same, the identical God, does not really act in that way. The transition from the *myth* of the flood to the *history* of the love of God culminating in Christ is there to tell us that this God who reveals himself *at the level of myth,* or *at the apocalyptic level,* or *at the parabolic level* as the one who execrates, judges, fulminates, and condemns is such only *at that level.* On the *historical* level of the real, the actual, the concrete relationship, he is the God of salvation, of pardon, of love and humility. He is the first poor man, he who, still humiliated, stands at the door and knocks. Such *is* the God whose terrifying glory is but a projection.

So this silence, this abandonment, this turning away is not a judgment and a condemnation of man. It is the expression for God, in God, of the judgment which man is pronouncing on God, of man's condemnation of God. This could possibly be intentional. It is much more certainly unintentional.

We have created a world in which words proliferate, a

world of "news" which tells us nothing. We are living in a deluge of bulletins, in an uninterrupted verbal explosion. All is talk all the time to all the world, and nothing is being said. In this flood of sound which comes at us, made up of endless repetition, empty curiosities, inner and intellectual vacuity, no word can really be a word. All is blended into an undifferentiated mismash, in which scientific information is drowned in news flashes; or a crucial political decision is a headline alongside murders and auto accidents; or the most agonized human appeal is obliterated by the musical alcohol of pop, and made the excuse for other kinds of talk to interest the viewers; or a key statement is used to spice up a release. No definitive word is any longer possible. There no longer are any final questions and answers. Tillich's Ultimate Concern is no more, and likewise Robinson's Depth. There is a superficial explosion of sounds which jolts and throws us in every direction. No word can be spoken under these conditions.

So God is silent. He could destroy Sodom and Gomorrah all over again, but his promise to Noah, and his still more radical promise in Christ, have permanently tied his hands. There are no trumpets of judgment to blare into submission the more sonorous pop festivals and the more thunderous political proclamations. Henceforth there is the silence of God, for he does not enter into a power struggle with man. He is the unfortunate, the deprived.[12]

By the same token, triumphant man in our day has decided to kill God, to get rid of the heavenly Father, to drive out this phantasm, or this embarrassing witness. God, who has let himself be put to death in Christ, with-

[12] We must not get out of it by the now current about-face, according to which, God, absent and poor, is really present in all poor and oppressed people. How convenient! How calming to anxiety! What a novel opiate! But it is merely a pirouette!

draws into his discreetness before the absence of love, the absence of filial relations, the absence of trust, the absence of gift, the absence of loyalty, the absence of truth, the absence of self-discipline, the absence of freedom, the absence of authenticity. God makes himself absent in this world of absences, which modern man has put together with enthusiasm. Man certainly has not killed God, but in creating this world of absence for himself he has brought about the discreetness of God, which is expressed in his turning away.

Now when God is silent, when we think we have killed God, fate is still there, and this is God, who can no longer be experienced except as fate. That is what Neher has marvelously shown in connection with Saul: "His tragic end underlines the awful nature of the tragedy of Saul, which the Talmud does not hesitate to characterize as a 'tragedy of fate.' Saul experiences the neutral silence of God as the supreme sign of the aggressiveness of the rejection." To this I must add that Saul is typical, for we cannot experience the silence of God in any other way. All theological reasoning, whether to explain God's silence or to assure us of its positive aspect and its depth of freedom for man, does not change the fact that when the God of the Word, who communicates only by the Word, is silent, he makes way for all the demons of the night and of death. They are the ones Saul struggled with, and which haunt both Churches and Christians today.

However, there is a point to be kept straight here. It is obvious that in an age of abandonment God's nearness is still experienced by certain individuals. God makes his word live in the hearts of some. That much is surely true, just as it is true that there still are miracles today, miracles of healing for example, brought to pass by God's grace and similar to those reported in the Gospels. It is collectively that we experience God's silence and absence. It is the body of Christians, the churches, people in the aggregate, who find themselves abandoned. The personal experiences of a few change nothing. Their testimony is not heard, is not received. God is silent to the Church. How could the word of one person who has experienced the active presence of God be received in the community as a Word of God?

In this catastrophic situation there are two reactions. One is to objectify the Word of God (a charge to which Barth was vulnerable). Objectivication says that there is no need to turn the word into an experience. The word *is*. That is all there is to it, and it never changes. The other reaction is the radical subjectivication of the Word of God (a charge to which Bultmann was vulnerable). Subjectivication says that there is no need to ask oneself whether or not there is a God who speaks. The important thing is "living as though." Unfortunately, these are interpretations of distress, when and because God is silent!

For the Church and for the generality of people, it is a desert. This silence of God can last one year or three hundred years, and all the well-meaning words, the authentic words, the living testimonials of the love and the presence of God make no difference to it until such time as God shall actually speak once again to *one* person *on behalf of* the others. "The word of the Lord was rare in those days," says the First Book of Samuel. There were no more prophets and the Judges were traitors. Then one day God again chose one man to carry that word to all the people, on behalf of all the people, one man who is to crystallize once again the entire revelation, Samuel.

It is not merely that he is commissioned to carry the Word of God (because every person who receives it and hears it *for himself* is commissioned to carry it for all!), but the time of God's silence ends by the fact that the people once again perceive in the speech of Samuel the very Word of God pronounced on behalf of all. Thus it is not a word addressed to each one individually, in his private conscience, which demonstrates the end of the silence of God, but the fact that the chosen people (the Church) *receives* the proclamation of one of its members (who has of course understood this as coming from God) as a word of God and sees in it the very work of the Lord. When that happens, the time of the desert, of the exile, of the abandonment is over.

But if that is the way it is (and that is the way it is throughout the entire Bible), then no individual who has personal and private communion with the Lord, and who reads the Bible as a living proclamation, can decline to express an opinion, thinking to let it go at that. No one can reason: "If it is true that we are in an age of abandonment, if it is true that this is a period of the great silence of God, then what good does it do to say anything, to communicate what I know and see, this burning love and this ineffable presence?" No one can claim the right to keep the mystical experience, the deep piety, the understanding of the revelation for himself alone. No such person can be sure that he is not the one commissioned by God to put an end to the age of abandonment. Many prophets have spoken in the desert without response from anything or anybody. Many prophets have exhausted themselves proclaiming that the time for renewal had arrived, and nothing came, even to the last one, who recognized that he was a voice crying in the desert. He had no more luck than his predecessors, but this time was the right time. The heavens opened and the Word of God was incarnate. So none of us can remain silent, using our age of abandonment as a pretext. On the other hand, to live in this age brings with it certain demands and decisions.

THE PROBLEM BEFORE US

I make no claim to having convinced my interlocutor. I am only saying what I see, what I have thought through, what I have understood, what I am living. From that as a point of departure, I must try to respond to certain objections, which we shall enumerate briefly at the start. The fact that Jesus is Saviour and Lord, that the work of salvation is completed, absolutely does not preclude that in actual history, at the level of temporary and temporal living, the Church can indeed know the drama of God's silence and can pass through a time of abandonment.[13] The

[13] Thus abandonment replaces the death of God. On that score I take the same line as Martin Buber. Speaking of "the eclipse of God," he criticizes the thesis of the death of God (*Werke,* I, 1962; Cf. *Eclipse of God* [New York: Harper Torchbook, 1957], pp. 65 ff.) and in particular Sartre's idea that the silence of God is proof that God does not exist, or at least does not exist for man (*Being and Nothingness,* trans. Hazel E. Barnes [New York: Washington Square Press]) and that rigorous conclusions are to be drawn from this silence. Sartre, in fact, puts these conclusions in the mouth of the hero of *The Devil and the Good Lord* (New York: Knopf, 1960), but Sartre's use of the thesis in a stage play allows Buber to answer the philosopher from the doctrine of acting. "Acting is not in fact performed in the I-It relationship, but in the I-Thou relationship. The eclipse of God is itself one phase of acting. It effects no change in the divine essence or existence, but it derives from the fact that we have erected a partition in front of being and existence, namely, the impersonal scenery of the It, which hides God's light and stifles his word" (as given in A. Neher). This reply to Sartre is, to be sure, correct, but if the concept of God's acting is acceptable from a philosophical or theological point of view, it remains nonetheless true that when we come up against the present, actual silence of God we experience his abandonment. It is not acting at all, whatever biblical wisdom one might possess concerning the silence.

letters at the start of the Apocalypse are there to witness to that. This does not call in question the eternal work of God in Christ, but it attests the fact that our God is at all times the living God, who as living is not inactive and bound. It is not a matter of an "everlasting" rejection, but of God's decision in history. That is small comfort, since we do live in history, and this age is hard to bear.

It would be giving way to a dangerous inflation of the present moment, to "everything right away," and to a harmful urge for rationalization, to think that "because there is this abandonment, therefore the work of salvation is not complete in itself. The Jesus of history has not finished all that there was to do." This is a *Miles Gloriosus* formula which one hears nowadays from so many theologians and philosophers. Yet once again they display their refusal to face reality in order to take refuge in theological innovations, in daring intellectual formulations and phantasmagoria. That Jesus Christ is God-with-us does not at all preclude the abandonment. We shall say simply that, for the time being, the presence of God is so secret and discreet that we no longer know who he is, nor anything other than our discourse about him. That he is there as though he were not there merely reminds us of his autonomy with regard to us. It also reminds us of the very essential fact that those who decree the death of God, or the incompleteness of the work of Christ, are, by that very act, doing what they accuse orthodoxy of always having done, namely, treating God as an object, manipulating him, transforming him into a thing at the disposal of our feelings and passions.

So let it not be said that it is I who am giving way to my feelings and my own judgment about this society which is not to my liking (I could argue at length over this estimate of what I have written!). As a matter of fact, it is not my estimate of the situation. It is, as I have tried to say, the general impression of the mass of the people in the Western world. All I am adding to it is the statement that, if man in our day is living in this anguish, it is because God is no longer present to him. An immense void is created, an unexpected wound, and abandonment in the midst of confusing change. This man is not my invention.

Nor am I making an undue transfer from observation of fact to theological affirmation. From the standpoint of faith, this transfer is called for by the need for further thought. The essential thing to remember here is that the initiative lies indeed with God, who is disqualifying himself and is silent. It does not lie with man, who one fine day made up his mind to get rid of God.

5

Signs of Abandonment in the Church

We can say that the man of anguish and despair expresses this abandonment secretly, and in a manner visible only from the outlook of faith. We were saying that this affirmation comes from faith and is understandable only to faith. On the other hand, if there is abandonment, it should be obvious in the Church and be seen as applicable to all.

The Church is the body of Christ. She is always that. But if the Lord withdraws from her she can be dishonored, just as God could withdraw from his people in spite of the continuance of the covenant. The Church is the bride, but she can be an adulteress. The Church is a community founded by the Holy Spirit, but she may become a community in which the Holy Spirit can no longer speak. Surely what I am seeing, and what everyone is seeing in one way or another in the Church, demonstrates on a large scale this abandonment and silence of God. What was merely interpretation when I was talking about the world becomes visible, tangible, and certain in the Church.

That is what I had attempted to explain in *False Presence of the Kingdom*, which was so badly received and misunderstood by so many active Christians who thought they saw personal attacks in it. I was certainly not aiming at them personally, but at the implementation of their ideas as indicative of a general trend of error which kept the Church from being any longer the Church. I shall take up some of the points again, but from another aspect, and only as signs of the abandonment.

THE MEDIOCRITY OF THE CHURCH

The Church was called to be made up of the weak, the poor and the lowly, and to have little power and glory. We know what happened to that. Yet it is not so much the fact that she is composed of the bourgeoisie and "the rich" (so obvious that it is futile to go over it again and condemn it for the three- or four-thousandth time). What seems to me important is the mediocrity, for she is just as mediocre where her membership is proletarian and antibourgeois. It is not the weakness or the small numbers, the decrease in the active membership, or the fact that she draws from a certain social stratum which troubles me. It is the mediocrity.

Big things are no longer being done in the Church, things that are striking, heartwarming, moving. One does little things. A small endowment is well administered. Scrupulous loyalty is exhibited toward little concerns. An amiable kindness is cultivated, which is anxious not to hurt anybody's feelings. No one dares set forth a confession of faith, because that might say something revolting which science has warned us to be suspicious of (scientific scruple has gained favor over moral scruple in our mediocrity, but nothing has really changed). Still less does anyone dare to declare that a given statement is heretical. The motives for refusing to declare a proposition heretical today are just as bad as the motives which would have produced its shameless condemnation two centuries ago. We have certainly not progressed since the loathsome days of Christendom, of crusades merged with colonialism and of heresy trials.

Obviously, our trouble today is not these excesses of our ancestors. It is mediocrity. We spit at the crusades or at wars of religion (which I am not seeking to defend or admire) in order to justify our lukewarmness, our impotence, our lack of faith. Then, just as we act superior in condemning heresy trials (a mere cover-up for our inability any longer to be deeply committed for our beliefs), so we also scorn the miracles as crude symbols for primitive minds, because we are incapable of performing any ourselves.

The entire Church is Petainist. She conciliates and collaborates with the world, accepting every compromise in the hope of salvaging a little something. She is only too happy when, thanks to her successive theological disavowals, she can say, "Look! At last there are some Marxist intellectuals, or some workers, who have been willing to listen to what we have to say." That is the perpetual justification of collaborators. There is Freudianism, which cannot be rejected because it is science. So we have to rearrange the revelation in order to come up with something which will fit in with it. When I say the whole Church is Petainist, I mean the whole Church. That is to say that the far left, our theologians of the revolution or of the death of God, our politicians of the challenge, are the prime Petainists.

In point of fact, the change in direction of theological or political opinion has changed exactly nothing with respect to the deepseated fact of Christian mediocrity. When I think of the general outlook, the speeches of Christian intellectuals, the work of the Church over the past century, I have the feeling of being in front of a very bad orchestra, made up of extremely poor musicians, each one incapable of playing well, and out of tune with the others. The orchestra could be that of a century ago, dressed in blue and playing *Veillons au Salut de l'Empire* or *Maréchal, nous voilà*. Now it is dressed in red and is playing *L'Internationale* or *La Jeune Garde*, but still playing just as badly, just as stupidly. It is just as mediocre, the same types with the same speeches. Given the exchange of a few terms, today's left covers the same ground as yesterday's right. That is to say that the vocabulary and the value references have changed, but not the fact that it is an insipid performance. Limited violence is substituted for syrupy charity. Cleverness of interpretation is substituted for orthodox imbecility. Presiding over it all is the master of ceremonies, the real conductor of the orchestra, the archangel of mediocrity and confusion.

We may as well resign ourselves to it. The Church does not exist, either at the level of freedom, or at that of the proclamation of the Gospel message, or at the level of intellectual responsibility, or at that of power; and let us not fool ourselves, the Church of the aggiornamento exists still less than the traditional Church. The Church of political involvement exists still less than the Church of the ghetto. True, the Church *is* in Christ. That I deeply believe. But nothing of her truth, properly so called, is making its appearance in the real world today. Everything is falsified. Everything in it is small. The music we are making—you can hear it in the Bergman films. The political action is infantile. The intellectual activity satisfies those who know nothing. The life commitment is completely neuter.

Is this due to the incompetence of Christians? Should we beat our breasts and repent? Should we pass resolutions and make inflammatory speeches? At the opening of Church meetings, of ministerial, regional or national councils, at the opening of the working sessions, one always begins with "prayer." Very often the Holy Spirit is invoked. I believed in it for a number of years and prayed fervently—then finally one has to succumb to experience. Our passive deliberations, our mediocre decisions, our petty psychologies, our meetings which are a deadly bore, our false problems, our serious concern for questions which do not exist, our inability to go ahead joyously and out in the open, our secret churlishness and our feigned composure, our justifications and our paralysis—it all bears irrefutable witness that the Holy Spirit is not there. However foolish it may seem, I am obliged to come back to this, "If the Holy Spirit had been there, the fact would have been evident." I have seen no such evidence at all.

So now, those prayers at the openings of meetings, in which I know only too well what is going to be said and what is going to happen, those invocations of the Holy Spirit which one makes right off in order to stifle the Spirit, those now appear to me to be pure and simple blasphemy. We have to make a choice. Either there is no God, and Jesus is a human model, in which case I see no reason to bother with the Church; or else we have come up against the stone wall of the silence of God, and our prayer is lost in the void of his decision not to be there any longer, in the void of his readiness to be the one who is turned away. All the assembling of biblical passages to prove to me that this is not possible does not alter one whit the easily observed mediocrity of the Church.

Let no one say that I am trying to escape by throwing the responsibility for this mediocrity on God and his abandonment, while the fault lies simply with Christians. These Christians are not so bad, whether politically involved or not, whether pious or loving, strong on righteousness or strong on charity, good managers or great preachers, philosophers or humble believers. Christians, as such, are mostly honorable, devout, religious, warmhearted, committed, and serious. No, it is not the fault of Christians, nor of a particular vice, that the archangel of mediocrity is the true master of the Church. The real trouble is that Christians are burdened beyond human power and capacity. In *another* organization, cultural, social or trade union, they would be wonderful fighters. They would be on top. But here they are burdened with a crushing load, with a responsibility courting insanity, which requires no less than the presence, the aid, and the immediate action of God if it is to be taken on.

It is a question of God's work, therefore who but God could do it, even when it is done through a chosen man? But this chosen man can achieve nothing of such a work by his own capacities. For this reason, I well understand the point of view from which the following reply is made: Let us abandon the Church and devote ourselves to human tasks, political and social, etc. To be sure, in that field one is at one's best. Yet that is, without more ado, to become renegade. It's the very opposite to that for which we were chosen, and heaven and earth will never make me change my opinion on that point!

Thus we have only this choice: either be mediocre or renegade, since we, the body of Christians constituting the Church system, are in the age of abandonment. If we are in the slightest degree aware of what that means, we surely cannot reason, "Good! We're no longer responsible if the Church is in a bad way." If we realize what this abandonment is, we can only sense it as the most fearful question ever put to us, and can only become responsible to the full extent of every human possibility.

THE INSTITUTION

This is a particular instance of mediocrity. Must we go back over what has been, here also, attacked thousands and thousands of times—the institutional Church, naturally, the rebellion against the institution of the Church, naturally. Yet, after all, I'm not so sure that this is obvious, for what I have frequently observed is that the greatest enemies of the institution find the latter quite normal, first-rate and well adapted when they get to be in charge. The Barthians held the institution in the greatest contempt, but once they occupied the leading positions . . . , and the same phenomenon is occurring today with the "challengers," who felt very comfortable in the institution of the Protestant Federation. Neither of these groups made the slightest difference to the importance of the institution, to the sociological rigidity of the organization.

A few years ago I indicated that, in my opinion, the Ecumenical Council meant the death of ecumenism because of the crushing dominance of the bureaucratic machine.[14] There has been nothing but confirmation of that over the past ten years. What was barely discernible then is now clear to be seen. The Ecumenical Council is the ecclesiastical point of concentration for all the sociological conformities, all the Christian mediocrities, all the organized superficiality and all the Christian reduplication.

[14] Unfortunately, Bieler's book on *La Politique de l'Espérance* has not convinced me of very much. I like his other works, but this one . . .

That does not come from the people in it, nor from the good intentions, nor from modes of procedure, but from the institutional crunch, from sociological fate. The Ecumenical Council was led to the same result that the Roman Church was led to when the Curia was established, and for the same reason. Having arrived at that stage, it is not surprising that the rapprochement with the Roman Church would be possible, even inevitable. Across institutions the two sides understand one another. In the long run they might even agree and merge, when the institution has definitely eliminated the very thing it was meant to implement, and when the message has become a tape recording. The growth and success of our Church institutions, and especially of the Ecumenical Council, is to me a striking, tragic, and glaring sign of the abandonment in which we have lost our way.[15]

There again, it seems to me blasphemous to invoke the Holy Spirit for that kind of progress, and to suppose that the successes of the Council are the result of the action of God in the Church. Any organization functioning as it functions, and under those same historical circumstances, would arrive at the same result. There is no need to invoke God, or to ascribe any progress to him. The development of the Ecumenical Council is a normal institutional development, and the lowering of the barriers between the churches is a product simply of a loss of interest in theological controversy on the part of the masses and on the part of intellectuals. No one any longer attaches importance to the differences between Baptists and Calvinists. Their rapprochement is normal, but this rapprochement

---

[15] Quite obviously my remarks here are of no use to the traditional enemies of ecumenism and the ecumenical movement. The recalcitrant Huguenots, the ultramontane Catholics, the biblical literalists, the hard core of all types, seem to me to represent such antiquated, outmoded, and trivial attitudes that they are not even worth mentioning.

is itself not very important. Since the differences derive merely from customs, organizations, and tradition, it is obvious that one works to best advantage at the institutional level in reducing them, but that is a matter of the sociological trend. The existence of that *kind* of obstacle, and of that procedure and its results, only proves the triumph of the institution in the Church and the unbelievable awkwardness of the nonspiritual system.

However, it is not to be concluded from this that I would argue for an anti-institutional approach, involving the dismantling of every institution, as though that were in itself a conformity to the will of God. That is angelism (the attitude of some modern revolutionaries in the Church!). We are not yet in the Kingdom of God. The point is, rather, that the church institution can be valid only if there is interference, shock, overturning, and initiative on the part of God, that is, if something happens. Without such intervention of the Holy Spirit, the church institution is subject to exactly the same laws as all institutions. It is a purely sociological body.

Henceforth, when we see the actual functioning of the churches, of the Ecumenical Council, of the Protestant Federation, of the large organizations, and observe that it corresponds exactly to that of any other organization whatsoever, we are compelled to say that we are quite dry of inspiration in the absence of the Holy Spirit. But no administrative reorganization, no political reorientation, no dismantling of institutions will make the slightest difference.

DRYNESS

The third observation which is obvious is the lack of outreach in witnessing, the lack of transmission of the Christian message. In the face of this incapacity for evangelization and mission, tons of literature have been published. Society is worldly and secularized. There is the modern scientific outlook, etc., etc. I shall not recapitulate the hundreds of explanations which have been dug up. It is all well known. I shall say just one thing: "If God doesn't speak, who will be heeded?"

In spite of modern research, I continue firmly to believe that it is by the action of the Holy Spirit (assuming, of course, that man has done his part for the proclamation and preaching of the Gospel) that people's ears are opened and they are made to hear. It is the Holy Spirit who provides the meaning and who brings about the reception of the Word. The Holy Spirit is no longer speaking. For me, the proof of that is not only the fact just indicated, the widespread indifference to the Gospel, but the combination of that fact with two others.

The first of these is the increase in religious mentality. At the very time when the Gospel is being rejected, flouted, and ridiculed, modern man is showing a keen interest in religious problems. Literature about God (provided it is not clearly and explicitly Christian) succeeds in the footsteps of erotic literature. Vahanian seems to be the only one to see that the "success" of "Christianity" in the United States at the present time is religious without being specifically Christian. The fact that man turns to religion, or to religions, at the same time that he rejects the revelation of God and of Jesus Christ is a plain indication that God remains strictly hidden.

The second fact is the great effort on the part of Christian intellectuals to make the message audible, understandable, and acceptable on the purely natural level, without the need of any revelatory intervention from God. That is the profound meaning of the immense, well-intentioned investigation undertaken in the areas of language and hermeneutics. If only one could manage to pinpoint the obstacles which impede man in his hearing of the word of the Gospel, if one could arrive at a linguistic analysis so that this language would be directly understandable, if one could discover the meaning in such a way as to make a restatement possible, then the revealed word would, in short, go over on its own.

The passion for language analysis and hermeneutics is the unintentional expression of God's silence. It reasons like this: "God is absent (we're not saying so, of course!), so we are going to get along without him. We shall demonstrate that it is not at all essential that God speak here and now in order that the witness be heard and received. We are going to denounce such an idea either as magism or as a path of least resistance which fails to meet the need. The Holy Spirit is not what we used to think, for he shows himself quite differently from the modes in which he was presented in traditional theology. We shall act on our own. We shall find out what the obstacle is which prevents transmission through language. With a language which meets the need, the transmission should take place. We are going to find out how the meaning of the text can be carried free of all miracle and of all ascription of meaning through the action of God. We shall stay within the domain of the human. That's where the problem has to be worked out."

This stoic stand is really a courageous bearing up under misfortune. It is evidence that God is not speaking, and that leads to quite obvious manifestations. On the one hand, we have a compression and a distortion of the texts. This did not begin yesterday, but with biblical structuralism and *Redaktionsgeschichte* we have reached the point of the evaporation of all possibility of meaning. With the text reduced to structures, it is interesting to play with the dismembered parts, but that is a game from which no message comes (and from which none *should* come). Or, on the other hand, there is a taking apart of what the Church thought significant only when the different parts were fitted together.

That, to me, is the important thing. There is a rejection of the radical unity which the thought of the Bible exhibits from end to end, over and above the diversity of authorship, schools of thought, and literary forms. It is a rejection for the sake of investigating the specifics of each sequence and of each compilation. This investigation will (perhaps) make possible the precise understanding of a paragraph. It will (perhaps) make possible a better grasp of the historical and cultural setting of this or that school of thought. But it radically separates this strictly isolated and particularized text from the sense of the revelation. The more a passage is dissected in this way, the less susceptible it becomes to a basic comprehension. My experience with that kind of exegesis over a period of twenty years in another field (the texts of Roman institutions) has taught me that the more one improves his formal knowledge of the text, the more its basic significance vanishes.

In biblical exegesis, we have now arrived at the point of a radical formalization of the text, which means the definite dissolution of the sense. Procedurally, the now classic formula, according to which it is important not to distinguish form from foundation in a text so that the sense springs from a complete analysis of the form, is a pure justification for the attempt to strip the text of its meaning. It is a reduction process which looks scientific, and which in this case is a process of spiritual poverty. It is indeed true that, with God absent, the only thing left for us to do in our real spiritual poverty is to keep peeling the layers from the textual envelope. We can rest assured, however, that that will lead nowhere. Its only effect will be to confirm our sterility and to make it more obvious.

To be sure, as is the case with the preceding question, it is not a matter of jumping to the opposite conclusion and saying: "Let us not perform any more exegesis. Let us stop this structural and cultural analysis, and in that way (by a *regression* to naïve and fundamentalist reading) we shall find the true significance of the Bible. Then we could understand it and pass it on to others." That would be absurd. God is not stopped by exegesis from revealing himself, nor is he coerced by simplism (confused with simplicity) and infantilism (confused with the childlike spirit) into coming back into the picture. The truth is that no reading is *possible* when God is silent.

What we need to realize is that the path of modern exegesis is the testimonial of our reaction to this silence of God. As such it is worth a lot more than the blind belief that everything is continuing as before, but it becomes harmful when we pretend to get out of the impasse by means of exegesis, and to do without the Holy Spirit while going after the same result.

Hermeneutics has pushed this to the limit. I make no claim to having plumbed the depths of the hermeneutic problem, nor to possessing adequate knowledge in it, nor to having understood the complexity of everything written on the subject. I know and have understood a little of it. I struggled in those quicksands for a long time, and I think I can finally say that the endeavor to recover "the meaning of the meaning" is a desperate, but total and totalitarian, attempt to make up for the absence of the Holy Spirit.

On the one hand, what we have is a gigantic and powerful effort to lay hold of the validity of the biblical message in all its aspects, and behind and beyond all its appearances. It is an attempt to do this in an age of suspicion, which attacks the proclamation of the Gospel more seriously than it attacks anything else. It is an attempt to do this while taking completely (much too!) seriously the standpoint of modern science and of philosophic comprehension, the current manner of stating problems. Finally, it is an attempt to do this while trying to locate oneself in the universe of nonsense and of the impossibility of communication of our society. Thus it is the most courageous facing up to the most important and profound difficulties that we know.

But on the other hand, we are looking at a strictly Babelian and Promethean enterprise (it is indeed interesting to observe the explicit rehabilitation of Prometheus by certain exegetes).[16] The hermeneutic enterprise probes tirelessly and ever more deeply into the mystery of the possible communication and recovery of meaning. It makes one's head spin. It is the exact equivalent, in reverse, of ancient metaphysics. Instead of trying to pierce the skies to lay hold of the mystery of being, instead of the ascent of the reason to the point of complete nothingness, it plunges into the mystery of communication. Its deepening is without defined limit, yet is pursued with the idea of attaining the final word. It proceeds in a hallucinatory manner, by a complex play of mirrors which keeps sending back ever more reduced and ever more numerous pictures of basic questions.

We are led to this by taking seriously, and as of "definitive" value, certain affirmations about the state of present-day science, affirmations which are accepted as conclusive

[16] Again, we must distinguish among the exegetes. I am not here thinking of Castelli, nor of Ricoeur, nor of J. M. Robinson, but of the overall trend manifested in so many minor studies, whose tendency we should be aware of.

and as posing a radical question. In imitation of the humiliation of Jesus Christ (the great passage in Phil. 2, together with Matt. 25, is *the* guiding text for all modern theology), we submit to our own humiliation before the supreme authority of science. But the fact is that it is the authority of God which we are humiliating! I am not too happy with these peremptory submissions such as, "Historical science teaches us that. . . ." Alas, I have been "doing" history for nearly forty years and I know how indecisive and how nondefinitive the lessons of history are, and how flimsy is any philosophy or theology which is based on those results. It is sand upon sand.

I likewise fail to understand why Freud should be looked upon as an undisputed authority, and why his word should be accepted by theologians as final and as requiring a given hermeneutic.[17] In other words, I fail to see the justification for accepting as legitimate all the questions about the revelation, more or less validly raised from different points of view, while at the same time refusing to question those systems, methods, and conclusions from the point of view of the revelation. The one seems to me just as indispensable as the other, but no more so.

Hence, on quite a number of points hermeneutics seems to me to be committing itself to paths which cannot possibly lead anywhere, and which raise innumerable problems, for the most part false. The tragedy of interpretation

[17] I can understand, to some extent, the sense in which Freud gives us a "reading," a hermeneutic, if you will, of the human phenomenon, and that one should make use of that perspective. What I do not understand is the need felt by Christian philosophers to "reconcile" analysis and Christianity at all costs. If the data are irreconcilable, why not just say so, instead of going in for roundabout proofs which convince no one? Such attempts are usually radically disputed by orthodox psychoanalysts. See a good critique by the psychoanalyst André Stephane, in *Contrepoint*, No. I.

is a tragedy, not because scientific interpretations enter in to overturn the traditional Christian interpretation, nor because procedures are highly sophisticated, but because God is silent. The Promethean role of hermeneutics is that of claiming to find a meaning as though God were speaking. Strictly, it is a matter of putting oneself in the place of God's decision. It is a matter of making Scripture alive and meaningful without God's making it alive and meaningful. It is a matter of effecting the transition from Scripture to word, or of making language into the word, by putting together highly sophisticated human means in order to economize on the use of the Holy Spirit. Hermeneutics is the business of interpreting revelation without revelation.

Of course, many people of my acqaintance will say quite the contrary: that in the end, and as a last resort, all will depend upon the certainty of the light of the Holy Spirit, and that one should not have recourse to that until the very end. They will argue that it is precisely through this hermeneutic activity that the Holy Spirit speaks, that is to say, that it is essential to the dignity, the sincerity, and the genuineness of the man before God that the latter make use of all the means available to him, instead of indolently resting back upon some miraculous act of God. Man must be responsible and must act, for that is what God expects of him. Anything that man is able to do we should not ask God to do.

If this approach does lead to great depth of hermeneutic research, we mustn't overlook the fact that it also motivates Billy Graham. Billy Graham's propaganda methods are the exact equivalent, at his level, of the hermeneutic philosophy, in that they use every last means to obtain results which the Holy Spirit is no longer giving. One can obtain conversions by propaganda, thereby economizing on the action of God, just as hermeneutics can obtain a meaning. I am aware that this comparison will scandalize serious researchers, but it is inescapable "by the nature of things."

As a matter of fact, the more the means are increased, the less the intervention of God makes sense. Insofar as we entertain no criticism of the means, but accept them a priori, what is rejected is God's discreet action, which does not impose itself. It might well be asked whether the prime moment is not the opening of the intellect by the Holy Spirit, then, in consequence of that, following upon that, a hermeneutic possibility opens up.

But the intellectuals and the theologians have deliberately chosen the opposite path. That quickly leads to a more radical position. If we combine this with what we were saying about exegesis and the modern manipulation of texts, we conclude that God must leave us free and independent in the pursuit of this "science," this exegesis, this hermeneutic. What a scandal it would be if a prophet were to appear who would crush these sciences by a manifestation of the Spirit of power. Thus God is forbidden to speak. It is not for God to speak in this business. It is up to us to make him speak. For his Word we must substitute our hermeneutic of the word. God's Word cannot come into the picture unless we recreate it and revive it. God must remain the inactive witness of what one does with his Word. Any other avenue save that of our knowledge is forbidden to him, and we look upon it as suspect. Such is the strict logic of the system.

But what we must realize is that such an attitude, such a philosophy, such a challenge (explicit or implicit) can take place only to the degree in which the abandonment has already happened. One shuts the door on God because he has already departed. One forbids him to speak because he is no longer saying anything. One claims to recover a meaning because the Holy Spirit is no longer supplying one. Such a theological position is only possible after, and from the standpoint of, the abandonment. The search for a general hermeneutic, of which the hermeneutic of Holy Scripture is a particular case, rests on the silence of God. Consequently, the condition for its existence is at the same time its negation, since all meaning found in God's silence can only be false.

CONFORMITY

Finally, while we are still dealing with these familiar signs, let us remember that, if the Church is thus conformed to the world, that is indeed in the measure in which she has been left to herself and all alone by her Lord. It is obvious that the only thing which might distinguish her and make her unconformed is the presence of the one who is the Wholly Other.[18] Without him she will necessarily be just another organism among many, in spite of her kerygma, etc. Conformity to the world is carried so far today that the Church is purely and simply negated in the interest of giving the world a higher rating. I shall not get into that outworn discussion again, except to say that this high rating given the world can happen only in the absence of the one who so loved the world (but one *always* neglects to quote the final verse in the context), and who, at the same time, judges it irrevocably.

Now, in the abandonment, the high estimate given the world means precisely nothing, since the only basis we have for this estimate is our own judgment, or a word from God which can no longer be actualized. There is no need

---

[18] I am anxious to preserve this designation as the only adequate one, even though nowadays it grates unpleasantly on the ears of our neotheologians who are drowning in the poverty of antiquated speech!!

to enumerate the obvious signs of the Church's conformity
to the world. It has been such a frequent object of criticism, and the signs are all around us. Whatever "research"
(of so-called centers of research) might be undertaken,
whatever efforts toward reorganization, whatever procedures (technique), at whatever points the Church's presence to the world might be effected, all conforms entirely
to the sociological order.

This is especially true of the oft-repeated declaration
(covered by a false reference to the Church as the *ecclesia,*
the assembly) that everything should be done by groups,
by assemblies, by teams—death to the individual, have
done with the lone operator. The great virtue is group
solidarity. In spite of his renewed authority, we are still
a long way from Kierkegaard:

. . . There is a nonsensical doctrine today that Christ saves *the
human race.* This is balderdash. I'll even say that if Christ had
wanted this he could not have done it, for the race is in the
category of perdition and salvation is outside the race. In virtue of race I can belong to this perverted race, but I cannot be
saved in virtue of race. Yet today we are almost ready to identify being Christian with being human. . . .
. . . The moment there is a crowd, God becomes invisible.
This all-powerful crowd can batter at his door, but will get no
further, for God exists only for the individual. That is his
sovereignty. . . .
In our day, the mass, the principle of evil, is promoted as
sovereign. . . .
. . . Mediocrity is the constituent principle of the compact
mass of humanity, and what the absolute, hence also God, has
to require as the prior condition for entering into contact with
people is to disperse them. . . .
Number is the most ridiculous parody of idea. In adding we
enter the absurd world in which adding equals substraction.
But number, of course, has the brute power. . . .
. . . Just as one cannot stand working without respite, just

as one has need of diversion, just so number diverts us, assuages us. The mistake is to have taken the diverting thing for the serious thing. . . .

. . . How ironic is the law which decrees that whoever needs number to become important is, by that very fact, insignificant. This is the more true the bigger the number one needs. Anything which is only done, set up or accomplished with the help of a big number, has the amazed admiration of mankind, as though that were the important thing. That is just what counts for nothing. True importance is in the inverse ratio, having always less and less need of number for its accomplishment; and for the prime thing above all others, for the thing which moves heaven and earth, one lone man is needed. If it takes many, that is a deduction. Wars, revolutions, art exhibits, big newspapers, etc., none of that, certainly, can be set up by one lone man. So one thinks those things important, whereas it is precisely their insignificance which makes them need crowds. It is their lack of importance which produces number in order to give them importance. But the prime thing above all others, and which intrigues angels and demons, the real intimacy of a man with God, for that, one lone man suffices. . . . (*Journals*)

However few they are in number, Christians today are impressed precisely by numbers, by plurality, by the ear of the public, by classes and parties. They conceive everything, the faith included, only in the plural. It is a sure sign of the abandonment. The need for the many is actually a defense against the feeling of emptiness, against the discomfort and uncertainty brought about by the silence and the turning away of God.

Conformity to the world is also expressed by the passion for politics, by the politicizing of Christian thinking, manners, and action. Today's Christians have adopted the very sociological slogan, "Politics is everything." The Bible is political, so the thinking goes, therefore morality is political as well! And how about the future of the common man, and incarnating righteousness? To think in that way is to be completely blind to the political illusion, to the political lie, to the ultimate ineffectiveness of politics in producing a human city. I shall not repeat the proof, which I have already given, of the biblical, theological, and sociological error of such a position. It has no other strength than its conformity to average opinion. Proof is of no avail in the face of the sociological trend which brings Christians irrevocably to do what everybody else is doing, and to think what everybody else is thinking.

If that is the real point of reference, however concealed, what a terrible sign it is of our abandonment. Moreover, it shows up immediately in life within the Church, as the passion for politics leads Christian intellectuals to practice those very politics at their lowest level. We have been quite critical of the Christians of past ages for employing methods copied from the politics of the monarchy, of the hierarchy, or of the episcopate, which were implemented by one-man rule, unlimited power, and the remote control of the faceless masses. Today we are going them one better.

Our Christian leaders, brought up in the maternal bosom of political parties or of trade unions, introduce political morals into the Church. There are sneak blows, the grab for votes, the quiet taking over of key positions, the forming of coteries and of pressure groups, the rallying of the hesitant by means of innocent-looking motions whose deeper meanings are hidden behind vague statements, the long-term strategies which become apparent only at the moment of their success, the disclosing of accusations against the opposition, the use of the weight of public opinion only sketchily certified, the maintaining of one's distance from those who think differently, the putting of political orthodoxy above every other consideration. When the Church acts in that way, she reveals the exclusiveness of her sociological dimension. She is completely colorless. In fact, when it is declared that horizontal relationships are the only ones which are theologically admissible today, this is a way of justifying the politicizing of relationships.

This is always done, of course, in imitation of the world. The Church's great concern is to justify what man and the world are doing.[19] This is just like olden times, except that it is no longer the same things which are being justified. Instead of the royal power, the patriarchal family, feminine servitude, worldly morality, etc., the things now being justified are science, technology, world management, politics, and the big city.

The latest fabulous example of justification is Harvey Cox's celebrated book, *The Secular City*. It is hard to believe that a book so feebly thought through, so loaded with historical error, so sociologically and theologically superficial, so ordinary, with its repetition of all the commonplaces about secularization and the profane, and lacking in any depth in the subject, that a book so dubious in its historical analyses and so generalized in its sociology—that such a book would enjoy such a success. Just one thing explains it: it offers the public a justification for what is going on in the world, for what man is in process of doing. It is true that modern man in his most fallen aspect wants exactly above everything else that someone should come along to tell him that he is right in doing what he is doing. That was the springboard for all the propaganda. From the standpoint of ideology and publicity, *The Secular City* is a great book.

[19] Here again, for the hundredth time, I call attention to the fact that to condemn the act of justifying is not, to my mind, the same as to condemn what is being done in society, in science, and in technology. I have never condemned these!

It supplies precisely the "solemn complement" (that Marx rightly accuses religion of supplying). Urban anonymity? That is great. That is freedom. Urban mobility is admirable, the very condition of progress. Pragmatism conforms to God's way of acting. The profane accords with God's will. The secular city is the meeting place of man and God. Since man's technological power is constantly increasing, the Church's message consists in giving assurance that it is up to man to create his own destiny.

This is a tissue of commonplaces, all of which are entirely nonbiblical, and are rooted in an *imaginary* factor in modern society. Here is where theology does indeed become a completely futile superstructure. Yet, as Marx rightly said time and again, no matter how futile and tasteless it might be, it nevertheless turns into a deadly poison, in that it prevents man from seeing things as they really are. It causes him to live an illusion and to turn his back upon the real. *The Secular City* is the prime example, for our modern society, of the opiate of the people.

When the Church spends her time blessing people's actual activities, when she is merely there to testify that they are on the right road and that what is happening is God's will, that is when she effects the great turning away from the revelation, the great imposture. But that is only possible to the exact extent to which God himself has turned away from his Church. The latter, sensing her extreme poverty and deficiency, is unable to live with the insecurity which results from her loss of contact with the Stronghold of Israel, so she has to cling to the world. She needs the confirmation which comes from society's approval. She needs number and multitude, and so only one path is open to her, that of supplying the world with justifications and reasons for thinking that what is being done is just and good.

The Church comes along to certify to a powerful world uncertain of its ends that which she herself does not believe. It is the blind leading the blind. Such is the great bravado—the double and mutual satisfaction of Church and society, the Church clinging to the power of progress, society and man, and society deriving its satisfaction from the Church as the still proficient guarantor of "spiritual morality" and of values. When the Church becomes the bearer of lies like that, she thereby renders the world incapable of a critical analysis of what is happening, and so is incapable of making true progress. How can we fail to see in this machinery the very expression of God's silence?

To complete this brief review of the signs of the abandonment given by the Church, we must go back to what we have already indicated above, namely, the mistaken diagnosis pronounced by modern theologians on the subject of man in our society. This diagnostic error necessarily brings with it an error in the prescribed cure, that is to say, that from the moment one is mistaken about the reality itself of our society and of our neighbor, one is mistaken as well about what has to be done. If the Good Samaritan, when he saw the man in the ditch, had concluded that he was sleeping peacefully and enjoying pleasant dreams, his charitable duty would have been to make as little noise as possible, leave the blissful sleeper alone, and continue on his way. The error currently being committed by the generality of Christian intellectuals on the subject of man implies that one should in no way do what is needed in our situation. Here, of course, is where we come upon the justifying machinery to which we have just alluded once again.

But the error alone is decisive, apart from its consequences, for the revelation is not only a disclosure on the part of God of what man is able to know, or by God's decision must know, about God's acts. It is also the disclosure of what man is before God. This clear insight into man derives from the revelation, and it is not an insight into eternity, but into the given historical situation. Now, what we find today is that the Christian has ceased to have a clear vision. He is completely obfuscated, and that can come about only when the revelation has ceased to be a disclosure.

When the light of the world becomes a darkened light, when the rainbow is reduced to the physical phenomenon, when the Ark of the Covenant is eaten by termites, when the empty tomb is filled with our hermeneutics, when the Kingdom of God is a political product, when the life in Christ is a mere symbol, when the dethroned King takes refuge in speeches, then the dead of night has won the heart and darkened the eyes. That dead of night is now.[20]

------

[20] To this analysis of the signs of the abandonment we must surely add that of the Jewish people, which symbolizes it obviously for all mankind. Can we suppose that God has not turned away from us after Auschwitz and Treblinka, after the genocide of which Israel (and Israel alone) is the victim? But I can only say over again, and not nearly as well, what Neher has said in his excellent *L'exil de la parole,* which I have cited frequently.

Self-Critical Interlude

We have come to the point where we must enter into a critique of this project. What am I up to?—for isn't there an attempt at an apologetic concealed beneath these proceedings? Do we not have here the traditional maneuver of an apologetic in three stages: man is unhappy (or wicked); that is explained by separation from God; this unhappiness or wickedness will be done away with by being reconciled with God, that is to say, by faith in God's action in wiping out the fault and the break.

First of all, I have to confess that I continue to believe in the truth of that schema, in spite of modern theology and the resulting arguments to the contrary. I think it true that man as we know him is both unhappy and wicked, that these two states are interconnected, and that each produces the other. It is indeed true that this is the condition of man who has rejected God's love, and who considers that he has come of age and has grown up, etc.

156

It is indeed true that peace with God in Jesus Christ does erase the evil in man, and does make it possible for him to live again. Therefore, when I repeat this schema here in connection with the theme of hope, that corresponds to what I am not ashamed to believe, even if it looks simplistic and comes under much criticism in our day.

But that debate bears on the question of validity, first of all, and second on the way in which we apply this three-stage "rationale." The mistake is, in fact, that of using those three observations in their barren dogmatism, and precisely as an apologetic. The error was indeed that of employing as a major premise the dogmatic concept that man *is* evil (in himself, of necessity and universally).

All we can do is to consider the actual state, the reality, of this man, of a given man or a given group, in a given set of circumstances, at a given period of time, to see *whether* he is doing harm and *what* his misfortune is. To talk in general terms and metaphysically about evil, sin, and human misery seems to me unimportant. However, should I be able to show that the maladjusted adolescents of my city in my day are basically unhappy, and that their misery far surpasses any harm they might do, should I be able to show that Western man in the 1970s is, actually and factually, a man without hope, who lives his life as though there were no future, that would not depend upon a theological presupposition.

I do make that observation. I am able to describe it. I have, of course, to seek the reasons and motivating factors for this situation at the psychological, or at the sociological, level. All I can say is that when I observe this and analyze it, it does in fact fit in with what the Bible tells me about man who rejects God. However, just as I cannot discover *causes* for this state of affairs, still less can I assign a metaphysical cause by proclaiming original sin. That is not a causality, especially since I'm operating on two different levels. I'm keeping two different sets of books. One is an attempt to observe the real, and if possible to arrive at some rational explanation. The other is in the domain of faith, of free affirmation and proclamation.

These two levels cannot be combined, nor do they go together naturally and objectively. For the person who lives on both planes, the two proceedings are mutually consistent. As a sociologist and a Christian, I can pursue this twofold quest. I am able to say that man is doing harm *and* that he is a sinner, that he is unfortunate *and* that he is separated from God. But that correlation is already established in my own thinking, by my own life experience. It is not something impersonal which can be passed around. For the person who shares the same faith as I, it can make sense, but not otherwise. Likewise, when I bear witness to the reconciliation with God, that is in no way a proof of a changed situation. I cannot deduce from faith the objective proof that man will cease to be evil and unhappy because reconciled. If such a thing should occur (because there are *also* some Christians who are less evil, or less unfortunate, than some non-Christians; but that does not follow necessarily), I cannot draw from that any argument for the validity of the faith, nor for the accuracy of the revelation. In other words, no objectifiable observation can be applied to progress toward or in Christ.

With that understood, how do we stand on that score in the project here being undertaken? The mere statement that I have no intention, and make no pretense, of presenting an apologetic is obviously not enough to keep me from doing it. Yet it truly is not my purpose here to prove that if modern man is without hope it is because of original sin. I do not mean to set a trap by promising the renewal of hope for anyone who will turn and be converted. But good intentions are not enough. I can, unconsciously and unintentionally, yield to the temptation to present an apologetic. . . . I would like only to make the following four observations:

First of all, I do not claim to introduce a logical relationship between the state of man without hope and the break with God. The relationship looks certain to me, but it is incapable of proof, and if it were proved it would become useless and unusable. The reason is that, if I could prove it, I have to know that the very hope I was talking about would then be a dead object, without substance or truth, and that the God about whom I was talking would have no connection with the one who reveals himself throughout the Bible. The more absolute and conclusive my proof would be, the more false and deceptive would be the point it was supposed to make.

Hence there can be no question here of bearing witness. I can show the person that which he knows better than anyone, namely, the extent to which he is living in an impasse, how gravely without hope he is, here and now. But I am not really showing him anything. He knows it and is living it. I can affirm, gratuitously and without proof, that the hope is in God through Jesus Christ, but I cannot guarantee anything. I am obliged to warn the person to whom I am speaking that there is nothing automatic or certain about it. The hope is in God, but whether *this* person will live that hope I do not know. His faith in God may be one of a lack of hope, perhaps a tragic one. That I know well enough, but at what moment the hope will be born I do not know. Yet I can attest that it is born.

Still less can I exclude other sources of hope. There are other religions and philosophies which can give a person hope. I have no reason to deny that, nor to argue that the Christian hope is superior, nor that those others are false and deceptive. What I should do is to give warning, whenever I see and know that a given hope brings evil, misfortune, and misery, worse than those which had gone before. The hope that the Germans had in Hitler, the hopes for tomorrow which were the theme song of Stalinism, those hopes I had the duty to declare not only false, but disastrous for humanity as a whole. Mao's hope of the red sun is one that I have the duty to designate as the greatest danger, the most atrocious, the most macabre delirium into which we have ever been thrown.

But I have nothing to say against a genuine, deep, and sensible hope, such as that aroused by Gandhi, or by Martin Luther King, or such as that described by Aldous Huxley in *Island*. In that case, what am I to say as a Christian? Simply that those who already have their hope have no need of the hope that is in Christ, if they are not Christians, and in consequence of that fact it is demonic to destroy their hope and futile to preach to them that of Jesus Christ. Yet it could be that they stand in need of some other aspect of the Gospel and that it is up to me to find out what that is.

This absence of logical and scientific correlation between the lack of hope in Western man in the 1970s and the hope that is in Christ is the more obvious and certain as hope itself belongs to a category which is not amenable to any psychological or sociological analysis. Everything uncovered by a scientific approach in this area is something other than hope. It is a facsimile of it (as belief is a facsimile of faith). What one is dealing with are external signs, factitious objectifications—not the thing itself. Briefly, I will say that, "in the nature of the case," there cannot be any convincing intellectual proof.

The second observation I would make is that there can be no apologetic because, even if there were convincing proof, it would be meaningless. In the first place, we must always bear in mind that there is nothing automatic in the return to grace through conversion. At a time when God is turned away, a conversion no longer suffices to bring it about that God is present once again. God's grace is not lost, but this God, now far away, is no longer at our disposal through a change of heart. Moreover, it is essential to remember (how many times does this have to be repeated!) that, even if I could furnish proof which was flawless, irrefutable, absolute, conclusive, and intellectually and scientifically irreproachable, I might possibly manage to obtain intellectual consent, but that would not cause faith to be born, nor hope. It is never because a person is convinced intellectually that he crosses over into the existential.

Now, in the case of hope, there is not even the intermediate step that one can experience for faith. Since faith involves an intelligible content capable of being formulated, there is the not unimportant role for the intellect to play. Thus one can argue the content of faith intellectually. There is available the possible step of intellectual consent. That is not faith, but it can prepare the way for it and perhaps approach it. But for hope there is nothing like that! The entire being hopes or despairs. No logical reasoning, no demonstrated truth, can in the slightest degree bring about the transition from emptiness to hope. Thus an apologetic is even more useless here than it is in the area of faith.

In the third place, I must continue to emphasize that the return to God through Jesus Christ, conversion, and faith are in no way "solutions." That was a frequent mistake of theologians: "Return to God, be converted, and your problems and difficulties will be resolved." Never does the biblical revelation make use of such language.

It shows, to the contrary, that faith in Christ involves one in incredible difficulties, without in the slightest providing an automatic answer to the difficulties which had gone before. If these human difficulties should be resolved, it would be, I do not hesitate to say, by pure illusion. Biblically, life is not a problem which will be *solved* by clear definition and a complete and particularized accounting. Until there is a problem *of that category*, there can be no solution. The Bible says nothing of a solution for sin, nor of a solution for the question of death, nor of a solution for collective evil. It tells us, on the one hand, that *all* is *changed* in Christ, and, on the other hand, it calls upon us for a decision, which is quite something else. God and faith are not solutions. To think that they are would again be to turn them into things and means.

The same principle holds in connection with hope. It is not a solution for despair. We *see* that hope is dead in our day, but we cannot put forth our own panacea of Christian hope. If there is no hope, there is no hope, Christian or otherwise. So what we are doing here is not in the category of apologetics.

My fourth observation is that we still cannot keep silent when we know that there is a living hope in Christ, a power which can cause hope to be born. We do not have the right to hide this and cover it up under the pretext that we are in danger of indulging in apologetics and that we have no right to influence people. When this person is in trouble, why should I not come to his aid? Why not bring him what he needs? I have already spoken of this, and of the need for the Christian to take to the other person what he himself has received and which the other person needs. "I believed, and so I spoke" (II Cor. 4:13), that is the first step. It springs from the core of my being, which is Christ. It attests that, yes, there is hope (but only if I have lived it, and it is not a theoretical "verity").

"Or what man of you, if his son asks him for bread, will give him a stone?" (Matt. 7:9). That is the second step, which derives from the first. But, it can be said, the other person asks nothing from Christians. He has been disappointed too often. This is true in part, but only in part. In a rhythm which is difficult to understand, questions are again being put to Christians. In the general confusion one *also* turns to the Christians (at least it is just possible they might have something to say). The worst situation, actually, is the one we are in at present, in which questions are being put to us and we no longer know what to say because the questions are not those for which two thousand years of Christianity had prepared us.

Then too, even if the questions are not verbalized and clearly set forth, we still can sometimes perceive that underneath it all an unexpressed drama is developing. An injured person does not always cry for help. He may simply be in a coma. Are we not to go near him? No appeal was made to the Samaritan from Jericho. He saw, and he provided the care. Hence, we too have to be neighbor to him whose hope is so dead that he doesn't even know whether he might ever hope again. He no longer knows even the meaning of the word, and possibly not even the word itself. In that case it is understood that we are necessarily beyond the point of transmitting anything directly. We are beyond a message to be mediated through the word.

So we began by attempting to show that there can be no apologetic here because intellectual proof is meaningless. We then arrived at the conviction that one cannot speak of hope to the person who has no hope (and therefore it is even less a matter of apologetics). Only the presence of a lived hope can eventually include a meaning (and certainly, for me, the *eventus* is the intervention of the Holy Spirit!). Also, we are talking about a meaning such as will incite the person, in whose presence I am living as a bearer of hope, to ask me the question to which I shall be obliged to answer by giving "an account of the hope" that is in me (I Pet. 3:15). Then, and not before, can that hope be expressed, mediated, and made known. Then, and not before, can the speech which is indispensable transmit the miracle of hope.

What, then, is the meaning of this effort if we have closed all the roads? It can only be an address to "Christians," to those who acknowledge Jesus as the Christ, to those for whom God has really revealed himself, for whom he has accomplished all in this man who is really his Son, to those for whom there remains, in spite of the scandal, the fact that Jesus Christ, God himself, is completely risen, those for whom this man has saved them for all eternity, is saving them now and will save them at the time of the final confrontation of man with God, because he is the Lord who humbled himself, gave himself, abandoned himself. Apart from that acknowledgment, this thinking has no import of any kind. This discourse has no meaning in itself, but only with reference to that prior discernment.

Yet at this point we are obliged to put the same question again (but in reverse): If the reader is already in the faith, if he knows all that already, what good is this discourse? The fact is, I observe that a great many Christians today, and myself first of all, can know and also try to live in the faith, yet without hope. In the midst of this world, in this occident, they are just as discouraged, depressed, uncertain, fearful, and agonized as everybody else. Hence, it is not to be taken for granted, it is not automatic, ob-

vious, and spontaneous, that faith should give birth to
hope, any more, as we were saying, than it is obvious,
automatic, and spontaneous that it should show itself in
love. Thus our thinking is located in that interval which
separates faith from hope. Its purpose is to close that gap,
and to arouse the Christian to hope.

To be sure, it can also be received and understood by
a non-Christian. I have no intention of erecting a barrier
here, of establishing a prior condition. I insist only on
emphasizing that there is here no recipe, no gimmick for
arousing hope, and that the reader can no more expect to
emerge from a meditation on hope equipped with hope
than I can expect to persuade him to "have" this hope.
What troubles me is to see a generation of Christians born
without hope (or with no hope but politics, which is
quite frequently the case and is still more serious than
not having any at all!).

But this always involves another dimension. We have
tried to show that no hope can be born except from a
hope lived by another, attested as lived and visible at
that level. It cannot happen otherwise. Hence, in a generation without hope, Christians would be seriously missing the significance of their faith if they failed to live this
hope. It is not given to them primarily for themselves. It
is for them in the midst of, and for, others. But if they are
not living it, there is nothing. They can in no way help
others, still less witness to Jesus Christ. A hope lived and
living is the prior condition for witness.

If (because we are in the faith of Jesus Christ) we believe that Jesus Christ *is* the living hope, then we would
be seriously and completely lacking toward others if,
through not having this hope, we canceled for them any
possibility of hope. In comparison with that, the various
aids which one might extend, such as economic assistance,

institutional reform, political action, all have no more value than did the former works of charity to which Christians were devoted for centuries.

But, of course, they have no less value either! Those things must also be done. Yet, however obvious the injustices, famines, persecutions, oppressions, repressions, wars, and tortures are today, that is not where the central disaster of man is located. Our business is to get to the center of the disaster, and not to its aftereffects or its periphery. We have to restore to man a possibility of living because there is a hope for living. We can do that only by living it ourselves, and we can live it only if we are exhorted to do so, and if we sense possible incarnations of this hope. We shall not succeed unless we perceive the bridge, the link, the relationship, which exists between this faith which we have received and this hope to which we are called.

PART III

Hope in an Age
of Abandonment

WELL NO! In spite of my known pessimism, in spite of the sociological studies I have made, which show the implacable nature of the evolution of systems, in spite of the lack of freedom which I see everywhere, in spite of the ineffectiveness of human potentialities in responding to the real questions, in spite of the sequel of fatalities, in spite of this abandonment on the part of God, I am not without hope, not at all.

Especially now. It is now, under these circumstances, in this very situation, that hope takes place. Otherwise it is nothing but a little spice on top to flavor the sauce. It is now, under these very circumstances, that hope is the indispensable force, that it has its reason for existence, that it really nourishes, that it supplies the bread and the wine with their meaning.

Hope . . . ah, we know what it means only too well. In a very orthodox way, of course, we have hope because Jesus Christ is risen, because there is God's promise and, as Jürgen Moltmann has admirably shown, we go from promise to promise.[1] Each promise fulfilled nourishes the hope in the new one to be fulfilled. We are well aware that it is a matter of the hope in the fulfillment of these promises. We hope for the coming of the Kingdom of God, for the return of Jesus Christ, for the forgiveness of our sins and for the resurrection.

[1] I have already cited the great work of Moltmann, and that of Ricoeur, but there have been a number of other works on hope in recent years. As a matter of recall, let me cite the learned studies of P. Schutz, *Parusie— Hoffnung und Prophetie* (1960; Protestant); Ernst Bloch, *Das Prinzip Hoffnung* (2 vols., 1959; Marxist); and the splendid meditation of E. Fleg, *Nous de l'espérance* (1949). I confess that I have read only reviews of the first two of these works.

Apart from those, A. Neher's brilliant study in biblical theology, *L'exil de la parole* (1970), should obviously be cited as well. This study of God's abandonment and silence appeared while I was completing the draft of the present work. The work of Neher fits in with what I was attempting to do, so much so that I abandoned a portion of the biblical aspects already studied, because one will find in Neher more competent analyses than mine on Job and Ezekiel, and on Abraham.

Yet I disagree with one of Neher's themes, which ends in treating the silence of God as a general, normalized situation, thus eliminating the tragic element from the absence of the Word, and bestowing on man a freedom such that, in the end, he is not lost in the break with God. It leaves the impression that it matters little whether God exists or not.

See also A. Maillot, *l'Epitre de l'Espérance* (1970) and A. Bieler, *Une politique de l'Espérance* (1970).

It is especially important not to separate those different themes of hope. It is important not to divide them, not to do a content-analysis on hope. That would be to ruin it, to distort it, to give it a meaning which it does not have, to kill it. That is to say that, if we think to lay hold of it by its object, we lay hold of exactly nothing, because it is only movement and life.

But when we have said that, we've said everything and we've said nothing. Certainly it is all very true theologically and biblically, but it cannot express hope today. The object hoped for can no longer give birth to the movement within us. It is when hope is present that the Kingdom of God and the return of Jesus Christ take on their full significance. It is by our hope that the power of the faith in these realities is nourished. It is not part of contemporary man's situation that hope should be born from the vision of, the prospect of, and the faith in those realities.

It is my belief that, while faith can be a subjective appropriation of what God gives objectively, it does not work that way with hope. It is not enough to announce the reality of the resurrection to modern man in order that hope may be born within him. All that meaning of hope is still true, but it is too weak, too lacking in vitality, to become a firm hope on the basis of which we can see and believe. We no longer live in an age when the sight of the heavenly Jerusalem could arouse such a disruptive hope that whole peoples would march to liberate the earthly Jerusalem.

Thus I have no dispute with the content of hope from the theological point of view. Those are the known verities. Neither am I looking for what is understood, or for what could be understood, by the expressions "Kingdom of God" and "resurrection." That insoluble and engaging discussion in no way throws light on the possibility or the impossibility of hope, either on its truth or on its dynamic. I am not about to elaborate a theology of hope. I shall keep to a much more lowly level (that of a person who had lived his faith without hope, and to whom hope was one day given), to a much more elusive moment (that in which hope is born), and to a less comprehensive outlook. What is the significance of hope when it is born?

6

The Response to God's Silence

So that leaves us with no possible theology or philosophy of hope. This theology, very patent, and taken up seriously in recent years, consists in a sort of constructing of hope. One gathers the biblical data and provides hope with a reinforcement, a sense, a raison d'être, an underpinning. In this way one perceives, with Moltmann, that the entire revelation is structured in terms of the promise, and that hope becomes an essential part of the Christian life because of the indissoluble relation between hope and promise. Thus one puts hope back into its theological setting, validates it biblically, and shows its relation to other elements of theology. It is no longer an isolated, erratic phenomenon, a more or less fleeting sentiment, an appendix to the Christian life. It becomes, to the contrary, the radiating center.

With this central reality of hope I am heartily in accord. To be sure, it appears to me obvious that the eschatological reality is also decisive politically, as I tried to show in *The Presence of the Kingdom* (1948). That seems to me the starting point for understanding the rest of the revelation, for establishing an ethic and for grasping the realities of the world in which we are living. It is now recognized that the preaching of Jesus proceeds from an eschatological background. Eschatology is not an appendix to a theology of the revelation. It is not the normal end-result (but as an end-result it is necessarily less important than the rest of the book or of the movement). It is not the terminus toward which we are advancing, but the force which is advancing toward us. We are not marching toward the Kingdom of God, but the Kingdom of God is bursting violently into our times, into our milieu. It is breaking up the balanced order of march, the timetables, and the organizations. It is alive in our midst.

Thus there is a dazzling presence of these last things, but the latter are not grasped, and do not become provocative, except by and in hope. This has been the focal point of all my biblical and political interpretations, and it is now being more and more confirmed by theologians and exegetes, who demonstrate that the theological concepts of the New Testament are centered on the preaching of the Kingdom which is to come and which is coming.

At the same time it is emphasized, with Buber, that the great contrast between the God of Israel and all the other gods is the contrast between the promise and the epiphany. All the gods of all the ages are gods who show themselves, who are visible at a given time. They interfere in the present, in the contemporary. They are "there." Thus, strictly speaking, they are "idols" (that is to say, images). The theophany is the act of the god who is there, at a given moment, in the present, and who manifests himself as God. The God of Israel, on the other hand, never shows himself, to put it briefly. He is the God who *speaks*, and his word is a promise, not a fulfillment at the present time.[2] He cannot be an idol because he gives only a name. He gives his name to Moses, but he does not show himself. Moses is able only to see his trace after he has passed by. Never does he show himself. All that is seen of him is a reflection, a symbol. He gives a sign. It is the burning bush.[3] He gives a mediator, and it is the angel of Jacob. When he is there, in Jesus Christ, it is not as God that he discloses himself. What we see is a man. Jesus is not a theophany, even if we could accept a theophany. There is no theophany of the God of the Bible, because he is the one who defers to a greater reality in the future.

Thus he opens up a "religion of the name," as opposed to the religions of idols. As Ricoeur rightly says, summarizing the thought of Buber, the religion of the name gives rise to a history. The religion of idols gives rise to a nature full of gods.

But if that be true, we can see that hope is indeed that which most completely expresses the will of this God. "History is a hope of history." We receive and lay hold of the promise, but the latter is inscribed in a possible his-

[2] It is of little consequence whether God discloses himself entirely or declines to do so, whether we know only an appearing of God which is different from his being. Surely we can say nothing of his being, but we cannot do other than consider the extreme importance of the appearing in which God reveals himself. In fact, if God chooses this appearing, that in itself confirms that this appearing is his being. But no speculation is possible beyond that. However, when God ceases to speak, the appearing which remains as a memory can no longer satisfy us. We are assailed by the lack. When the morphine addict lives in his illusory world, an appearing seems to him more true and more desirable than anything else on which he is prepared to take a chance. When he runs out of morphine, he experiences a lack in which his whole life is at stake.

[3] We must remember that it is never said that Moses *saw* God face to face, but that God *spoke* to him face to face.

tory because we bring about a tension in every actuality by our expectation of fulfillment. We cannot sit comfortably in an established situation. We are living by a promise which is to be fulfilled (and toward the fulfillment of which we have to put out an effort), and by a staggering invasion into our life experience of last things. So nothing can be settled and nicely organized.

Each time a received promise is fulfilled, it obviously is experienced as a confirmation of what had been announced, as a pledge of the more complete fulfillment to come, and as a raising of the level of hope which is nourished by this actualization. Thus we come upon the movement from the "already" to the "not yet," and the nourishment for this "not yet" is firmly planted in history by the "already," which loses its importance in and of itself because its true significance is to refer us to the plenitude of the "not yet." Thus, in brief, is formulated a theology of hope.

All this is undoubtedly right, and a good and an important thing to say, but, in the final analysis, is it possible? Is hope still hope once it has been given a motive and accorded its place in the intellectual system which justifies and explains it? If, as it seems to me, there is an indissoluble relationship between faith and the object of faith, so that in speaking of the object of faith one is speaking of the faith itself, the same is not true of hope. The thing hoped for neither defines, nor arouses, nor in any way limits hope. To show it constructed on a theological ensemble is not to show it, or, more exactly, is to attempt to insert into a system that which is antisystem, and which explodes all situations and all explanations.

Actually, to want to produce a theology or a philosophy of hope is to transform hope into the opposite of what it is. One can only treat it as an object. In spite of all in-

tellectual precautions it is bound to be objectified, that is
to say, it is no longer hope. Neither can it be fixated, and
consequently a discourse on it does not give an account
of what it is. Nor can it be treated as a constructed, justified, and explained object placed in relation to other
theological data, for anything manipulated in that way
is the opposite of what hope is. Here also, this is to take
the vestiges of that which no longer exists for the actuality
of that which is. Hope is the antiobject, and the anti-
discourse as well. Thus it can neither be explained nor
defined. A theology of hope is unavoidable, to be sure.
It is fine that Moltmann should have written what he has
written and that Ricoeur followed him, but every theology
of hope is an expression of a concept of hope. Still, we
should rejoice in these works which call the Church to
hope, because they do point to the way of life which has
now to be adopted.

If there are so many such works today, that is surely not
mere chance. These rediscoveries of a central Christian
theme never come about by chance. From one point of
view, one can say that it is a sociological necessity which
has led in that direction (and in that case I will say that
it is the abandonment which has incited us to hope). From
another point of view, one may also see in it the hidden
work of God, who is speaking still in calling us to hope.

What I find objectionable is the theological structuring.
In reality, one is treating hope the way the dogmatists are
accused of having treated God, by transforming the living
thing into a corpse for autopsy, the subject into an object,
the one doing the talking into the one talked about, the
elusive into categories. If there is such a thing as hope, it
is so close to the truth of God that it cannot be delimited
in any theology. What we are attempting here is in no
sense either a theology or a philosophy of hope (which,

moreover, I would be incapable of producing), but it is, if I may say so, a sort of mirror to reflect the source.

TO BE CLEAR ABOUT HOPE

If I were to give a "definition," I would say that hope is man's answer to God's silence. What good is hope when God is talking? What meaning would it still have? Paul's statement about faith applies to hope *as well:* "For now we see in a mirror dimly, but then face to face. Now we know by a flash in the dark, but then we shall understand, even as we have been understood" (paraphrase of I Cor. 13:12). When God's Word strikes us with its flood of light, when it bursts in upon our lives or upon the world, when it is transformed from dead Scripture into a disruptive, living thing, when the disruption is translated back again into a work, into Scripture . . . of what use is hope? Even if the word is that of a promise, of a designation of something beyond, of a reference to what is to come in the future, the fact that it is a word from God gives it such a value, such a presence, such a fullness, that man is no longer in a state of hope, but in a state of assurance. He is in the mood of power and daring, in the joyful activity of the unshakable martyr. When God speaks, what possible significance could hope have? The Kingdom of God is *here*, the resurrection is achieved, the eschatology is realized.

Perhaps, also, that is why we find throughout the course of the Church this unconscious movement back and forth between a theology of the presence and a theology of the promise. When the Word of God is present strikingly and unquestionably, what need is there for a theology of promise? What counts is not the possible future but the incarnate present. Under those circumstances, the Church produces a theology of the presence, forgetting somewhat the decisive eschatology. When, on the other hand, we find ourselves in a period of silence and sterility, when the Word of God is rare, incommunicable, and incomprehensible, then we are thrown back upon the eschaton, and the theology of hope becomes a necessity. The one is not more true than the other, but the alternation depends on the times.

Hope comes alive only in the dreary silence of God, in our loneliness before a closed heaven, in our abandonment. God is silent, so it's man who is going to speak. But he is not going to speak in God's place, nor in order to decorate the silence, nor in taking his own word for a Word from God. Man is going to express his hope that God's silence is neither basic nor final, nor a cancellation of what we had laid hold of as a Word from God. This Word has now ceased, but its object, content, and reflection are still in our memories, and we accept it because the witnesses who received it and transmitted it were worthy of trust.

Hope is, first of all, this absurd act of confidence placed in those who declared that it was the Word of God which they had received (and which we are no longer receiving). Though we no longer know the Word, we believe their testimony that it was living, active, and disruptive. The hope is that this Word of God might once again be spoken, might again be born and might again be decisive. But it is more than that. It is not only expectation, or certitude. It is demand. When God is silent, he has to be made to talk. When God turns away, he has to be made to turn back to us again. When God seems dead, he has to be made to exist. It can take the form of an anguished appeal, a complaint, a lamentation, or a prayer of repentance.

It can also take the form of daring protest, of violence against God, of accusation.

These are all valid means for hope in the face of God's rejection, in the face of his silence and his turning away. It is a challenge directed at God. Hence, in a sense, it could be said that hope is blasphemous. It actually rejects the decision of God's silence.[4] It refuses to give in to the new situation in which God has placed man. It does not acquiesce in the idea that the Word could be a thing of the past. It does not ratify God's will to turn away, knowing that this God is he who was, and is, and is to come. It appeals to God against God. It demands an accounting of God, who is not acting the way he had said and had shown that he acts.

For there is that as well. Hope is not only the reaction to a promise of God fulfilled (though it is that too!), which spurs us toward a new promise to be fulfilled. It is also the testimonial of a promise not fulfilled, and a demand that God keep his word. The whole secret, the genuine expression and the essence of hope are stated for us by Isaiah: "Truly, thou art a God who hidest thyself, O God of Israel, the Saviour" (Isa. 45:15) and, "I will wait for the Lord, who is hiding his face from the house of Jacob, and I will hope in him" (Isa. 8:17).

[4] For it is hope, not man's silence, which is the true answer to God's silence, in spite of Neher's splendid pages: "God has withdrawn in silence, not in order to avoid man, but, on the contrary, in order to encounter him. But it is an encounter of silence with silence. Two beings, one of whom tried to escape the other in the face to face of the lighted stage, find each other in the silent back to back of hidden faces. . . . The dialectic which links God with man is no longer positive. . . . It is a negative dialectic. Silence is no longer an escape. It becomes the place of supreme aggression. Freedom invites God and man to an inevitable rendezvous, but it is a rendezvous in the opaque world of silence." Undoubtedly that *can* be the case, but then the only outcome is death, the return to nothingness, if the person who knows God ratifies this absence.

Hope is the shield against defeat, against God's rejection —"freedom's shield against death" (Neher). Everything is said openly, the fact of the silence and the abandonment, man's shattering affirmation that, in the face of God's rejection, hope is alive. It is the confession which binds even God, "Thou art the Saviour." We find exactly the same proclamation in Daniel, in connection with the awful story of Daniel's three companions who were threatened by Nebuchadnezzar with being cast into the fiery furnace, and who declared that, on the one hand, "Our God . . . *is able* to deliver us . . . , and he will deliver us." That is the first declaration, of a hope humanly perceptible. But then comes the most essential: "But *if not*" (if God doesn't save us), *in spite of all,* "be it known to you, O king, that we will not serve your gods or worship the golden image which you have set up" (Dan. 3:17–18). That is the true affirmation of hope, like that of Isaiah. I remain faithful to God, even if nothing, absolutely nothing more, comes my way from him.

Thus the attitude of Job is par excellence the attitude of hope.[5] He dares to declare God unjust because he fails to show himself as he said he was. When Jesus Christ says that he is with us even to the end of the world, hope consists in demanding that that is how it should be. When it becomes clear that that is not the case, hope refuses to take refuge in drugs and in abstract explanations. Instead, it enters into conflict with God, and untiringly demands his presence.

And when it is told us that miracles will accompany us through life, that serpents will not bite us and poison will not kill us, hope refuses to accept that as a mere manner of speaking, as a symbol of a purely spiritual reality. It

---

[5] Ecclesiastes seems to me to be the book of hope above all others.

rejects the idea that interest in miracles shows us still slaves to the primitive, magic-mongering, and materialistic mentality, which preserves the less important things (miracles) while neglecting that of which they are the sign, a mentality which emphasizes the thing signifying while neglecting the highly spiritual thing signified, that is to say, the thing not made flesh.

Such a theology and such explanations are really a coverup for a fundamental hopelessness, a resignation. Even if the miracle is *relatively* of little importance (which it is), even if it is really only a sign of a much greater reality, and even if it is true that we should be interested in the more important things, nevertheless miracle was the object of a promise which is not only spiritual, but very tangible.

It has especially to be understood concerning these stories involving signs, things signifying, and things signified, that where there is no sign neither is there a thing signified. If you live without signs, you strictly cannot claim to be going directly to the thing signified. If there were other clear and striking signs of the spiritual reality revealed in Christ, I would accede, in the absence of the thing signified in all its fullness. But not a shadow of any such sign is to be seen. Therefore the sign which has been shown us and assigned to us in the Gospel (the miracles) is the one we have to lay claim to and demand of God. After all, that is what was promised—and how do we know that the "rest" of the promise (the Holy Spirit and the Kingdom) is realized when we have no sign, and when it is rather obvious that the external things signifying are nonexistent?

Hope is a protest before this God, who is leaving us without miracles and without conversions, that he is not keeping his Word. Thus it is not a nice peaceful confidence that things are going to get better and that the situation is going to change. It is a real indictment of God in the name of the Word of God. It is Job's great declaration, "my eye pours out tears to God, that he would maintain the right of a man with God" (Job 16:20–21). It is still from God that we look for this realization, this fulfillment, but a God turned in man's favor. That was already done, once for all, in Jesus Christ. It has been achieved. The union is brought about. "God has crossed over to man's side," as Karl Barth says. Well and good, so let us see it. So let God show that he actually is maintaining our right, that he is walking with us, that he is all around us and is going before us.

Speaking for myself, what I see is that we are abandoned by God. Oh, I do not say forever, or that we are excluded from salvation, but that here and now, in this moment of history, in this night which perhaps has refused the light, no actual light is shining any longer. God has to agree that he's wrong to turn away like that, and to shut himself up in his silence. He has to hear man's protest. That word of Job is of the essence of the word of hope. We have the right to say it, and to say it again, in this age, even if we are sinners (and we are), even if we have deserved to have God abandon us (and we have indeed deserved it), even if the Church is a parody of the Church, unworthy of God (and she is a parody of the Church), even if our contemporary theology is a heaping of vanity upon discourse and of discourse upon misunderstanding (and it is that). After this has all been acknowledged, and much more besides, we still refuse to accept God's leaving us and ceasing to speak. We walk toward the crashing storm which surrounded Moses. Hope means running the risk of really being struck by the lightning of God's anger which we may arouse rather than of molding in his silence.

But more than that, hope is the accusation that God who is silent cannot be the true God, our Father. He who is silent is related to the idols, those idols the Bible makes fun of. The hope of God's Word, in order to bring out the Word, is offensive to the God who no longer speaks. It says to the silent God: "Only idols are mute. Only the false Gods are incapable of speech, and you, O God, inscrutable now after having revealed yourself, are putting yourself on a par with the idols." Hope never ceases to shout in God's ears, like the woman in the ears of the unjust judge, when she summoned him not to be unjust because he is judge, when she summoned him to be the judge. Hope says: "I summon you not to be an idol, not to act like a false God, since I know that you are God. I summon you to speak, since you are the Word."

Thus hope creates an attitude just the reverse of the one we would naturally adopt. As good and obedient Christians, we are always ready to accuse ourselves and to humble ourselves. If we see that God has turned away, our first reaction is one of an examination of conscience and self-accusation. God had a "reason" (yet he is the one who acts beyond all reasons and without cause!). We are guilty of very serious sins. That is true enough, but our sins are no greater than those of the first century or the sixteenth century.

So we must repent and humble ourselves and confess our sins. That is an excellent thing to do, but when one has done it one has done nothing. Heaven is just as empty and the Word is just as absent. When one has done it (and, of course, it should be done!), one is left open-mouthed at the end of a dead-end road. After all, God has said that our sins were forgiven in Jesus Christ. Therefore, if this procedure does not work, it means that something else is wrong beside our sins, and it is not for us to sit in weary resignation by the side of the road waiting for things to change.

Hope is the opposite of resignation. Hope alone (not revolution!) is that. Perhaps in wrapping up all our little sins we should wake up to the fact that the sin which really counts is precisely the lack of hope, the loss of the conviction that God opens the way, the readiness to resign and sit down. It is true that "things have to change," but it is not "the situation" in the abstract which needs to change, nor is it we who are called upon to change things by our decisions and actions. It is God who needs to change. It is God who must return to enlighten his Church and to make our hearts shout with joy. All the other things, our works, our commitments, our theological constructs, and our political and sociological agitation, are so much eyewash. It is God who has to change, and hope is the resolute will to make God change (because, beginning with him, every concrete situation is modified). It is to bring about once again the implementation of that wonderful statement of the Old Testament, "and God repented. . . ." [6]

To be sure, it is always up to us to repent for our part (without crocodile tears or fruitless brooding!), but hope pushes God to repent along with man, who in Jesus Christ is not separated from God even when God is turned away.

[6] In his semantic analysis of the silence of hope, Neher offers the following noteworthy observation: the same word (*nehama*) designates God's *repenting*, his regret, his weariness, the miscarriage of his expectations, and it also means *consolation*, recovery in the face of failure, determination to resume the task, and hope. Likewise, the word *azav* signifies, on the one hand, abandonment, and on the other hand, the fact of being gathered in. "Abandonment and ingathering do not depend on the compensating and healing effect of the passage of time, but on the internal dialectic of their unbreakable relationship." Thus hope is biblically linked to abandonment.

That is the meaning of Jesus' famous statement, "The kingdom of heaven has suffered violence, and men of violence take it by force" (Matt. 11:12).

Yes, the violence (it is often said that love is violence) is that of hope. To enter into the Kingdom of heaven you have to want it the hard way. You have to knock on the door to the point of exhaustion. You say its doors are open, and we are invited in? Yes, of course, I agree, in eternity, in the perfected plan of God. But in the tangible world of a period in church history, as in that of a man's life, the doors are slammed shut, barred, and padlocked. Hope means the rejection of this real discrepancy between the eternal plan revealed in Jesus Christ and the concrete situation of the present time. Hope means to be invited, to find the doors shut, to be offended by that, to put in a claim that God operate in accordance with what he had said. Hope uses the most violent means to enter into the Kingdom of heaven, which is our passion, our expectation of joy, our abundance, our reason for acting, our every breath, more precious than each beat of the heart, our assurance of justice and our inner light of peace. If it means that to us, how could we acquiesce in the doors being shut at this moment of time?

Our hope is precisely that this Kingdom of heaven is all that; and because it is, hope is violence in order that it may be in our midst. If the Kingdom does not mean that to us, it may just as well remain closed, because basically it doesn't interest us. That means that we have no true hope, and everything may just as well stay the way it is, a matter of little prayers, little political actions, little theologies, little lives Christianly cozy and pledged. Wherever there is not that human and spiritual violence in the face of God's silence, there is no hope, and in that case we cannot hope for what has been promised nor that the Kingdom of heaven might be in the midst of us. So what's the use? But who is it who is saying this "What's the use?" In the end it is God himself. Hope is the refusal to acquiesce in God's being reduced to this "What's the use?" and in his having given his Son for nothing.

THE UNSHAKABLE

But that is only the first face of hope, for hope is also the expression of the final, complete, and unbroken confidence in this God, even though one is attacking him and asking him to explain. It is still Job (first of all) who recites it to us (19:25–27):

> For I know that my Redeemer lives,
>   and at last he will stand upon the earth;
> and after my skin has been thus destroyed,
>   then from my flesh I shall see God,
> whom I shall see on my side,
>   and my eyes shall behold, and not another.
> My heart faints within me!

That is indeed the other visage of hope. It, too, burns with impatience. But the two faces are united in one, for who is this Redeemer, this avenger of blood? He it is who is to take up Job's defense, and even his place, in his combat with God, who is to avenge him. But avenge him of whom? Of none other than God himself, since it is God whom Job accuses of having reduced him to the last extremity, of having tortured him, pursued him, made him a laughing-stock and abandoned him. Job demands to be avenged of God. And he voices his absolute certainty that he will indeed be avenged. Yet this Redeemer can be none other than God himself. In other words, as a sequel to the great cry, the decisive issue, "my eye pours out tears to God, that he would maintain the right of a man with God," there comes the affirmation of a no less decisive confidence that the answer is indeed "Yes, that is the way it is." God is the avenger of man against God himself (not against Satan, or against human enemies).

It is useless, at this point, to refer to Jesus Christ, and to the fact that all has actually been accomplished. We are in the stage of hope. We are still in Job's situation in this current abandonment. Hope is not an embittered zeal, a futile rebellion. It is also a confidence that things are happening and will happen in that way. It is the resolute certainty, in spite of all the absences and seeming treacheries of God, that these latter do not represent the truth, that the truth is that at last God will stand upon the earth and will be favorable to us.

We cannot dissociate the three aspects: the observation that we are abandoned, the refusal to acquiesce in this decision of God with its combat entered into against him, and the confident certainty that God is still "my God." We find this very progression in the words on the cross, "My God, why hast thou forsaken me?" (Matt. 27:46). This word, in which we see abandonment as a possibility for each person and for the Church, since Jesus did not escape it, is also the word of hope in its fullness. God has abandoned me. *Thou* art *my* God. There is a reality which cannot be suppressed, and which exists because I say it, namely, that thou art still my God. He is mine, just as Job could say "my Redeemer," he who was willing to give himself so that I might say "my God," he who is so tied to my life that he has become "mine."

The exacting metaphysician will surely say that this means nothing, since the Being of beings cannot be "mine." True enough, but this is a situation which no metaphysician can grasp, and which cannot be accounted for by rationalizing. God has made himself mine. God has willed to be in my life in that manner. Hope means so to be aware of this that I could not possibly think of God otherwise than as he who is mine, fully and without reserve.

This God is silent? God has abandoned us? Yes, but by the rejection of that abandonment I can still say "my God." Perhaps there is now no thing or person to receive that word, but as long as I say it I know of a certainty that this God is not breaking the relationship, has not withdrawn for good. When God is silent, we ourselves have to speak his Word. When he no longer reveals himself as our Father, we ourselves have to claim him as such. The Word by which Jesus finds himself forsaken is the same by which he declares that God is his God, and that it cannot be otherwise, since his Word is the Word, and that Word is creative of all reality.

Our word, no. Yet our word still takes this reality into account. That is why, as long as I can pray those words with the full commitment and consent of my whole being, the abandonment is not closed, decisive, and complete. In the end, all the trouble has to do with this stammering. It takes the courage of hope to begin again, and still again, to make that confession of faith, all appearances, all rationality, and all experience to the contrary, to fill the void left by God with this single attestation that he cannot, under any circumstances, be other than my God. That could just be what will bring God to repent.

But the genuineness of this prayer resides precisely in the fact that it goes with an awareness of the abandonment, and with the violence against God in order that he might be what he promised to be. Apart from that, it is another vain repetition and a too-easy appropriation of the one who cannot really belong to anyone. As long as the battle is not fought, with its twofold aspect of the violent person who batters the doors of the Kingdom and of the trusting person who, left in the lurch, insists that God is his God, there is in fact no hope. There is nothing to look forward to, nothing to believe. Indeed, there is no reason to hope for the fulfillment of the promise.

Especially is it important not to let a theology of the promise beguile us into a false position. We have said that it is the only theology possible at the present time (even if there cannot be a true theology of hope!). Moltmann's antithesis between a religion of the promise and a religion of the presence (of God), corresponding to that of Buber, does not mean that, in a *theologia perennis*, a theology of the promise is more true and correct than a theology of the presence. It means only that in an age of abandonment and of God's absence there is nothing else to do but to attempt a theology of the promise, since hope is the only possible approach. With faith impossible in the end, everything—life, ethics, and theology—has to be based on hope.

So this theology of the promise is essential but dangerous. I said earlier that there is always the risk of reducing hope to an object (and so of letting it get away!), but a theology of the interplay of hope and promise is likely to encourage us to think, in brief, that the promise is fulfilled surely and as a matter of course—that it fulfills *itself*. In other words, it can lead us to suppose that the promise possesses a sort of intrinsic power which brings it necessarily to fulfillment. As opposed to this, we should realize that in the Bible the promise is contingent. It can be carried out in diverse and cryptic ways, and its fulfillment can be put off to a much later time. The promise never fulfills *itself*. God fulfills it, and he does so as a conclusion to the harsh and difficult struggle of hope. Hope is not one of the pieces in a well-ordered game. It is, rather, the

violence which lays hold of the promise with fury, so as
not to let the Almighty get off any longer without blessing
us.

When man picks up the conversation in order to force
God to speak, when he never leaves off crashing God's
silence, when he refuses to put up with God's going back
on his Word, when he lets his hope burst forth, that is
when he is obeying the Word of God addressed to Abraham, and which Neher translates: "Go before me" (Gen.
17:1), walk ahead, go forward and show the way. "He is
ahead of God." It is hope challenging God's silence which
opens the road of the Word of God.[7]

MAN'S CAPABILITIES

Is that the same as saying that the promise is to be fulfilled by man himself? According to this, man would
really be the one to carry out the promise. God gives him
a certain number of means, and man takes the action.
That theology, very popular today, is manifestly anti-
biblical, and in our area of interest it is the opposite of
hope. If man can carry out God's promises by himself,
there is no hope. The latter means exactly nothing. How
can you hope for what you are able to do yourself? We
will come back to that in the next paragraph.

Hope is not self-fulfillment by one's own powers. It is
not addressed to man and to his capabilities. It is focused
on God. Hope even implies a complete rejection of de-

[7] This is my interpretation rather than Neher's. He takes it to mean: "Go
forth into the world, proceed with your life without reference to me, without concerning yourself whether I exist or not." It is one of the places in
which Neher insists on the unlimited freedom which would be given,
in this way, to man.

pendence on man and of confidence placed in man's capacities. Hope also consists in the complete refusal to hope for anything at all from man himself. It is opposite to the attitude frequently adopted today, that, since God is silent, man who is now grown up will get along quite well by himself.

Man is capable of great things, positive as well as negative. That is obvious. But he cannot fill the void left by the withdrawal of God. In the midst of this silence, no other response than hope is possible. In particular, the ways in which we are trying today to put up a front—like the theology of the death of God, theological research, and the asking of questions—are false appearances out of which man erects the scenery to give the impression that he is still in charge, that he is in no way abandoned, and that it is he who decides the fate of the Word of God. But it is a farce, as is also the substitution of "service" for faith, the claim of uniqueness for horizontal relationships, as opposed to the emptiness of the vertical relationship.

The only honest and courageous attitude is to see things as they are, then to respond to God's decision with hope. Only after that decisive turnabout, after having taken up the combat with God, after having tried to force the doors of the Kingdom, can one consequently give a concrete (however secondary) form, and an ethic, to this hope by involving it in human decisions, let us say in revolutionary action. If there is certainly no "theology of revolution" which is valid in and of itself, the revolutionary involvement nevertheless *can* be one form of the hope as lived.

But if we are firmly convinced that hope has nothing to do with falling back on man's capabilities, on his greatness and efficiency, or on his so-called vocation as demiurge (based on a mistaken interpretation of Psalm 8), then we have to understand that not only is hope the only response to the abandonment, but in addition to that it can take place only in an age without hope.

Monteilhet, in one of his splendid novels (*Policiers pour la forme*), speaks of a child who was cruelly beaten by a brute:

I can still hear his cries. It's unbearable. It almost makes you believe in God. . . . Cries like that seem to call God back to life, much more surely than all the happiness in the world. There's a rare quality of silence surrounding certain atrocities, an end-of-the-world silence, more frightening even than instant justice. One has the impression that a presence has been withdrawn which could one day fill everything. That total absence of charity takes the form of the low-pressure areas which bring storms.

I know of no passage which more clearly expresses the feeling of hope.

If our good Christians could read world events from the standpoint of hope, they would not cry out against injustice, ignominy, inhumanity, imperialism, exploitation, etc. (new forms of protest against sin, which are just as moralistic and just as futile as the old). They would be able to see in the atrocities of our time what Monteilhet is able to see, the presence which has been withdrawn, the barometric void filled with nothing, the silence beneath the cries of the victims. Then they could recognize in it a gigantic impulse toward faith, for it is this human misery crying to heaven which can "call God back to life," that is to say, can move his heart to stop abandoning us. But when that day comes, it will really be the cyclone drawn in by the complete vacuum of love. All of that can be spoken and lived in hope. Apart from hope, the only thing left is childish indignation, pompous proclamation, and fruitless agitation.

7

In a Hopeless Age

HOPE AND THE THING HOPED FOR

Just as hope is the response to God's silence, so it takes place only in a hopeless age. At this point a distinction has to be made, even an opposition, between hope and the thing hoped for. That implies, to be sure, that I do not go along with Emmanuel Mounier's point of view, nor with his interpretation of events, in his *L'espoir des désespérés*. Of course the thing hoped for makes no sense unless there is some foreseeable outcome. But let us be serious. We are living in a situation which we think has no way out and is hopeless. We really face two possibilities: either there is no foreseeable outcome, everything is unpredictable and there is no way to gauge the chances of success, or else the chances of success and of failure are equal. We can only say we hope "this" will succeed, and that the situation will come out all right.

Unfortunately, hope is too often identified with that state of affairs, with the little absurd and childish leap into the irrational assumption of a happy outcome, of profit and success. Consequently it is easy to understand why hope should not enjoy a good reputation and why one does not quite know what to do about it. It is easy to understand, also, that one would want to replace it with action. The hope is encased in an inconsistent statement that "it can come out all right." This is summed up in the popular saying, "While there's life, there's hope." In other words, give us a little time and our luck can turn. The intellectuals, in recent years, have been putting it in terms of "the worst may not happen." Even in one's darkest moments, the outcome may not necessarily be catastrophic. The storm which looms on the horizon may not strike.

It was that kind of something hoped for, as Jean-François Steiner has shown in *Treblinka*, that made possible the wholesale massacre of the Jews. The latter let themselves be massacred as long as they retained the hope, the hope that, as prisoners, they were being taken to prison and not to death, a hope kept alive on their arrival in Treblinka by the warm welcome at the little railroad station, the hope of finding some scheme to get them out of this, the hope that if one were careful to be unobtrusive one might slip out of the net, the hope of clinging to life (because while there's life there's hope!), rather than risk immediate death in savage revolt.

The thing hoped for is the curse of man, for he does nothing as long as he thinks that a way out will be supplied him. As long as he imagines that there's an exit from a terrible situation he does nothing to change the situation. That is why, for many years, I have tried to shut the false escapes of man's false hopes, an effort which is taken for pessimism. To continue to live with the thing hoped for is to let situations deteriorate until they really are without any way out. The dreadful hope precipitated by Marxism, that history runs a course which necessarily ends in a socialist (or a communist) society, the hope at the beginning of the war in Algeria, that it was not as tragic and extensive as it looked and that it would work itself out, the hope that, after thirty years of talking about it, pollution is not as serious as they say—all these obey the formula that the worst may not come to pass. It is the best possible formula for permitting the worst to develop as a certainty. True hope, to the contrary, has not a grain of sense or of logic except when the worst is considered certain.

Still, it is important not to mistake minor situations for the really essential ones, not to mistake problems which are as good as solved for the problems which are insoluble and tragic. This misunderstanding about the "what" which our desperation should focus on is the thing I condemn the most in the Maoists and various leftists who are acting desperately. Unfortunately, they address themselves to situations which are not at all desperate. They act like real, authentic Don Quixotes in a death struggle with windmills, on the assumption that the struggle is a desperate one, whereas it is just silly (even internationally, silly is still silly). It is a confusion concerning the object, and it leaves the thing which really is desperate free to develop elsewhere. Yet it is good that they act energetically, since their desperation is genuine. They simply are mistaken in their diagnosis.

The thing hoped for appears also on another level, that of acting on the basis of the possible. In a given situation it seems possible to act in such a way as to find an adequate answer. Hope would commit itself in that direction, but here again it is better not to confuse this with the thing hoped for. If we calculate our chances and find a certain reason to expect success because a certain development is probable, then we can have the hope that such an action will succeed, but hope itself has nothing to do with that. All reasoning about the outcome gives birth to a reason-ableness of the thing hoped for. The whole thing is a hope because one is never sure. There can always be an accident.

When I get into an automobile to take a trip, I can reasonably bank on the car's working all right, and that the trip is possible. We will arrive at our destination. Is that a hope? Hardly. It only enters my mind when I say to myself that there is the possibility of an accident, an idea that I dismiss immediately, hoping that such a thing will not happen to me, that the proportion of accidents to the number of cars on the road will not include me. That is where the hope is located, but it is superficial and futile, a vague sentiment having nothing to do with hope itself. It is just a little sacrifice to the mentality of magic.

We can say that reasonableness of the outcome gives a quasi-certainty, on which it is useless to graft a supple-mentary impression that a hope should be entertained concerning the accident which might spoil the outcome. Therefore it does not seem to me that you can define hope as a "passion for possibles." [8] If it is a matter of possibles

---

[8] This formula was repeated by Kierkegaard, but there would appear to be a certain misunderstanding. Actually, when Kierkegaard gives this defini-tion of hope, he does it in *Either/Or*, but, as we know, he presents it in the first, explanatory part as the aesthetic position. Thus, for the aesthetic decision there is this passion for the possible which sets the bounds to, and characterizes, hope. But that definitely cannot be seen as an expres-sion of the Christian faith. Quite the contrary. The exploring of all the possibles is the act of the aesthetic approach, not of the ethical, still less is it that of faith. The determination to actualize the possible is the atti-

196 · *Hope in Time of Abandonment*

really known and discerned as such and adequately calculated, one can in that case have a passion for actualizing
them. That has strictly nothing to do with hope. The
evolution of a technical system, for example, rules out
hope. It is possible, or it is not possible to perform a
surgical operation. One does not engage in such a thing
merely by a spurt of hope, but only after the most minute
experiments and the development of a rigorous technique.
To have an urge to make use of all the instruments, to
have a taste for long journeys, now interplanetary, to ex-
plore the possibilities of a political situation—all that is
the reverse of hope.

I am well aware, of course, what some mean by it.
Hope pushes us to act in all possible directions, not to
stay put, not to fall asleep, satisfied with things as they
are, not to spend our lives in mediocrity. But for this let
us appeal to the spirit of power, to the spirit of self-interest, to the spirit of the will to dominate, to the urge to try
out new things, to the exaltation of an ideal, to enthusiasm
for a myth, and that will be quite enough to push a person
into all the possibles.

---

tude of the person *without* hope, precisely because that possible is never
more than a duplication of the present. Very explicitly, at the end of
Either/Or, in "Ultimatum," Kierkegaard shows that to do everything one
can is the reverse of faith. There he goes counter, in the ethical stage, to
what he has set forth in the first part, and he shows, without, however,
using this formula, that faith in Jesus Christ presupposes the passion
for the impossible. So there is need to clarify the source of this misunderstanding.

If one refers hope to the possible, then the computer is the true figure
of hope, for it contains the totality of all the possibles in each sector. It
possesses all the eventualities. In a given situation, nothing escapes the
computer which has been programmed for it. But is it not clear that hope
is precisely to escape from that predetermination, and to depart from
the field of the possibles? The choice is a radical one. The computer
places us in an impasse.

Hope is not there, because hope is the passion for the impossible. It makes no sense, has no place, no reason for existence, except in the situation in which nothing else is actually possible. What it calls for is not a person's last resort, nor some second breath, but a decision from without which can transform everything. It exists when it is up against a stone wall, faced with the ultimate absurdity, the incurable misery. Thus it never expresses itself through a concurrence of means, but through the absence of means. As long as there is a chance to employ the same kind of means, means of the same category as those encountered in the problem (even if they are totally different and of unequal strength), hope has no place in the venture.

Therefore, if one uses violence in a violent situation, or puts out "counterpropaganda" when faced with propaganda, there is really no hope in that at all. It is a mere matter of quantity and efficiency. If a person becomes involved in such activity, either it is because, unable to find a way out, he rebels; or else it is because he has a hope of winning. Rebellion is not an expression of hope, but of desperation. It takes place in excessive suffering and misery and it feeds on the illusion of the possible. But in an improving situation, as when the State is growing weaker, or class domination is diminishing, then the oppressed person hopes to be able to change the situation radically in his favor. In that case there exists a hope which is reasonable. He can count on friendly allies, on weapons, and on the weakness of the enemy. There is a chance of winning.

Hope has no place in those instances. It takes place when it calls upon and brings a radically different factor into the situation. In the face of violence and oppression, or of repression, hope is nonviolence, which, be it remembered, is in no sense a passive resignation and weakness, but the affirmation of another dimension of the person and of a higher requirement, as when the condemned person judges his judge and his executioner. The model is well known. The debate is not over.

To those who seek immediate results, violence seems to pay off, and of course it does pay off by causing the innocent person himself to turn murderer, and become an accomplice in all the world's violence. At that point, the question about who started it becomes totally and fundamentally absurd. The current game of excuses and justifications on the part of those who take the path of a "just" violence is indeed irritating. It is at the level of children's squabbles. When mother scolds them they say: "I didn't start it. He started it." If I murder a policeman, or an ambassador, or if I set fire to a department store, it is not I who did it. It is this repressive society, this capitalistic oppression, or the cops, who started it. There is no hope in that, only pitiable self-justification.

Take another example. Various types of propaganda are being let loose from all sides, by the pseudo-realists, the utilitarians, the instant-action people, those who think they possess the truth and who cannot conceive of a struggle against propaganda except in terms of another propaganda, called "counterpropaganda." Actually, as I have shown elsewhere, that is just one more propaganda. The effect is cumulative, and man is possessed, manipulated, and alienated all the more by two contrary propagandas.

Hope is a work of deconditioning. It is the opposite of every propaganda of whatever kind. It causes the acting person to reject propaganda as a means, since there is real hope that genuineness and freedom alone are livable, and that they are capable of bursting forth in spite of all past experiences. It commits whoever is willing to having everything which comes his way passed through the screen of an exacting critique.

But if we evoke this critique as an expression of hope, then let us say that the cultural revolution is the negation of all hope, since it has as its motive and object the greatest possible conditioning of man. He who lives in hope and has its power vitally in his life, who has caught a glimpse of what it can be in reality, can in no way believe in and participate in the cultural revolution of our time. What has occurred in China under that name is a gigantic political maneuver of manipulation, propaganda, and the eradication of the opposition root and branch. It is an implacable mechanism of conformity. We have seen the cultural revolution of Nazism, with its impugning of the liberal bourgeois culture, the burning of books, the vilifying of professors and student self-government (staffed, to be sure, by party members).

The cultural revolution bears a singular resemblance to this springtime of youth. It is a matter of substituting a new orthodoxy for the old orthodoxy. When, in May of 1968, I was debating with students on the project of the critique of the University, we obviously were not giving the same meaning to the word. For them it meant a Marxist university with an orthodox and dogmatic instruction of a different kind from the orthodox and dogmatic bourgeois instruction they accused it of having. There was not a shadow of the idea of critique in the enterprise. The cultural revolution is neither a sign nor a creator of freedom. It is a power method for still further enslaving those who are subject to it. In this sense it is indeed the opposite of hope, or rather, hope can only try to destroy it, not in the name of a past to be preserved, but for the sake of a future which needs to be opened up, and which the cultural revolution blocks and terminates for good.

All acts of counterpropaganda, of political involvement, or of cultural revolution have their dosage of hope. It is a human hope which could indeed be characterized as a passion for the possible, but which is based on an impenitent idealism, on a blindness with regard to the real and on a powerlessness to get beyond the most ordinary dialectical reactions. Now in the precise measure in which it is a question of possibles actually foreseen, hope has strictly nothing to add to the calculation of the possibles nor to the forecast.

THE SPICE OF HOPE

At this point we encounter what appears to me to be another error with respect to hope: Hope is an excess in relation to knowing and acting. By reason of this excess there is no concept in it, but only a representation.[9] In other words, hope supplies us with a supplement. Through knowledge one can zero in on the real. Through action one can influence the course of events up to a certain point. Hope adds a plus to all that, a plus which cannot be strictly nor exactly defined and conceptualized, but which one represents to oneself. It is the myth (in Georges Sorel's sense) which incites us to action because it is a rich and inclusive image of the goal. Once again, that can mean that hope is of the same genus as knowing and acting, that it is on the same plane and of the same register. It is *merely* a plus.

Yet everything we have been able to say about it tends to show that it is other than that, that it is not a little something which would come along to fill out an understanding, an action, or an enterprise, but rather that it is the source of another knowledge, of another action. It arouses us to an ethos which is not the same as that which

[9] Ricoeur, at least if I understand him correctly!

would have existed if it were not there. It changes the indicated realities. It is not "in excess." It is sufficient of itself and is destructive of other works. It is when there is no more knowledge or action apparently possible that hope is born, and that it evokes another knowing, another acting, which moreover are plainly and realistically impossible. It is that or nothing. That is to say, if it contents itself with being an excess over the possible, it plays the part of a dream in the midst of the action. It is an open gamble. I can win in the National Lottery. If it enters the impossible with the firm determination to blow it up, to reduce it, to negate it, then it becomes part of reality.

I am well aware that the normal impression is the opposite of what I am writing. Normally, one considers that if a person has a passion for the impossible, that means he is a dreamer. It is only when he is engaged in a concrete action (for which one has added up all the technical reasons for success) that a bit of a hope, over and above, is the dash of pepper or the spoonful of mustard which adds a certain flavor to what he is doing.

But no! The hope of Jesus Christ is never a dash of pepper or a spoonful of mustard. It is bread and wine, the essential and basic food itself, without which there is only the delirium of knowledge and an illusion of action. It is essential that hope be the all. It has to commit us to those insane actions which alone are reasonable, to that critical knowledge which alone is constructive, to the relentless scouring of the real which is the only realism.

The same is true with respect to sense. It is when there is no sense, when all sense seems absurd and worthless, that hope plays, or that it can play, its part. When there is a sense already given, received, shared, exchanged, and believed, when it emanates from the society, from the "collective unconscious," from a philosophy which be-

comes the accepted thinking, from a revelation understood and accepted, from a political commitment taken for
truth, from a revolution—no matter where it comes from
—if there *is* a sense, hope has nothing to do. Here again
it would be only a gratuitous addition. When the person
sees no further sense to his life, when the social group has
no further meaning in common—*then* hope has power,
value, and significance.

Strictly, it is the act of mediation between delirium and
sense. It is located at the hinge of the door between. It is
the power which brings about the transition from one to
the other; or again, it is the discovery of sense in what
one had supposed was nothing but insanity and bitterness.
Thus in our day, in this age of abandonment, the discovery
of a meaning cannot derive from a philosophy or from a
political action, or from man's knowledge, or from a collective ideal. If there is still a meaning to be given us, it is
in and through hope that we receive it. But we must stick
sternly to that principle. That is to say, we must know
that it all slips away the moment one tries another route.

Here we must connect hope with the promise once
again. This trust in God's promise is exclusive of other
trusts, yet it articulates into two motifs. On the one hand,
because there is a promise there is a history (a possibility
of history which is only *attested, given* to us, not calculated rationally). Hence there is a possibility of action
(but remember always that it is a possibility of that which
is, humanly considered, impossible!), and there is a commitment to make this history, to open it up, to "implement" it at all costs.[10] But conversely, because everything
depends on the sole and exclusive promise, because the
one decisive and deciding reality is that promise, this

[10] In all this section, I am indebted to Castelli, *Le temps invertébré*.

history already has a meaning. It already has an established and assured goal headed our way. At that moment man's indispensable work is at the same time useless. In history, as in the Gospel, man remains the useless servant who nevertheless is necessary and wanted, since the fulfilling of the promise excludes man's work by embracing it.

Thus we see what the exclusive possible of hope is. It is the impossible which is the sole creator of true history. God's impossible is the only real. The possible of human means is always without interest because it is actually unreal. (In other terms, it *always* achieves and *always* brings about the opposite of the intentions and goals which had been set forth. In that sense it is unreal, foolish and blind.) Such human history is the history of "mortality."

Hope, on the other hand, wants us to write another history, that of the impossible life, of the true life, which the mind of man never conceived. Here is where we find "sacred history." So true is this that the messianic hope, in no way to be confused with class struggle or with revolutionary or technological projects, is the creator of history. It is at the same time a rejection of every human attempt to construct paradise by means of a reason which is always deceived and insufficient (yet the only thing we have available). Thus hope, essentially productive of history, is also a critical power and an ability to reject. It closes the escape routes.

We shall sum up under two headings, on the collective level and on the individual level.

I repeat that it is because, and when, a situation is hopeless (in our age of abandonment, man and society are without hope) that hope not only is important, urgent, necessary, but that it is in truth possible, that it has a raison d'être. Apart from that situation it is not hope. It is a search for means, for a solution to the problem, for a rational decision, for personal commitment, which is quite another thing.

In this area I am in full agreement with Ricoeur, with the "in spite of." Hope is the challenging of a concrete situation held to be obvious and certain. It affirms a way out, in spite of all the roadblocks:

If the link between the cross and the resurrection is of the order of a paradox, and not of a logical connection, then freedom, according to hope, is not merely freedom for the possible, but still more basically freedom to give the lie to death, freedom to decipher the signs of the resurrection under the contradictory appearance of death.

Thus hope is always an "in spite of death." It is a "giving the lie to the real of death." All hope is always in that category. At whatever level it is encountered, it is always *this* giving the lie to something *obvious* which man considers unimpeachable, to a *fatality* to which man bows. It arouses man to go beyond that. This is indeed why it has no place except in a situation without hope.

Finally, and this is the second point, for a person without hope, or for a person fundamentally called into question (in fact, what greater calling into question could there be than abandonment by God, when God is silent? and it is true also of all the other ways) hope exists. It is when a person is questioned, when he has no further justification, when he is no longer "right," when he is no longer protected, that hope *has a place*. That is the meaning of the "forty" days (or years) which recur throughout the Bible, in which, at the very time when man is bereft of every security, the reality of hope opens wide before him. It is "the way of all the earth" which, in the ambivalence of Hebrew thought, embraces in a single expression both death and hope. So it is in the midst of doubt that a person can experience hope.

Faith, hope, and love are not three things which can be superimposed on one another, nor are they even direct complements of one another. We have already seen that hope and faith do not overlap. Now we have to go further. Doubt (which in this context is the existential aspect of the critique of which I was speaking above) is also the possibility and the form of hope. The person who is plunged into doubt is not the unbeliever, but the person who has no other hope but hope.

From another point of view, Castelli, in a splendid statement, shows us the same relationship:

The myth of Eden is the paradise of living space. Hell is the paradise of essences, of pure forms. The *doubt* that it [hell] exists is the possibility of deciding against it, of reconquering being through an existential contact, in which "discursiveness" becomes a means of communication (not communication *itself*). The doubt is the hope.

This passage throws light both on the fact that the doubt is about hell and also on the importance that "deciding" has for hope, which we shall come upon again later on.

To be sure, it is hard for the person dispossessed of himself, the person who has no further justification, the person with neither weapons nor armor, the person plunged into doubt, still to hope. And yet he has to realize that it is he in that, not some other situation, who is filled with hope, since there is no other possibility for him but hope.

8

Questioning

HOPE AND APOCALYPSE

If hope is indeed man's response to the silence of God, it has no place nor reason except when the situation is actually desperate. One can say that it is the Yes pronounced by God on a world *otherwise* condemned, rejected, and going to its death. It is a Yes pronounced by God while God is turned away and is silent. It is actually a Yes which the bearer of hope causes God to pronounce, which he pronounces in the name of God. By running that risk he indeed commits God, according to his promise.

But hope cannot assume that "things will straighten out," that peace and justice ought now be established on the earth quite normally, at the price only of a few political and institutional adjustments. Hope is not confidence in the virtues of history, any more than it is confidence in the virtue of the noble savage or of man's nature. To the extent to which it reduces itself to that, it means nothing. Whoever nurtures that kind of belief is merely an idealist, and hope is, in that case, a vague, pleasant feeling.

Hope is that act whereby a person becomes aware of the distance of the Kingdom, and it clings to apocalyptic thinking. If the Kingdom is there, within easy reach, if the Kingdom is *quite naturally* within us, there is no need for hope. The latter is the measure of our distance from the Kingdom. Certainly the saying which attests that the Kingdom *is* at hand, that the Kingdom *is* in our midst, is truthful, but it is truthful as a saying of hope. It is not the report of an observable, measurable reality, complete with tangible consequences. It is an affirmation of a counter-reality. Humanly speaking, it is not true that the Kingdom of God is present.

The complaint is so frequently heard that Christianity has been trying for two thousand years to solve the problems of society and has failed. It has not brought about the reign of peace and justice, etc. Very simply, there is a basic misunderstanding contained in the question whether Christianity was created in order to establish peace, or political or social justice, whether it is the organizing factor in society. That is the medieval approach to Christianity. I think the Kingdom of God became confused with a satisfactory politico-social system, and that we must not make that mistake again.

In any case, that confusion brings out the misconception about hope. If there were hope, it alone would make clear how far we are from the Kingdom we are expecting, toward which we are working, and which remains secret, hidden, and mysterious. Hope allows us to catch a glimpse of the invisible signs of the Kingdom actually at work, but which are visible only to hope. Only for hope are they signs and carriers of the future. The moment the Kingdom of God is confused with a just and peaceful politico-social system, there is no more hope, because one is walking by sight and by tangible fulfillments, by the obvious. Hope is situated precisely beyond those obvious things. If it discerns secret signs, it also knows that it will be done away with when the Kingdom actually comes. As long as there are only signs, hope is the one reason for living and for keeping going. Since the Christian is called upon to live in hope, he is, by the same token, called upon to declare that the reign of Christ is not present. He takes his stance in relation to that. As in the case of God's silence and the abandonment, hope is the positive act in the face of the absence, which it measures and knows.

Hope also can be situated only in an apocalyptic line of thought, not that there is hope because one has an apocalyptic concept of history, but rather, that there is apocalypse because one lives in hope. Those who reject that interpretation of history are saying that they have no hope and that they do not know what it is about, those, that is, who reject the vision of a radical judgment, of a collapse of the world in its own destruction, in order to pass over into a new creation and the resurrection and the recapitulation of history. For to fight the battle on the two fronts, as hope requires us to do, faced with the silence of God, on the one hand, and with the evil which dominates the world on the other, implies, since there is hope, that God will break through, both unexpectedly (like a robber) and explosively (like a hurricane drawn in by a low-pressure area), and that this will really call everything into question.

Like it or not, if we have the idea that the world develops through the wonderful works of man, that it goes from progress to progress in that way toward the Kingdom of God (and, at best, only by political and social revolutions!), that there is an unbroken continuity between this world and the Kingdom, that the way is prepared for the latter through political, technological, and scientific action, then one is dealing with a motionless object-God, a God who is no longer a stopgap, but a porcelain vase set aside in a corner: "Wait for us. We'll take care of it."

The Apocalypse is tied to the thought of a God who intervenes in history, who makes his own decisions and acts as sovereign, creating the world he wants through his almighty Word, whose fiery approach melts mountains and causes man and his works to collapse. It is to take the living God seriously. Now hope is that work which incites this God to come and reveal himself, no longer in his discreetness, weakness, and humiliation, but also in his glory. If one doesn't hope in the glory of God, of which the Apocalypse is a translation, there is no hope. There is only human progress and the hatred of those who obstruct it.

THE SIN AGAINST THE HOLY SPIRIT

If hope is this response to God's silence, if it finds its place and its reason in a despairing age, I still can ask myself whether in our day the sin against the Holy Spirit isn't precisely the rejection of hope, or the inability to live by it (that is, the requirement of wanting *something else*). I say "in our day" advisedly, for it seems to me that this sin against the Holy Spirit, which has caused so much ink to flow, and which has been interpreted in so many different ways, is not just a fixed category. It is not presented as a simple, single thing. What is given us is its structure, not its living reality.

This sin against the Holy Spirit varies in content according to the times, according to the period in question, and

the spiritual events. It has to do with the possible relationship with God in a given cultural context. Therefore we
have constantly to reassess the question here put to us
whenever we change our religious form or our metaphysical interpretation of God. We have to reassess the question
exactly in order to try to discern what this sin is.

In our day, if what we have attempted to perceive is
correct, the sin against the Holy Spirit is pessimism and
anguish. It is the theology of the death of God, and the
gloomy, or the joyous, acceptance of the fact that God
has turned away. It is the stoicism of the Christian condition without God. It is fatalism before the God who is
silent. The Holy Spirit is he who leads us to this hope
which challenges God's decision, as well as to the discovery of the meaning which is given to all things by that
very hope. To reject it is to go against the work of the
Holy Spirit.

THE POWER OF MAN

Hope in action is the opposite of the theology of the death
of God, even though it arises in the theological context of
the death of God, and even though there is a seeming
identity between what I am writing here and the theologies of the death of God. We are bound, here, to have a
closer look at hope. Is it the advantage man gains through
God's giving way to him? Is it man's striving to have God
give way to him? That is the problem. One could roughly
outline the theology of the death of God as follows: the
further ahead man goes the more ground he gains, the
more he knows how to manage by himself, and the more
God is removed from the picture, or, the more God withdraws, or again (according to the various viewpoints), the

more the image of God which one has constructed for one-self collapses. Concerning hope in an age of abandonment, that is progress precisely because God has withdrawn.

On the one hand, we are told that God decides his own *impotence* and that henceforth he is *powerless*. On the other hand, he is the secret God, the invincible one, the mighty fortress, the Almighty,[11] who is withdrawn into his incognito and who abandons us. One side tells us that this powerlessness of God brings out the joyful, victorious freedom and the glorious autonomy of man. On the contrary, I am saying that this abandonment results in despondency, anguish, and the sense of being abandoned (*Sometimes I feel like a motherless child . . .*).

On the one hand, they tell us that by remaining faithful to man and to history, by putting the second commandment in place of the first, man remains faithful to God. I say, on the other hand, that you can be faithful to man and to history only through, and in, a prior loyalty to God, that is, in hope, which is primarily a relationship with God. It is that hope which *consequently* applies to man.

It is declared, on the one hand, that we are witnessing the legitimation of the power of man. I observe, on the other hand, that this power of man accumulates as much disaster as it does progress, and that it reveals itself finally as illegitimate in essence (for example, in man's relation with nature!). The Italian theologian Mancini surely is very ambiguous when he speaks of this power of man. While telling us that it is power as such, without bounds

---

[11] And who remains such, even though he chose to manifest his love in Jesus Christ by becoming powerless. By what right do some continue to split the passage in Phil. 2 apart, by seizing upon verses 7 and 8, while excluding verses 9 to 11: "Therefore God has highly exalted him, etc." Why would Paul have seen revealed truth in verses 7 and 8, only to act like a poor fool in falling once again for the cultural images of God in the lines which follow?

and affecting everything, he also tells us that this power is that of "being for the other." It seems to be taken for granted by this theologian that if man becomes powerful it is in just such an abandonment, and that there, in that way, the very power of God resides. "The being of God's presence in the world rests on the omnipotence conferred upon man, in order to accomplish the divine *katabasis* [descent] of being for the other."

Actually, this idealized view of things corresponds to nothing at all. When one speaks of power in this century we know what is involved. Mancini's assigning of a meaning and a purpose to "power" is in truth a simple lapse in his thinking. Once again, the theologian constructs a system with skill and logic, but takes no account of the real. In fact, we have here the same motif as that of the most hackneyed of the theologies of the death of God, with the little supplementary title to legitimacy thrown in that all this conforms to the will of God.

When I was saying that man advances by hope in all the domains that God seems to abandon by his silence, the diametric opposite was implied. It is not a question of any domain of power and effectiveness. As far as power is concerned, exactly nothing has changed since Genesis. When we take into consideration the actual facts of human power, how could we be so absurd as to turn the biblical myths upside down? Man's power is always a consequence of the break with God. It is always the deed of Cain, of Babel, of Nimrod, and of Mammon. There is no other. It is the demonic pride of putting oneself in God's place, of hunting him down and vanquishing him. It's always characterized by blood, murder, and the degradation of women, by the triumph of money and power. I know that in writing this I am going counter to the contented purring which justifies the "greatness" of modern man, but what can I do?

Torture, exploitation, dictatorship, and the universal destruction of nature constitute the essence of the power of man. The blind sycophants ignore fact. They ignore the concrete reality of the facts as well as the internal structure of the phenomenon. When they talk about a valid step forward for man in replacing God, they comprehend nothing of what is happening, that it is not man who is taking the step forward but the technological system and the system of state control, both of which expand in autonomous obedience to their own laws of growth and give man the appearance of success!

Hope, a sally into the territory abandoned by God, is the contrary to all this. It is the calling into question, not of God but of the power of man. If it is hope, it is "by nature" that which plays upon an "unachieved-unachievable." It is not fulfilled by the methods of power. It does not actualize itself either by techniques or by administration. It is hope precisely because its purpose surely cannot be attained by the instruments of power. What the powers of man achieve is in no sense the object of hope, for the very reason that it can be attained through the internal logic of the system.

Hope does not rejoice over the fact that God is leaving us free to act. It wants, to the contrary, to have a pole of reference which is God. It demands that God speak, because without the presence of the God who is the Wholly Other, the Almighty and the Lord, man can only go from disaster to chaos. There no longer is any light or any way. Hope is the negating of the powers and successes of man, since it cannot be fulfilled except by God's presence with man, who never takes that path.

Yet it actually advances to root out God from his turning away. It advances into the unknown territory which God abandons to it. It advances into the Word of God which is dead and done with. It advances into the past works of God in order to find there a recovery of strength. It advances into the desert of the Church (not to reform it, but to draw from it a witness of the Spirit). It advances into the devastation of the world in order to make worn-out man go forward, to get him (him, not the system to which he has surrendered) to take one more step. It advances into the inflexible, the morbid, and the frenzied in order to catch there the unlooked-for, the unsuspected, which would give evidence that God still is not entirely absent.

Hope is on the lookout for every sign. It cannot accept the conclusion that God is gone, that he's dead, and that man is abandoned (while calling himself grown up). It advances into God's territory and, if necessary, replaces God's Word with the echo of its own word. It occupies the places to which God has to return, to which it will ultimately force him to return. It is the march toward, the march into, that promised land, but without God any longer to lead the way and do the work. All illusion to one side, this march toward and into the promised land is one that hope alone can make us continue.

9

Hope in a Time
Without Faith

Since it is a matter of the combat with God, since it is a
matter of putting in a claim against the absent God, hope
can only be the lifestyle of those who suffer so intensely
from that emptiness that their entire lives are centered
around it. It has no connection with those who easily
accept the death of God or who justify it, with those for
whom God is no longer even an issue, for whom life is
horizontal, for whom everything is wrapped up in the
daily and the historic event. Those people, to be sure,
can nurture hopes for the near or the distant future. Nothing is to be had from such hopes.

Hope is different in kind. Hence, however scandalous
it sounds, it has to be said once again that only Jews and
Christians can be the bearers of hope in the midst of men
by taking as their point of departure the refusal to accept
God's absence. They alone can provide the power to make
man go ahead with his history and the fulfillment of him-

self, which is actualized solely by the grace of God. Thus hope, in fear and trembling, becomes a sort of sacrament of that grace, a sacrament and a substitute during the period of the absence. I will go as far as to call it a placebo.

Is hope, then, an illusion which creates illusion? Certainly not! The physician who makes use of the placebo does so on the basis of a science which is real and not illusory, and he obtains a result which is real and not illusory. The placebo is only a means to an end. The illusion has to do only with the substance of this means. I am inclined to say that the same is true of hope (and, after all, of every sign, every miracle, and every word the Christian speaks!). The Christian and the Jew know, of a knowledge which is more sure than anyone's, that God is the Living God, the Comforter and the Father (terms which are foolishly being disparaged today in the new theology, yet their reality is still experienced, not through habitual, cultural images, but by the most profound and enduring hope). The Jew and the Christian know, on the other side, that modern man needs, above everything else, to recover his relationship with the Father, and that this relationship actually puts an end to anguish. Thus, in the silence and absence of God, hope can continue to say and to affirm that God is there, that he is the Living God and the Father, that he saves and heals.

Is this a lie, when we know that God has abandoned this age? Not at all. Surely it is not a lie, but a stronger certitude about whence we came and where we are going. Yet will it still be through an illusion that man is to receive this word? And if his anguish is assuaged it will not be by God, but merely by the word of another person. Certainly not! When hope speaks it is indeed a Word of God which is involved! Here is where we go beyond the crucial question, namely: Isn't Christian hope illusory, and as an illusion doesn't it drag people into illusion? The answer is Yes, if it is a matter of a leap into the absurd, into the unknowable, into paradise or heaven, into an unforeseeable future. In that case it would be a matter of illusion (yet no more, nor less, so than the Marxist hope for a communist society, or the Hitlerite hope for a society of the millennium, or the hope of the cultural revolution, or the hope for a solution to man's problems through the humanistic sciences). But here we are in the presence of an entirely different dimension. Hope starts with the knowledge of the revelation of God. It exists through the combat with this God, and it discovers the only possible meaning of history and of life in the reciprocal Yes-No/No-Yes relationship between man and God. This discovery supplies man with just what he lacked, and this discovery alone.

In this discovery, the word of hope which a person can speak to others is not uncertainty about God, but an attestation that, in his very absence, this absent God is the one who gives meaning. The person who says this on behalf of others is actually transmitting the word which God is not speaking here and now. The person himself discovers it as a word of God when hope's violence assigns God as "my God." In that context, and only in that context, do we have the right to talk about a God who abases himself, humbles himself, and gives himself. All the rest is an approximation produced by the political concerns of the time. So that principle applies to the testimony of hope, just as it does to the theological word on the subject of the unknown God.

The opposing argument is well known. It has been developed at length, for example, by Francis Jeanson. It goes like this: "Christians say that God is the Wholly Other, that in himself he is unknown and unknowable, that he is ineffable. Yet Christians write tons of literature

on what they say cannot be known. How plainly absurd."
Unfortunately, this argument, as logical as it is simplistic
and elementary, makes an abstraction out of the relationship which God establishes with man, a relationship which
is outside of that logic, and which formal reasoning cannot
grasp. It is a relationship in which everything rests, as far
as man is concerned once he has grasped it, on the extra-
rational phenomenon of hope. God has to be the one revealed in Jesus Christ. The Unknowable and the Absent
has to respond to the appeal of the unpronounceable
name, which hope persists relentlessly in repeating. The
thrust of reciprocal relationship has to be lived to the full,
and the Unknowable, so says hope, corresponds to what
the person has grasped of him in the revelation. But if
the unbeliever elaborates on the contradictions without
taking this dimension into account, no matter how powerful his logic, he is examining the star with a magnifying
glass.

Thus, because they have had that relationship with that
God, the Jew and the Christian are the sole bearers of
hope among men when God turns away. This hope is not
an illusion, but the final and only effective reality which
subsists. Hope has the outrageous audacity to affirm that
which cannot, or can no longer, be known or tried out
(and this is often the case with the preacher. That is why
all preaching *is* a test of hope, and is possible only as an
act of hope). Hope does its trying out in the situation, in
the condition, in the will of man abandoned by God. It
never ceases repeatedly to lay hold of this God, and it
obliges him to be on man's side once again. That God
should go into hiding, that he should refuse, that he
should keep silence, is the occasion and the condition for
hope. There has to be an unknown for there to be hope.
The reason hope also exists when God reveals himself

is that, as we well know, he only reveals himself as the Unknown. Only the unknown has a content of hope. This brings us back to what we have already said about the fact that certainty excludes hope. Hope is tied to revelation by the fact that the specific Christian revelation is neither a proof nor a display. It consists only of symbols, of mediation, of indirect knowledge and word. Thus this God remains unknowable even though he reveals himself, and that is why his revelation is necessarily productive of hope. It is hope for the time when what has merely been heralded will be actualized. Hope is tied strictly to that relation to God.

Hence its place in the Church is a permanent one, and it belongs at the center of the life of the Christian. It is not only for the age of abandonment, although that is the time when it enters its acute and active phase. In an age of revelation, in an age of the presence of God, and when his activity is felt through the course of history in people's lives and in the Church, hope is tied to the charter itself of the Church, to the mode of revelation which God chose.

Hope should give meaning and direction to the Christian life, but it very often fades out and grows weak because all seems to be stabilized and normalized with God. That is when the formulation of a creed is the great issue. Before this God who reveals himself and acts openly the only approach is that of faith, and the only problem has to do with the content of that faith. The expression "to have the faith" then gains general acceptance. In the attempt at stabilization, of which the disciples at the time of the transfiguration are the typical example ("I will make three booths here, one for you and one for Moses and one for Elijah" [Matt. 7:4]), the thought is quite naturally that of proprietary responsibility for what God has granted us.

The process of appropriation is never anything else than the process of stabilization.

So even when we know very well that we do not possess God, and dogmatics and the confession of faith drill into us constantly, nevertheless when God actually reveals himself, when it is given to us to become once again contemporaries of Jesus Christ, when God is the living center and is present to the Church, then, in spite of our good intentions and our spirit of poverty, we can hardly do otherwise than to settle ourselves in. We are rich. At such time, although hope is still recognized as a theological virtue, it is always pushed a little to one side. It becomes something slightly unnecessary, slightly "surprising" (that which takes me by surprise, otherwise known as God).

On the other hand, when God is silent hope returns to the center of the stage. It becomes the burning issue, the approach without which nothing else is possible. Settling in, satisfaction, and appropriation are out of the question, and this is what we now see quite clearly in the Church. We have become poor once again. We actually are beggars for the Spirit, since the Spirit has been taken from us! Hope, and hope alone, becomes the state of standing or falling, not only for the Church but for each Christian life.

It can be said that this hope is, in a certain sense, anti-information. When we are well informed, when we are acquainted with the record of events by an adequate communication, when we know the reality itself of what has happened, what would we hope for in that? Information as a process of keeping one abreast of the facts leaves no room for hope. The more exact and complete the informative process, the more it makes possible an adequate comprehension and a correct decision. This strange act of hope can have no part in that, for it takes place only in connection with the indistinct, from the intellectual point of view, and with the uncertain and the wretched on the existential level. Hence hope is tied to the revelation because the latter is never in the category of information.

I will not go back over that issue, which has been so frequently contested, nor over the terrible errors of biblical misunderstanding which have been introduced, and are still being introduced, by the confusion between revelation and information (the obvious absurdity of thinking that Genesis gives information and instruction on the manner in which the creation took place, or on the manner in which the break between God and man came about). What is revealed to us is never in itself objective. It is what is judged by God to be necessary to our lives, to our salvation and to our freedom. Hence we cannot speculate on what is revealed in the same way that we can on facts garnered from information. We cannot build it into an adequate system, since we know that nothing objective or objectifiable has been said to us (albeit God, to be sure, is still objective in relation to us!).

We cannot resolve the enigma of God, nor find a solution to the problems of life, death, and the creation. We can only come to a decision with respect to a revelation which engages our existence, and which has no content for the person who does not commit his existence to that decision ("if any man's will is to *do* his will, he shall know whether the teaching is from God or whether I am speaking on my own authority" [John 7:17]). The debate is well known. I limit myself merely to a recall of it, since Bultmann has repeated the principle in the wake of many others, notably Kierkegaard. I mention it here solely for its bearing on hope.

Conversely, objective information, like science, has no use for hope. The more information we have the less there is of hope. One is tempted to think that it is the puritan objectification of the content of revelation which produces this closed-off life without hope which we have experienced. Even so, revelation in the true biblical sense has also its share of information (even when finally it comes up against the unknowable God), and the more extensive that share of information the less is the role played by hope. When a theologian thinks he knows all, there is no more hope. What place would there be for it? It is made for the hazardous, the uncertain, the obscure, and the inexpressible.

The more scarce the Word of God becomes, the greater is hope. It eagerly latches onto the few scraps still visible, onto the whisper, of which it seems that everything in it has been said. When God is turned away, then, in the desert of information, nothing more is possible but hope. That is the only path open to us today. Philosophical or theological dissertations no longer have any possible meaning or substance for us. Surely hope is a theological virtue. It is the virtue for a time which has no faith, no word, and no escape.

PART IV

And in the Beginning Was Hope

(Tentative Proposals for an Ethic of Hope)

THE CREATION was God's act of hope, as well as of his love. The Word is hope each time it acts. At the beginning of the incarnation there is hope, and hope manifests itself at the beginning of every life in Christ. At the beginning of each human life the person is urged onward and made to grow by a secret, hidden, and obscure hope, not discernible as true hope.

10

Pessimism and Freedom

BEYOND THE DEBATE

The age of abandonment—the day of hope—that is where we are now. This is bound to express itself in a formula which is at the juncture of theological investigation and spiritual need, on the one hand, and the search for signs and for an ethic, on the other.

For there can be only signs. Discourse has exhausted itself. You cannot *talk* about hope. The further I advance in this book the more I am aware of that. As I have already said, you can live it and bear witness to it for another person, or for a number of people. You can transmit the living sign, attesting the profound action of this power, so different from, and not really commensurate with, any other power.

But the question is how to live it. I think, in the last

analysis, the best formula is one of pessimism in hope. The lively debate which took place between the exponents of active pessimism (de Rougemont) and the exponents of tragic optimism (Mounier) is well known, in which the attempt was made, both to fix upon the coloration and the climate of the Christian life and also to formulate the intermediate term between theology and ethics. I believe that, when all is said and done, both formulas are incorrect.

In the first of the two, pessimism is far too much the dominant note. God is taken to be a sort of supposition. The whole burden is put on man. God is a supplementary factor which we do not need to talk about because it is understood that he saves, forgives, resurrects, etc. Man has only to act. Ultimately, the only principle insisted upon is simply that man should not be discouraged by pessimism, which is a permanent and constant attitude based on original sin and the total depravity of man. Man has only to act. He *knows*, on the one hand, that all is wicked and, on the other hand, that God is with him. The action lacks openings, joy, and human flexibility, and it is without spiritual risk.

Yet the second formula seems to me to be worse. There is nothing in revelation, nor in the observation of history, to encourage us in optimism. Let us be clear about it. Optimism and pessimism are human impressions, which sometimes derive from value judgments. They are ways of looking at life. One person takes it negatively, while another takes it positively. To be sure, optimism is entirely legitimate in the Christian life if understood as a will to "keep an open mind toward everything and to judge nothing in advance." Optimism carries with it this openness and joy, which are excluded by pessimism. But optimism is just as false as pessimism in the degree in which it implies a sort of final judgment that everything will come out all right.

It is indeed true that in and through grace everything will come out all right, but really *through grace,* not on an assumption, nor through any human assurance or conviction. Grace does not authorize optimism, which is a humanistic interpretation based on a too-secure assurance. It certainly is not good to use Paul's famous statement in an ethical sense: "where sin increased, grace abounded all the more" (Rom. 5:20). What we have here is a revealed truth about God's action. It is a theological statement, but we cannot construct a philosophy or a theology on that base, still less an ethic, since it has to do with grace. It has to do precisely with something which cannot be grasped, pinpointed, guaranteed, or incorporated. There can be no intellectual construction of any kind based upon grace. That is why Luther was right in insisting on *faith,* a discernible and structurable human capacity, and in not constructing a theology of grace (although that was the driving force of his life and of his theology).

Grace is a pure act of God. Precisely because it is grace, it is beyond our grasp, and beyond our ability to structure and to assimilate. It cannot give rise to any speculation. We certainly cannot say to ourselves on the basis of Paul's thinking that *if,* under these present circumstances, sin abounds, we are quite at ease, because we know that it is under these conditions that grace will abound all the more. That would be a horrible manipulation, a taking possession of the living God. Grace abounds all the more through grace, but it is through grace, and not through some constant, some guarantee of an automatic recurrence. It is a decision, and not a physiological or sociological law. It is a miracle from which my faith can take its source, or my hope can find its assurance, but on which I cannot count with serenity. I cannot speculate about it intellectually or morally. That is to say, on the one hand, that I cannot make of this superabundance of grace a principle of construction or of intellectual interpretation (in that case grace would cease to be grace). On the other hand, neither can I quietly take it for granted that everything is going badly, that my life and the world are tragically overrun by evil, but that, in the last analysis, it is unimportant because grace abounds even more. This would be another normalization and rationalization of the cross.

"God will take care of it." As a statement made in connection with a given tragic situation in the here and now, that could be an expression of the most complete faith and of genuine hope; but as a systematized formula it could also represent indifference for the sake of a bit of intellectual and spiritual comfort. We have no right to play upon the superabundance of grace. Since the Spirit is free, it blows where and when it wills. We can only be ready to receive it when it blows. God gives grace to whom he gives grace—and when he gives grace—no more. We can only pronounce the so-be-it at the moment when, and if, we receive this grace; but precisely because it is a matter of grace, there can be neither constant nor universal. Even the knowledge that at the end of time, in the Kingdom of God, all is grace and God's love will encompass his justice, does not allow us any appropriation, but only the lively impetus which grows out of hope. There is no chance for a fixed translation in human terms, for an integration of this revelation into life, no chance for a theology, a history, a politics of grace.

So I think the only acceptable formula is that of the pessimism of hope. As far as pessimism is concerned, we surely don't have to go far. Look at the reality of our society and of man. I look at myself. What cause is there for satisfaction or optimism? There is no need to emphasize it. Do we have to recall what the Bible says about man or, in words which are outmoded today, how God sees man? In any event, for Jesus to have been crucified (whatever be the interpretation of the crucifixion, whether we are thinking of the righteous man whom people did not know how to treat otherwise, or whether we are thinking of the Son whom God gave for our sins), the evil, or the sin, in man had to be unfathomably powerful beyond all human virtue. The fact that the new theology puts great emphasis once again on the crucifixion should lead inevitably to a recognition of the *radical* evil in man. Otherwise this crucifixion would have absolutely no meaning. It is useless to keep insisting on these themes which are so well known, but which are rejected today (because we are living in the abandonment).

However, nothing in the revelation allows us to remain in this pessimism and nothing takes us over to the other side. Nothing transforms this pessimism into optimism. Yet everything obliges us to go further than mere "action," and this "further" is hope, of which we have said that it has nothing to do with optimism. Hope is in no way a sort of compensation or counterpoise to pessimism. So I am not saying that the situation unfortunately forces us to be pessimistic, and we need a little sunshine. That is not the point. There is a strict and indissoluble link between pessimism and hope. This follows from what I tried to show in the preceding chapter, in connection with hope as the response to God's silence, and as the truth of the despairing situation. What we are getting into here is that same principle, the link between pessimism and hope, translated into ethics. Since now we are dealing with two human dimensions, it is possible to engage in reflection about behavior and about signs.

Hope makes no sense except in relation to a pessimism concerning the real. If we are optimists, there is no need to appeal to hope. Conversely, the pessimism implied by the observation of the real and by the judgment of God is bearable thanks only to hope. Faced with the radical nature of evil, we would be driven to suicide were it not for hope. The latter makes it possible to look at reality without turning our eyes in some other direction. All the signs of the incarnation of hope are to be found in this reciprocal relationship.

We can go further. If pessimism provokes and evokes hope, it is also true that hope provokes pessimism, for it assigns us our place *far* from God. It locates us so far from God that hope is the only thing still possible. So here we are, in reality right back at the beginning of things, back at the first day for man and for the creation. We must remember that the act of creation does not graft itself onto an absence, a nothing, a nonbeing. It is not a matter of a creation *ex nihilo*. It is the affirmation of the hope of God *against* the aggressive power of nonbeing, against the invasion of that which normally should win, prey upon, contaminate and pollute, against the aggression of the negative.

Thus hope is necessarily committed to a hazardous undertaking. It is the opposite of morality and theology, which provide answers and solutions, and introduce schemas (if you do this, the result will be that). It is the opposite of the theatrical role, in which each participant knows in advance how everything is going to turn out. Hope is a firm advance toward a masked future. It forces the future to show its hand, to become future and to become history, but it cannot know what it is. Nothing is done in advance. It accepts all the responses and all the chances, provided there's a thrust forward, provided there is creation. No past event inevitably dictates or determines what we can live. Hope affirms only that we can actually live it.[1]

HOPE AND TIME

This relation between pessimism and hope leads us first of all to locate ourselves with respect to time, and it actually produces a restructuring of our time. It brings an ordered time to what Castelli calls an "invertebrate time." It does this by a recapture of the real. We must insist on that fact. If hope occurs when God turns away, nevertheless it is not an illusion, nor an ignoring of the real. To the contrary, we have already seen how totally different hope is from the thing hoped for. A thing hoped for rejects the real. It is an escape from seeing it. Hope is the opposite of that. We shall see later on that it is tied to the most rigorous realism. As we have said, it is an attitude of conquest and of a decision to fight. It is an entirely positive, constructive, demanding, and vigorous value. Hope involves an ethic, and it produces in us the appearance of

[1] Obviously, I can in no way share the proclamations of Harvey Cox, according to which "Laughter is hope's last weapon" (if he had said "humor" I might have agreed), and "In the presence of disaster and death we laugh instead of crossing ourselves" (shades of Catullus, Priscus, and Tibullus), and "Its [hope's] Christ is the painted jester. . . . Its [hope's] Church meets *wherever* men lift festive bowls to toast joys remembered or anticipated." (Harvey Cox, *The Feast of Fools* [Cambridge: Harvard University Press, 1969], p. 157; Ellul's italics.) As always, there is in Cox a bit of true insight which he sends astray through lack of intellectual rigor and a facile use of words. One could say it is bad Alfred de Musset, bad because de Musset's theology was far superior to that of Cox.

power. It orders time. I cannot help quoting this splendid passage from Castelli's *Le Temps invertébré*:

All *modern* philosophy has prepared the way for *technique,* and *technique* is presented as: a) the technique of sleep (no longer having any spare time); b) the technique of the aggression of the subconscious, an aggression which has led to an iconoclasm against the *intimate* . . . on the part of forces interested in making it impossible to recover full freedom of judgment, after the hypnosis brought about by the growing suppression of pauses. . . . If *unplanned sleep* led to *tedium* there would be no diminution of hope, theologically speaking, but boredom's metaphysical principle is time in disorder.

Nothing in the time of our technological society any longer has order, ordination, nor any qualitative reciprocal variety. Everything flows with insipid liquidity. Yesterday and tomorrow are meaningless. Time is invertebrate. In this invertebrate time there can be no hope, for hope is constructive of true time. Hope is, in fact, a remarkable motif in time. As we have already said, it does not consist of projecting the present situation into the future to give the present a happy ending. Still less does it consist in counting on the future as such. That can all constitute a thing hoped for, but nothing more.

Hope already implies an extra-temporal relation, for it is the meeting place of the future with eternity (the latter obviously not understood in the sense of unlimited or infinite time). Hope demands a sort of preemption of eternity by the future, and the taking up of the future by eternity. But that implication and that requirement are lived in the present. In other words, hope causes this future-eternity relation to intervene in the present instant *and* in the current event. Hope, then, is that which establishes the right relation between a future (other than a succession of moments) and a present, at the same time that it is the force through which the eschatological power of eternity comes to us and intervenes in the present.

So true is this that we must affirm that hope has the effect of structuring time, of giving it both a value and a continuity. It is the only human force capable of this transmutation of times. If Christians can live hope, then that could give rise to a renewal of time. The great difficulty is to find the ways and means of this life of hope. Once its importance is discovered, the question remains what to do, and what to be, in order to inscribe it in time.

Here we encounter anew the conflict between hope and the dominance of technology. The latter can neither tolerate the future-eternity relation nor the intervention of a future composed in the present. Technology is expressed by means of necessity through cause and succession. It is incapable of entertaining any other prospect. We now are called to another prospect, but that in no way implies a condemnation of technology! It implies simply the observation that salvation is not to be had from that source, since technology unstructures time and blocks the movement of hope.

What we have eventually to do as Christians is certainly not to reject technology, but rather, in this technological society and at the price of whatever controversy, we have to cause hope to be born again, and to redeem the time in relation to the times. This mysterious expression of Paul (Eph. 5:16 and Col. 4:5) is frequently commented upon. Here we need only remember that it refers to wisdom, but that the latter is never a knowledge or a morality. It is, rather, a discernment, a choice, a "policy," and it implies the foresight of hope. We can redeem the time only if we conduct ourselves in these times, which are evil, with a wisdom rooted in that hope which comes from the distant horizon of the revelation. Then, and only then, is time set on its true course, toward its authentic unfolding.

THE GLORY OF GOD

But here we are confronted by a more exacting task. We have said that hope, during the abandonment, during God's silence, not only brings us into combat with God, but makes us bear witness, in the face of all that is obvious and certain, that God is still Lord of all things and of all humanity. That implies a manifest turnabout on our part in relation to the generally accepted outlook.

First and foremost is the matter of the glory of God, but this glory of God cannot be made present by means of words. Still less can it be brought out by any supposed prestige of Christians, of the Christian life and of the Church (which it is useless to hope for in our day). It is much more a matter of turning the things of this world to the glory of God. Hope leads us to seize upon these "secular," desacralized, profane, demythologized things, surely not in order to render them sacred once again, nor to reduce them to a religious status, but in order that they might manifest the glory of God, which is their true, if not their only purpose.

Christian life and thought are dying for having forgotten that! Paul tells us that the whole creation witnesses to this glory (Rom. 11:36), and this is a constant affirmation of the Old Testament. It is not for us to turn the creation in the direction of that glory. It is there already. But perhaps we could have avoided turning it the other way! —which is what we have done. If in using, enhancing, even in exploiting the world's riches we had maintained the primary vision that, prior to our utilization, prior to

234 · *Hope in Time of Abandonment*

our comfort, prior to the raising of the standard of living, the important thing was to maintain this creation to the glory of God, it is probable that technological insanity would not have debased and disintegrated that creation.

One is amazed at Christians who justify technology by saying that it is man who is to the glory of God and that, since technology opens the way to man's development, it is good that it be used in that direction. Must we remind ourselves once again that man in the technological society is not much more "happy," nor probably more developed? He has had to come to grips with ever more insoluble problems from the very fact of technology. We might, in a pinch, concede the point if the results of science and technology were completely and solely positive and favorable. A fair estimate indicates an equal increase of the good and the bad.

Moreover, even if everything were positive, it is not certain that such a position would be right theologically. It is not only man who is to the glory of God. It is the *whole* of creation, which does not have to be sacrificed to man. And can it really be said that technological exploitation is the way to reveal that the creation is to God's glory?

Actually, there are two possible attitudes with respect to the world's goods. One is to seize upon them, use them exclusively for our own benefit, turn them our way and exploit them as efficiently as possible in accordance with the principles of technology. But in that case we separate them from God. We turn them back on ourselves. When the things of the world are oriented exclusively toward man and subjected to the laws of technology, they lose their profound meaning, and their future at the same time. We cut them off from a possible development, and that not only in the spiritual sense but in a very material sense.

When we restrict things solely to the service of man we condemn them to extinction.

Can it be said that there is glory to God and hope for the world when we waste the reserves of coal and petroleum, when we disrupt the ecological balance, when we pollute the waters and the atmosphere, destroy the forests and devastate exploited lands, when numerous species of animals disappear in our wake? Again, is it in this nature which is polluted, pestilential, rampaging, and covered with dead bodies that the glory of God can appear? Yes, of course, if the glory of God expresses itself in the destructive pride of man, but who would dare to claim that? Do not the proponents of the theology of the glory of man and of his demiurge loftiness see that man's glory implies his solitude in the midst of a nature turned barren? When man subjects everything to his own utilization, it all disappears, truly annihilated. We are putting an end to the hope of the world.

But there must be another possible attitude, which would consist in making the things of the creation share in our hope. In consequence of the break between man and God known as the fall, which has dragged the whole creation into man's catastrophe, the constituent elements of the creation are no longer directly and spontaneously to the glory of God. Though they still allow us to see, as with the naked eye, the invisible perfection of God, they no longer are the incontrovertible and manifest expression of God's glory. Man would have to intervene for them to become once again what they were. Man's first act, obviously, is that he himself, in consequence of the revelation, should discern God's glory in those things (without, of course, making them the theme of an apologetic!).

Now, however, we are faced with yet another problem.

We no longer are in a natural universe. The things which surround us are no longer the things of the creation. They are our own technological products. If the things of the creation were called to manifest the glory of God, technological products express the glory of man. They really manifest nothing by themselves. They are not of the same nature and have not the same meaning nor the same aspect as God's creation. Nevertheless all must be turned to the glory of God. Nothing, either in the natural world or in the system created by man, can be left outside that glory. To leave it outside would be to consign it to nothingness.

Thus we have to restore the meaning of God's glory to the natural elements, on the one hand, and to technological creations, on the other. This is their one possibility of life, and it can be done only by bringing both of them into the way of our hope. Just as this hope pushes us to live for God's glory, by the same token to turn things Godward and to cause them to express the glory of God is to restore hope to them. It is to give them a meaning which is no longer exclusively that of utility. It is to give them a future, to cease to consign them to nothingness. It is to open to them the way of the heavenly Jerusalem. That is already a beginning in what the Apocalypse refers to when it says that the nations will bring their riches and glory into this heavenly Jerusalem.

This obviously calls for a tremendous reversal of all our habitual concepts and of the collective technological trend. To treat things as expressive of the glory of the Lord is no longer to put the meaning of human life into them (possession, use). It is no longer to take man as the measure of the use of things. It is to grant them a value independent of man (because referred to God) and to take from them their mythological prestige as a new creation.

From then on it is a question of not giving way to the desire for increased consumption, to the zest for technological exploitation, and to the belief that man's destiny is linked to a raising of the standard of living, etc. "Man shall not live by bread alone." The increase in the consumption of goods and in technological production prevents turning them to the glory of God. That is, it kills the possibility of a future for things and it destroys the hope of man. That is decisive, but the first point is not less so. To give to things, to nature and to technology, a specific value, considered in relation to God and not in relation to man, is to treat them with respect and caution. It is to put a stop to exhausting them, exploiting them, annihilating them and degrading them by making them serve just any purpose.

Only with that outlook, and on the ground of hope, is the utilization of the world's riches validly possible. In that case it is not a matter of setting man up in surroundings of his own fabrication, still less is it a matter of humanistic progress. It is a movement toward the Lord who is coming, in which we include things as well. That is the only possible answer to the famous problem of the "good use" of technology. There is no moral use of technology, still less a good use according as it serves "progress," and less still is there a possibility of its serving a final end.

But there is a legitimate use when it is put back into the movement of hope. That is the only place from which one might, with a great many difficulties moreover, rethink the whole problem of technology and come up with the true import of man's tremendous discovery. This position reverses that of Teilhard de Chardin and of the theology of the death of God. The latter delivers us over, bound hand and foot, to the technological system with its implacable growth. The former transforms technology into the driving force which propels us toward the omega-point. Both put the human phenomenon (scientific and technological) in the foreground and make it the determining factor for all the rest.

We are claiming here that everything is determined beforehand by man's relation with God, a relation which in our day is to be stated in the "abandonment-hope" couplet. It is my contention that it is there that man can perceive a meaning in his technological development without becoming enslaved by it, without being subordinated to it. I am fully aware that such a concept can now seem fuzzy, uncertain, and lacking in any practical answers.[2] Indeed this is not a description of *what ought to be done*. No purpose would be served by laying down a new law, a new circumstantial ethic. It serves no purpose to state in terms of hypothetical action what we first have to live as a relation with God.

Our sole effort here is to provide a point of departure, with indications of paths to be opened up, and to formulate the contemporary relation with God, on the basis of which the central issues of life in these times, and of our society, can be picked up and lived. But I emphasize: from that standpoint. It is not the other way around. It is by understanding the phenomenon of technology as inscribed in the abandonment, and as it is to be inscribed in hope, that we have some (slight) chance of finding an answer to it. The answer will not come by revising our concept of God, or of our relationship with him, from the

---

[2] But it should be noted that it is no more fuzzy and vague than the best proposals made by the greatest specialists in technology, such as Jouvenel (*Arcadie*) or Friedmann (*La Puissance et la sagesse*).

standpoint of the phenomenon of technology. The moment we do that we condemn ourselves conclusively to remaining totally enslaved to the technological mythology, and the only thing awaiting us then would be agony, followed by death.

FREEDOM

I shall not resume here the relation between hope and freedom. For the Christian that is one of the most basic truths of our age. Freedom is the ethical expression of the person who hopes. Hope is the relation with God of the person liberated by God.[3] "The link between freedom and hope is marked by a new ethic, which Moltmann calls 'the ethic of mission'." The promise of God, which is the theological basis of hope, implies mission. "In mission, the obligation which commits the present derives from the promise, and it opens up the future. Yet mission precisely signifies something other than an ethic of duty." And again—"All hope will henceforth bear the same sign of discontinuity between that which is headed for death and that which denies death." There indeed is where freedom plays its part. "The Luther who has won me is the one for whom hope is hidden *sub contrario*. What we live every day, what appears to die, is what prepares the future. It is the hope of the cross, the freedom to share in this reaction of life." By these statements Ricoeur sums up admirably the relation between the two, granted that for me freedom can neither be a postulate nor a field of

---

[3] This has been abundantly treated by Ricoeur in his article in *L'Herméneutique de la liberté religieuse* (1968) and in *Le Conflit des interprétations* (1969) and by me in *Ethique de la liberté,* to appear shortly.

philosophy, but *uniquely* an ethical expression of the liberation effected by God for man in Jesus Christ.

Right there we confront a major problem. Freedom does not exist as long as God does not speak and does not emancipate man who, without that emancipation, remains tied and predetermined. Yet here we are in a time when God is not speaking. We must absolutely renounce any appeal to the past (God spoke in time past, hence we are liberated), or to objectification (the continuing Word of God which continually liberates us; that is nothing but a dead word), or to the all-embracing *opus operatum* (all mankind has been liberated once for all in Jesus Christ; the human condition underwent a mutation on the cross). Those are very convenient interpretations from the spiritual point of view. They are indeed necessary to the elaboration of an intellectual system, but they are strictly the reverse of what is shown us in the history of God with man in which everything, whether we like it or not, happens in the here and now. Systems and interpretations are even sterilizations of God's action and of his Word. They are the negation of the *living* God.

God is now silent. How shall we be free? It is not enough to want to relate to the emancipation of the cross and of the resurrection. God's spirit is no longer manifesting itself. How shall we be free? It is not enough to believe that Jesus is the Lord. We cannot call our own selves free, for our freedom consists essentially in the emancipation by the Lord who is coming; *who is coming*—that is to say, he on whom our hope is centered. So we see how this impossible, yet indispensable, freedom is the very expression of the pessimism of hope. God is silent. I cannot call myself nor believe myself free. Yet hope is the act itself of freedom. If I were without exception caught in the toils of predetermination, of fixation and fatalism, I could not hope. That would be unthinkable intellectually, psychically, and spiritually.

Hope is that extraordinary moment in which man, abandoned by God, presses (God willing) his demand upon God by the one act of freedom possible to man. All other acts of freedom are actually derivative of man's emancipation by God. But this one act, hope during abandonment, the hope of pessimism, is man's attestation that the fall was not absolute, that the break with God was not irreparable. Of course, man is no longer the image of God. He has no remedy for alleviating what has been done. He has no possibility of saving himself. He has fallen into the circle of fate, but he still has this unbelievable contrivance of hope. He resumes his true authority (that which God had willed for him in Eden), not when he multiplies his techniques, but when he impresses his hope upon God, when he decides to hope.

For it is indeed a matter of decision. To be sure, like everything else, hope is grace. It is a gift of God. But there would be nothing (and the gift of God remains terribly hidden in this time of abandonment) if man did not of himself decide to hope by engaging, through a free act, in the combat with God. But all has to be lost for him to make that decision!

If we are indeed in the presence of the one freedom possible to man, then we have to say that this freedom in this age has no social or political dimension. One can always expatiate on the fact that "the ethic of mission," as an expression of hope, has community and political implications (Moltmann). Of course that is possible theoretically, but in the extreme anguish in which we now find ourselves that is not the real issue, and it only ends in abstraction.

In the sphere of philosophy I would be more than

happy to see opposition to a too subjective view based on personal inwardness, etc. It is always possible to say that a freedom open to the new creation is focused less on the subjective than it is on social and political justice. But that is no more than a statement which contains no measure of reality. The sole tie between hope and freedom depends on this slender thread that all freedom is summed up in the wish, the declaration, the perseverance, and the combat of hope. Alas! (but how can it be otherwise?) that puts us in the domain of the subjective. Every other interpretation of hope brings us back into the situation of the predetermined, reinserts us into the socio-political machine and thus finds itself cut off from freedom.

RELATIVITY

Hope, or the immediate presence of the eschatological, brings with it still another decisive and specific ethical dimension of the Christian life. That is the relativizing of all things *and* a total seriousness applied to the relative. Separated from each other, these two attitudes are trite. The relativity of all things is a sermon theme as worn out as can be, based on the Absolute or the Transcendent. The serious treatment of the relative, on the other hand, is the heroic and despairing witness of Stoicism, of humanistic skepticism and of the doctrine of the absurd.

Neither one is true. The absolute of God does indeed relativize everything, but God's Word tells us to take absolutely seriously this relative, which he himself took seriously enough to give his Son. It did this from the moment of the incarnation in time and space (which, for all that, do not cease to be relative) and it promises to continue to take them just as seriously in creating his

Kingdom and in recapitulating our history, the history of our relativity.

In the face of all that, we see the radical impossibility of man's living the relative seriously. Since Camus's crest-line is untenable, man knows only two alternatives. On the one hand, he rejects everything, plunges into radical skepticism and attaches no value to anything. At one time he renounces something or other, at another time he does almost anything, both equally lacking in sense. Yet, in the opposite direction, he elevates some aspect of the relative to the status of an absolute. The person who is zealous for what he is doing and who wants to find meaning and value in it, who throws himself into an action, cannot help making an absolute out of it. He believes absolutely. One cannot believe relatively. The cause becomes the measure of all things and is worth the sacrifice of everything to it, just as it is worth the devotion of oneself.

Whatever the great thing may be that one absolutizes, whether it be peace, love, freedom, or justice, the final result is the same as when the state or the revolution is involved. Whatever the political goal, a totalitarian qual-ity is always tacked onto it. You pronounce a final judg-ment on the person who does not agree with you, and who therefore represents absolute evil. There is no es-caping it. Man cannot continue in this action-approach with fervor without believing in the absoluteness of what he is doing, without claiming to be radically right and without excommunicating others. Secularity has never lasted long without turning into its opposite: secularism.

Again, that is the fundamental failure of Mao's cultural revolution. It could be carried out against the ideological bind, against bureaucratic rigidity, against the economic debasement of man, on behalf of virtue and unselfishness, but it could not set its troops in motion by maintaining the relativity of those objectives, which it was well aware of. Mao was able to carry out the cultural revolution only by absolutizing its thinking, by bringing blind passion to the flash point, by glorifying an implacable intransigence, while at the same time insisting on a psychological and ideological conformity more absolute than mankind has ever known. He could not set a whole people in motion behind such a tremendous undertaking by telling them that it was relative after all.

All wars and all revolutions involve absolute belief on the part of the people. But the moment there is absolute belief then massacres, exploitation, oppression, torture, and concentration camps follow immediately. It is not economic interests which are to be feared, but rather, absolute convictions. It is that which shuts man up within a narrow scope and organizes him in terms of total polarization.

The *sole* important task in the liberation of man is the relentless relativizing of all great causes, of all beliefs and ideologies. But that relativizing can be accomplished only from the standpoint of some absolute point of view, certainly not from the point of view of some other value which we would absolutize, and which would only bring about the same situation all over again. It would have to be from the point of view of an absolute which exists of itself. Otherwise we have no way out of the vicious circle. Relativizing is possible only on the basis of a transcendent.

All theology of the horizontal leaves man to choose his own absolutes from among human values, and by that fact, precisely because these are not really absolutes, it causes him to affirm them and assure them through violence, restraint, and oppression. In fact, we have to be clear about it that the Transcendent, existing of itself, has its being without the need of any oppression, violence, or victory. To the contrary, any relative value worshiped as an absolute can be declared absolute before men only at the price of a material victory over men. My God is stronger than yours, and the proof is that I beat you. Thus the theology of the horizontal, with the good intention of liberating man from a cruel Father and of encountering God in the other person, leads inevitably to crusades and to burning at the stake.

It will be said, however, that it was precisely in the name of the trinitarian and almighty God that Christianity oppressed mankind and set crusades and religious wars in motion. Yes, to be sure, but that only goes to prove that one was not taking seriously the almightiness and the absoluteness of the God of Jesus Christ. It was a constant temptation. He was not effective enough, so one had to bring human effectiveness to bear. That meant that God was demoted to the rank of an absolutized value. That is what the Old Testament never ceased to declaim against, but man always falls back into the same trap. He of course wants Jesus Christ, but with the addition of science, politics, power, etc. Only the rigorous insistence on the Transcendent, maintained, believed, and obeyed, assures the relativizing of everything in the name of which man kills and oppresses other men. As long as one is dealing with facts, values, and theories known to be strictly relative, passing, uncertain, and inadequate it is much more difficult to kill and oppress others.

But then another problem presents itself. Does not the relativized Transcendent lead to a completely negative and skeptical attitude, as was the case with the Cathari? Here we must be clear what Transcendent we are talking about. That of the God of Jesus Christ is that of the God who comes into the relative and takes it with entire seriousness. Henceforth, if we believe in him, we are led also to take this relative world, this world of politics and of economic activity seriously, *but for that reason.* We do not do so because those things have the slightest importance in themselves, nor because the future of mankind hangs on them, but exactly because God has become incarnate and has died in the relative in order to save it. Then we can take it seriously.

Just because it is God who has come down into the relative, the latter is all the more relative. Man, as man, does not become divinized because Jesus was incarnate in man. To the contrary, what the incarnation makes clear is the completely sinful character of man. Yet, as God took the relative seriously, we do the same. Now it is an extraordinary innovation to be willing to work with zeal, love, joy, and interest in something which is entirely relative and secondary. We have to realize that man cannot do it left to his own resources. He cannot give himself to something he knows definitively as relative. He can submit to working in the relative only if he knows there is some absolute motive for acting and for getting involved, a motive which, as a matter of fact, is not embraced within the action itself. To take the relative with entire seriousness implies some anchorage in what is not relative. It implies a justification not absorbed by the thing itself.

There is yet a final step to be taken. Who can guarantee that this Transcendent, this absolute point of reference, will not in its turn become the alienation of man? Here we have to admit that if the Transcendent is in effect the absolute God without more ado, he does again become a source of alienation and sterilization. But it is a matter of the Transcendent who reveals himself in Jesus Christ. So, since he is love, he is himself the guarantee of the nonalienation of the person to whom he reveals himself. Thus, because he is the Transcendent he assures the disalienation of man with regard to the absolutized relatives, and because he is love he assures the disalienation of man with regard to himself (himself, the Transcendent). Finally, he assures man's presence to the relative world because he is the absolute motive who is present to the world in his revelation.

After this long detour we have to come back to hope, because the Transcendent in question is obviously not in some particular place. It is neither "in the heights" nor "in the depths." It is the eschatological presence here and now (or, just as well, the presence of eternity). It is that, and only that, which relativizes, yet at the same time also brings about a zealous involvement in this relative which one never absolutizes. With regard to the eschatological presence, it is not an essence of itself, or rather "in itself." It is not lived. Relativizing is not a magic operation, nor is it valid once and for all. It is done by the person. This presence of the eschatological takes place in and through hope.

Henceforth hope, as one can see, has enormous ethical and politico-social consequences. It calls for a way of life which combats the absolutes. It calls for radical and relentless relativizing, leaving nothing illusory to survive. Thus it is the reverse of what in current speech is called "hope," which consists in throwing a little halo around realities that are ordinary, relative, and uninteresting, giving them a future and a grandeur with the glow of a purely romantic hope.

Yet, at the same time, hope involves us in this relative in which the whole of man's life is acted out. It sternly rejects skepticism and the absurd. It participates in the game which is only a game, but it testifies by the buoyancy of hope that there is nothing more serious than a game! Thus hope achieves an ethical mutation leading

248 · *Hope in Time of Abandonment*

man to assume a role which, in each occasion, is the opposite of what he naturally would have played. It guarantees
a freedom incommensurate with that of socio-political endeavors, for the reason that it is the only freedom not
based on other slaveries.

THE CHALLENGE

In any event, this is not without its political and social
consequences, because that hope, the only act of freedom
possible and linked to pessimism, produces a challenge at
all levels of every organization and of every category.

At this point we must be on our guard. It is not a question of revolution, nor is it a question of just any challenge.
While freedom in our day can be expressed only in terms
of the act of hope, that in no way means that we "hope"
that with some political reforms, or some revolutions,
things will turn out in such a way that men will be free
and society will be just. That is just the opposite *both* of
the pessimism of hope *and* of the freedom expressed by
hope. The sole challenge is that of hope—that is to say,
not of a theoretical, thought-out, systematic, doctrinal
construct opposed to an organized and oppressive present
reality for which it is to be substituted.

The challenge of hope is the introduction into a closed
age, into a tight security, into an autocephalous organization, into an autonomous economic system, into totalitarian politics, of an opening, a breech, a heteronomy, an
uncertainty, and a question. Let us be careful about that.
It is not at all a doctrine or a concept of man, set up in
opposition to those which are dominant today. When one
orthodoxy combats another the only result is to confirm
the exclusion of freedom and the extraneousness of all

hope. No matter whether it be Marxism, Stalinism, Hitlerism, Maoism and the dictatorship of the proletariat as opposed to the bourgeois and imperialist society, or whether it be liberalism, democracy, participation and the cooperation of the classes opposed to dictatorship—in *all* these cases, without a single exception, the inscription over the door leading to the future can only be: *Abandon all hope, ye who enter here.*

The revolutionary act of hope is, and can only be, the opening up of situations which want to stay closed, and the contradiction of systems. Its purpose is not to replace them with other systems, or other organizations, or other ruling classes, or other governing parties. That is why hope is radically different from all revolutionary movements, albeit it can give rise to such movements and can live with and in them for a certain period of time (for as long as they are revolutionary, only to abandon them when they are established). For this reason hope is never incarnated in an organization, in an ultimate goal. It is power in action, never satisfied and never incarnated.

It is all very well to point to the leaven and the dough in order to say that the leaven does not end in an independent existence, that it *should* blend with the dough, etc. The important thing is not the bit of yeast. It is the raising action. After the leaven has done the raising there is no more leaven. You can then justify the recommendation made to Christians that they blend with the world and disappear into it. But that is the whole problem. Will there be no need of bread again tomorrow? If there is, will there be no need of leaven? If today's leaven disappears into the dough, there is none any more, and there can be no bread tomorrow. Hope incites man to be the leaven in a given batch of dough. It requires that he be in a certain organization or a certain group.

But make no mistake, the leaven is specific in relation
to the dough. It is only of value because it contains a
power not in the dough. If the Christian ceased to be
specific, if he acted out of the same motives and in the
same way as others, he could of course blend in with them
and become involved along with them, but in no way
would he be leaven. Leaven has a function which no person fulfills. It introduces an active power into the dough.
That power is neither conviction, nor good will, nor intelligence, nor devotion, nor knowledge. One can find all
those things in even greater measure among non-Christians. Nothing *in* the person can be useful to a revolutionary
movement. The revolutionaries already have that in themselves, so if Christians just add their numbers, that means
that they have added a supplementary batch of dough,
but nothing will rise.

Or indeed Christians, making use of their title, will
bring to a revolutionary movement the Christian label,
"The Christians with us," a propaganda of very feeble influence. In any case, the Christians cannot then claim to
be transforming the revolutionary movement, to be giving
it a new meaning. That is to say, they are not the leaven
in the dough. Unless they are bearers of a dimension
which no one else has, they are incapable of playing the
role they are meant to play. Like the leaven, they are
meant to have a power which is external with respect to
the dough, a power which cannot be discerned a priori,
and which only makes itself felt when the leaven is mixed
with the dough.

Moreover, that power of the Christian is not his, nor
does it come from him. In order to be truly effective it
has to be qualitatively different. It is a matter of the
Kingdom of God, of which the Christian is the bearer. It
is as a witness, as a bearer, as a guarantor, as a living sign

of the Kingdom of God that it is important for the Christian to join a revolutionary movement. But in order to be that he has to be in relationship with the Kingdom, and we have seen that this is where hope comes into play.

At the same time that the Christian has to be related to the Kingdom he has to be driven to enter into this action. Here again it is hope which acts. Thus hope appears as the link which joins the two external poles of his person. One is the divine pole, the pole of the Kingdom of God. If hope does not rivet us to that power we are not the bearers of anything. We represent nothing but ourselves. We are of no use in a political or revolutionary movement (except to be one more voice howling stupidly with the band of wolves which has seduced us). The other is the pole of socio-political action. If hope does not rivet us to that action, then the Kingdom of God within us becomes a meaningless, sterile contemplation, a repetitive automatism, and we abort the Kingdom.

In order to commit ourselves in this way we have to live this hope. It is the hope of the Kingdom of God which can give meaning and truth to any revolutionary movement whatsoever. Apart from that, revolution is nothing but savagery, illusion, useless devastation, accumulated injustices and revenge, and it always ends in its own reversal by a necessity of history which never fails. As long as Christians take part in revolutionary action on the assumption that everything depends on the horizontal relationship, on the search for social justice, on the struggle against imperialism, they are nothing, they count for nothing. The dough remains dough. It hardens and cracks, becoming a spoiled lump of flour. No bread will come of it. Hope alone, that exclusive hope bound to the God of Jesus Christ, can transform the dough into bread.

Thus hope inside a revolutionary movement becomes

the source of *another revolution,* the same as it must when inside established and vested situations and institutions. Hope leads necessarily to a radical revolutionary attitude *irrespective* of the milieu in which it occurs—revolutionary, that is, in relation to social conformity but just as revolutionary within a revolution. It is not merely a force driving us to sign up and belong to some other revolutionary movement. That certainly is always a possibility on the human level, but having done that, we still have not done anything—not the shadow of a beginning of what could be considered Christian.

Hope requires that we bring about a raising of the dough, of every human dough with which we are blended by an action of which the dough can never have the slightest idea. The bitter proof that hope is dead is afforded by the sight of the very best Christians either renouncing their title in order to mingle with the revolutionary crowd indiscriminately and without more ado, or else renouncing the transcendence of this God whom they want to get rid of because he is an embarrassment in their relationships with others. They are becoming revolutionaries out of despair. They contribute their stoicism and their greatness of soul without realizing that they have lost everything, that they do not mean a thing, not even to the movement they are supporting, that by their very presence (since they have renounced their faith) they are the inscription of condemnation within the revolution. Historical adversity is not what causes the failure of all modern revolutions. It is the denial of the hope of God, even on the part of the Christians involved.

It should be understood once and for all that God's revelation is not an object among other objects. Like the Ark of the Covenant, it authenticates life but it also carries the thunderbolt. If it is not the source of the presence of the Kingdom of God borne by the hope of a Christian to the bosom of the politicians or the revolutionary, it becomes annihilation, the unleashing of the power of death in the movement itself, a sort of reverse image of the Kingdom of God brought about by the Christian's denial, by the failure of hope. Whenever the latter is not the leaven in the dough, the presence of the faithless and hopeless Christian becomes the corrupting agent of the dough. If revolutionaries had the slightest awareness of the meaning of their revolution, they would exclude all Christians who do not bear with audacity the witness to the God who is wholly other, almighty, holy and just, to *that* God who humbles himself in Jesus Christ and who comes among the poor, bringing them not his powerlessness but his power, to the God who is silent now but whom hope arouses and of whom it declares that he is that God.

Thus hope throws us into a revolutionary movement, but it also throws into it the God who is silent. We know very well that hope's provocation can be the decisive factor in his coming back to be present, to be the active and radical God who will enter once again into history, on condition that it be worthy of being made and lived. God, who is silent in the midst of the diminution of life, in the midst of the prevalent phagocytosis effected by the bourgeoisie (the latter has in fact devoured the Christian religion, has turned it to its own ends so that, of course, the God of Jesus Christ is no longer in it), this God is also silent in the revolutionary lie of the holy quaternity, Marx-Lenin-Stalin-Mao, in the revolutionary farce of the third-world activists, in which the participating Christians betray Jesus Christ just as much, but in the reverse direction, as they do in the bourgeois magnificence.

I am not saying that these are *causes* of God's absence.

We have already said that there is no cause. That is simply the way it is. But we do know that for it to be otherwise Christians must live a burning, fierce, excessive, overflowing, and questioning hope, not one which is timid and ready to tiptoe out of the room. We know it is up to us whether the capitalist regime will be transformed by the presence of this hope, as well as the revolutionary movement. Apart from that there can be nothing but dreary repetitions of well-known, outworn, banal, and useless historic scenarios, which we know in advance will wind up in ridiculous epilogues. Apart from this Christian hope, and from that alone, Fidel Castro can become nothing but a little accessory to the Soviet Union. The challenge of 1968 and of Maoism can end only in mad dictatorships, to which they are inexorably a prologue.

When will Christians wake up to the fact that history is not a series of throws of the dice, with each throw a pure chance out of a clean slate? When will Christians understand that there is nothing more stupid than a false human hope? The entire youth of 1933 believed in the Hitlerian revolution, which was a dreadful miscarriage, as we know after the fact. Yet later: "Sisters, if we get a fresh start it goes without saying that Stalinism has nothing in common. It's beautiful." Then we see its horrible miscarriage after the fact. "Sisters, if we get a fresh start it goes without saying that Maoism has nothing in common, etc." When will Christians realize that history has known only one absolute novelty, the incarnation of God in Jesus?

History is made up of the balance of power, of reciprocal conditionings, of series of predeterminations, of blind intrigues, of structures and factors, in which there is scarcely any place either for the freedom or for the originality (in the etymological sense) of man. The latter is the carrier of these predeterminations, the agent of these forces, but he is unable to play upon them. He gives expression to them in the same way in which an actor plays his role. He neither creates nor originates them. He brings nothing of the unforeseen nor of chance to the sequence and groupings of factors. He repeats his "miscalculations" without having learned anything from those of yesterday. He thinks he is demonstrating his independence by saying that the situation is novel. Of course it is always novel. History never repeats itself, but it is never anything but a novelty of combinations and the expression of a tautology which man is incapable of penetrating.

When will Christians see history in that light? When will they understand that the independent, the surprising, and the unlooked-for factor—that which introduces initiative and the possibility of a fresh start, that which overthrows and changes the basic principles of the game—is the intervention into this dreary course of events of the Word of God. Only if and when the Wholly Other cuts across history does history have a chance of modifying its course. Only then can a novel situation be created.

But that intervention does not take place through some resounding, extrahuman miracle. More often it is the nonconformity of Christians, accepted and assumed by God, which changes history by its own authority. If Christians run the risk of being nonconformists, they do this in terms of the hope that God will in fact assume their action.

In relation to this world, this Western world given over to its demons and the third world given over to our demons, nonconformity today is hope itself. But it is the rigorous and particular hope of which we have spoken, not some vague discourse or unwise political commitment. It is a question of hope boldly proclaimed before men, in the sole and exclusive power of the Holy Spirit, bearing witness to Christian particularity. Apart from that, Christians can agitate, demonstrate, sign manifestos, take part in protest marches or guide unions, and they only corrupt the revolution they think to serve. Hope is a creator of history, since it opens the closed, hardened, and self-contained situations. Just as the resurrection opened the grave, so the rigidity of history is broken by hope.

But this comes to pass only if hope consists in a contradiction—in a contradiction of God who is silent and in a contradiction at the same time of the political movement and of the normal course of events. Only then does hope open up a future. Only then does it give man a possibility of expression and a chance to seize the initiative. Thus the Christian, as the explicit and declared bearer of *this* hope, which devalues all the others (most certainly by explicit declaration), works alone on behalf of all men, in order that *those* who are not bearers of the hope might benefit, in order to bring about an upheaval of history which would then become once more a workable clay in their hands. This contradiction is the expression of the freedom of Christians and a condition for the possible action of others.

If Christians are not bearers of this hope, they contribute to the even tighter closing of situations, to the hardening of institutions, and to the transforming of history into a fatalistic process. Disengaged from the combat of hope, Christians are the ones accountable for the closing of the iron doors of fate. So the golden rule often put forth today, "among and with people," "at the risk of being lost oneself," "politics first," that golden rule is the diametric opposite of hope. It means actually that Christians should be *today's* leaven for *today's* dough. It presupposes that when this bread is made and this society rebuilt, the last and final goal shall have been attained, man's work shall have been completed, and that henceforth it will never again be necessary for Christians as such to fulfill the function of leaven.

That golden rule confuses socialism or the secular city with the Kingdom of God. It rejects the necessity of continuing within the Church to transmit the deposit of faith, the necessity of relentlessly pursuing the specific and unique revelation of God, so as to ensure that there shall again be a possibility in human history of a transformation, of a calling into question, in other words of a future indefatigably open through hope, of a possibility of history. To mingle in politics, *before all else*, is today to kill hope and to turn back God's gift. It is, strictly speaking, to take the name of God in vain.

11

Hope's Human Base

This hope is expressed in and rests upon three attitudes which do not appear to be active ones. One is psychic, another intellectual, and the third spiritual. They are: waiting, realism, and prayer, three forms of hope's pessimism. Faced with the pressing tasks to which we are summoned by the world's ferment, by the urgency of the situations and the decisions to be made, in short by the present human misery (the solution for which cannot be put off until tomorrow), hope certifies to the fact that commitment in the immediate and the current is nonsense. It tells us that the first step is to take note of the impotence and the futility of our so-called revolutions, that the effective fundamental attitude is another one, which will be translated into involvement secondarily.

WAITING

The person of hope is the person who waits, and with a pessimistic waiting, for *normally* nothing should happen. The only thing we can reckon on is frustration and derision. How could it be otherwise in God's silence? Job waits, and his friends never tire of proving to him that this is absurd (which it is), that he is wrong (which he is), that God will not come (which is true). They take pains to explain to him *why* God will not come (Job is guilty), and to make fun of him, since his attitude either is one of a godless rebellion or of an absurd expectation. Still Job waits.

Just as Job is the one who attests that a person serves God for nothing, so he is the one in whom the fullness of waiting is actualized. His whole life is filled with waiting. He never lets himself be diverted to the right or to the left by his own attempts to transform the situation. He has penetrated to the bottom of the problem with lucidity. He knows that in the last analysis it is an affair between God and himself, that all the rest, the things that happen, are only the outward aspect of the quarrel with God. He does not work hard and courageously to recover his riches. He does not set out in pursuit of the brigands, or the foreign soldiers, in an attempt to get back his oxen and his camels. He rejects all those human reactions because he knows that the root of the problem is not there. Nothing of serious consequence can be done until satisfaction is had from God. He leaves activity and work to one side, since the one important thing is to wait for God.

I know very well that the modern exegete will say that Job's attitude is specifically "cultural," since for one thing the culture is oriental, and for another thing it is dominated by the conviction that everything comes from God, that all is subject to a destiny, before which one merely bows and waits. Thus it is a simple passivity on man's part based on *that* concept of life, a concept derived from the milieu. According to that theory, Job's attitude expresses a fatalism toward events and is in no way exemplary.

Now I contend that this explanation is totally inadequate. Oriental passivity is a legend. No one was more activist than the oriental from the tenth to the first centuries before Christ. That was true of the Tyrians, the Phoenicians, the Chaldeans and Sumerians, the Hyksos, and the Persians. It is the same with fatalism. All those peoples had developed antifatalistic religions, especially Israel. The entire Old Testament abounds in reactions, decisions, and attitudes which were extraordinarily activist. Each time, without exception, that we are told about brigands or foreign pillagers and destroyers, the immediate reaction in Israel, on the part of the patriarchs, the judges, the shepherds, and the kings, is one of setting out in hot pursuit in order to get revenge, or to recover the stolen goods. After every natural disaster the damage is repaired. Job's attitude is not at all that of "the culture." To the contrary, it is quite heterodox in relation to the typical reaction of the times.

If he bows before these disasters, that is not through a natural passivity or a fatalism, but through a discernment of the underlying truth, through the requirement that the root of the problem be brought to light, that the answer to the ultimate question be had before going on to the superficial matters of family, money, and politics. Therefore, Job is exemplary precisely because he goes against the cultural schema.

We know what it is to be waiting today, waiting for the return of Jesus Christ, for the coming of the Kingdom and for the Word of God and of the Holy Spirit *here and now*.

But the important thing is that this is not an empty, passive, hollow, drowsy waiting, the kind that one settles into. The waiting is a hundred thousand times more difficult than action. It demands much more of the person, and especially in our times. In this lost age, the person cries out constantly, untiringly, every day and a hundred times a day: *Maranatha,* just as one cries S.O.S. when in imminent danger. But the S.O.S. is kept up for a certain number of minutes when all is lost, whereas *Maranatha* has to be repeated with the same force and conviction as S.O.S., as though one's life were in imminent danger, yet kept up every day of a person's life without stopping, without his becoming discouraged, without his falling back on a hollow repetitive formula, without his seeing anybody or anything.

The person of hope is a person of a demanding, wide-awake (the two things inextricably go together: "Watch over us" is constantly being said), tensed waiting, which does not let itself be diverted or taken in, either by the game of the serious things of politics, economics, technology, and science, or by the seriousness of the games of eroticism and philosophy, art and leisure. Stubborn, firm, unassuming, the person of waiting rushes into the dark of God's silence and of the abandonment. He has a stature over and above those who hurry about in their automobiles and their unions. He has chosen another field of battle, and he knows that it will be as a result of his own combat that all the rest will get its meaning and its possibility. He openly rejects the action constantly being proposed to him, in favor of the waiting for the moment when all will have become possible again. He concentrates all his forces on this waiting, which is in itself a concentration of forces, through its silence and its avoidance of scattered action.

This waiting is decisive, since we should know that nothing will come to pass without it—nothing. There is no return, no Kingdom, if we fail to live in this fervor of eyes lifted up to the hills awaiting our help, the fervor of the watchman, trembling with fear, awaiting the dawn.

Still we have to realize that these promises of God are not fulfilled mechanically nor arbitrarily (according to a plan fixed from all eternity, or according to a whimsy of God). The promise is fulfilled every time in connection with a person who bet his whole life on that promise, that is, in the expectation of its fulfillment. I have often written that it is of the very foundation of the last things that Jesus is coming again, that the true motif is not our forward motion *toward* these last things. It is the motif of these last things *in* our history. Except that the eschaton does not speed our way on rails. There is no automatic, mechanical movement comparable to the onrush of time. There is no capricious coming of Christ similar to a return from a journey (obviously, the parables of the return are not to be taken literally!). The Kingdom comes, and Christ comes again, through the person who waits with unmitigated hardness, with a demand without loopholes, with an exalted fervor, and with a persistence which refuses to be diverted by anything. The Kingdom comes and Christ comes again through that person alone, but not *for his sake* only. It is for the sake of all, as the prophet watches for all.

The treason of Christians and of the Church was to settle in, to wait contentedly for something for which one hoped less and less, to organize so as to wait as comfortably as possible, and finally no longer to expect anything at all, but to put oneself to sleep in the feverish activity of organizing society, the world, the economy, and of discovering science. In that terrible time God continued to speak. He pressed his appeal. He kept up what was no longer anything but a monologue, so that there were two disconnected monologues. Now it is abandonment.

Christians must understand that the one thing useful to the world, and indispensable, is to recover the fighting and the burning expectation. It is not the pursuit of justice, nor the defense of the poor, nor political activity, nor the third world, nor hunger, nor the renewal of the Church, nor hermeneutics. Those things are simply diversionary traps to turn us aside from exclusive, central, stubborn, and enthusiastic waiting. In spite of all the apparent Christian validity of those useful activities, and in spite of all the disappointments, on the other hand, of an expectation which sees nothing come and which is never realized (and for how many generations yet to come), the waiting person has the hardness of a rock, and an absurd firmness and fixity of purpose. He is completely absurd, and deaf to all the beautiful promises and philosophies, as well as to derision and argument (Where is your God? . . . You said he was alive and active!). He knows but one word: "If any one says to you, 'Look, here is the Christ!' or, 'Look, there he is!' do not believe it" (Mark 13:21). Do not believe it when someone tells you there is some other Christian duty than the absolute, ultimate, and energetic waiting. Do not believe it when someone tells you that the good of mankind demands of you something other than that waiting.

It is a perfectly ridiculous attitude, I know. It is exactly that described in *Waiting for Godot*. One cannot stop talking. One can see many human types and be a witness to tragedies (and also the tragedy of exploitation). One can try to decipher signs which are not there. One can think that Godot has come when he has slipped away. That changes nothing with respect to this rigorous, re-

newed waiting, which is always just as radical. If you are
not flayed alive by God's abandonment, if you are not
torn apart in the very depths of your being by the delay
of his return, then it is useless to play at waiting and to
talk about hope. In that case keep building expressways
and fighting against shantytowns, keep stirring up revolutions and creating theology. Very well, but then it would
be better not to talk about Jesus Christ and all the rest
of it. It would be more honest. Let us be fully aware that
nothing comes except through him who waits. Take all
the other directions and nothing will come. It is the *word*,
spoken and spoken again by tireless hope, striking the
empty sky throughout the years, which suddenly one fine
morning of flame is taken up by God, is assumed by him,
and becomes truly a Word of God.

But, of course, such a waiting is not an inward, hidden
affair. It is not a simple petition in the depths of the heart.
Job had his witnesses, who were his accusers as well as his
friends. The waiting person must make his waiting "e-vi-
dent." He should call others to witness, risk his reputation,
risk being called a stupid literalist, feebleminded and
under apocalyptic influence, neuropathic, obsessed. He
has to know that the judgment against him will be as radical as his waiting, for if there is one thing our society
cannot accept, since it is all for efficiency, production,
action, politics, and victory, it is just that very attitude. It
can accept *anything* (troublemakers, revolutionaries, sur-
realists, Christians), it can swallow anything except precisely the person who is firm in his attitude of the radically
other, who has anchored his boat in outside waters, who
hopes for what no historic development can ever bring,
who at the same time rejects historical materialism, political idealism, and fatalistic structuralism—and who, from
that very fact, has nothing in common with the building
of this age, but who serves the world by waiting, by that

approach alone, by that decision alone, which cannot be assimilated and is from outside.

He must call to witness all those he can reach. But he must know that the first to accuse him will be his friends, the members of his Church. O Christians, rational and active, full of good works and strategies, constructive and positive, when will you be sensitive to the fact that all your history and your faith and your life rests only on a foolishness, that the cross is an absurdity, a folly, in spite of all the theologies, and that if we do not behave foolishly we are not faithful to the cross. When will you realize that, in this society (so activist and efficient), and in relation to this abandonment by God, the only folly you should be guilty of is a folly obvious and visible to human eyes but the only one accepted by God, the folly of rejecting everything which is not waiting.

I have praised indolence, and I can stick to that. Indolence is exemplary in a civilization of work, but only if it is the visible face of this intense struggle of waiting, of this commitment indescribably more total than political commitment. The waiting person will of necessity not be understood by his brothers in the faith, by his friends rehearsing the role of Job's friends. He will be charged with having a watch-and-wait approach, with threatening our charity toward the rest of mankind, and with bearing useless witness to a useless cause. Yet it is essential that this waiting be expressed and exhibited. Every act, every human proceeding, whether intellectual or charitable, should be carried out in relation to the coming Kingdom and to the cause of that Kingdom (it is good eschatological logic that the end should be the cause). The works are chosen for the fact that they are only understandable (and exclusively so!) in relation to the return of Christ. They are there on account of that return.

It is obvious that the virgins who kept their lamps lit

and provided themselves with oil acted in a way that was absurd and ridiculous to those who ignored the actual possibility of the return of the bridegroom. There were a hundred thousand more useful things to do around the house. Their attitude could be explained only by the importance they attached to the master, by their conviction that nothing was of any consequence in the face of the joy at the expected return of the master, and the joy of the eventual meeting. It is obvious that Noah, in building his ark on dry land, acted in a way that was absurd and ridiculous to those who ignored the actual possibility of God's judgment on us all. There were a hundred thousand more useful things to do in the village and in the fields, the local administration and the cultivation of the crops. His attitude could be explained only by the importance he attached to the Word of God, and by his conviction that the only thing of any consequence was the possible fulfillment of that declaration.

So we have to choose our actions and decisions, not only in relation to the personal, social, and moral context, but in relation to this eschatological reality. In that way, and only in that way, can we say that our works tend to actualize the Kingdom of God we are hoping for, tend to render it present in our midst. Now this action, which is marginal, disquieting, off-center, eccentric, anachronistic, and timeless (if it is not *all* of that, it is not expressive of the waiting), can only be begun endlessly over and over again with perseverance. It is an indefinite waiting, an inexhaustible perseverance. The epistles refer to it often! (Rom. 5:3–8; 15, 4; Eph. 6:18; II Thess. 1:4; Heb. 6:12; James 1:3), yet theology and preaching pay scarcely any attention to it! Perseverance, as a quality of the waiting, is one of the tangible aspects of hope. It is hope's response to failure and suffering. It is constancy in the inner life, and it is action in the face of appearances to the contrary, in spite of the refutations thrown at us by facts and events, by the state, by science, by technology and by history, by all the gods.

Perseverance never counts on success, on a possible outcome. It is not because the situation might get better that one keeps on going. To the contrary, perseverance completely repudiates all the success-criteria of action. This is decisive, for we are not hoping for any success, but for the return of Jesus Christ and the establishment of his reign. The return and the Kingdom are indissolubly linked to our tangible acts, but these have no need of a present success, that is, they have no need to attain their rational objective in order to have their own meaning, in order to be successful when Jesus Christ comes. Here again, as is the case with nearly all action taken in accordance with biblical instruction, there is a disengagement of the action from its "rational-concrete" effectiveness, since the reference of the action is not to the obtaining of a result. It is either obedience to a command or a waiting for the return. Consequently, we should be able to keep on indefinitely renewing these acts, economic, political, cultural, etc., without receiving the slightest human satisfaction or encouragement. It is only at the end of time and in the Kingdom of God that our action will have its final outcome.

But that can lead to laziness, to a lackadaisical attitude, to mere waiting without doing anything. Perseverance is just the attitude by which we continue to act with maximum earnestness and down-to-earth devotion, in spite of the absence of temporal effect, because there is no cause-and-effect relation between our acts and the coming of the Kingdom. There even is no visible, rational relation between them. Neither is there a relation between the success of these acts and the possibility of the return. There is no continuity from one to the other.

On the other hand, the hope and the waiting which are

incarnated in these acts as a matter of obligation are in strict correlation with the return. Thus perseverance teaches us not to attach importance to failures, because the important thing for us is Jesus Christ. Through perseverance, the failures cease to be sources of upset and despair, for it persuades us that failure is a necessary part of the Christian life (through the disengagement between the immediate objective of the action and its true ultimate). By the unity it gives our lives, it is the practical demonstration that the whole of our work (thought, prayer, action) is entirely related to the Kingdom of God, to the last days, and that it is not subject to the criteria of human activity.

Perseverance is truly an absurd attitude in the eyes of men, but it is the gauge of those who "inherit the promises" (Heb. 6:12), since the continuity it gives our lives is temporal and at the same time extra-temporal. Thus perseverance "in all good works" is the active aspect of waiting, but it rests on the vigor, the stubbornness, the determination of that waiting. All is oriented toward the eschaton, toward the return (including also the judgment, of course!). I am well aware of all the danger this involves. I know that the fervor of waiting is looked on askance by our theologians and Christian intellectuals as a source of absurdities and strange behavior. Throughout history, and to this day, groups of impassioned Christians are revived periodically who are a bit neurotic, paranoid, and schizophrenic. They live among themselves in a state of incredible tension, with the inflexibility of a block of cement. They speculate about the end of the world, and are sure it is the day after tomorrow.

These illuminati have a bad press with our rational Christians, and they are also made ridiculous by the fact that their predictions never come true. Jehovah's Wit-

nesses, Watchtower, Watchmen, Darbyites, etc.—all these
heretics look to us like unfortunates, and be it noted that,
in a period when there is a general refusal in the Reformed
Church to establish any criteria whatsoever which would
make it possible to draw the line between orthodoxy and
heresy, there still is no hesitation in calling these poor
fools heretics. At the same time, the proponents of the
good theology also do not hesitate to come up with the
following nonsense: "The great heresy of Christians of our
day consists in their refusal to take part in the revolutionary struggle of the peoples of the third world," a proposition which seems to me just as heretical as the nonsense
of the illuminati. But let us leave these mutual accusations
there.

It is indeed true that these people, burning with hopes
and fixated in a fierce expectation, do not provide us with
the trustworthy model of the Christian life. They are "psy-
chics." Yet there are a number of elements in their attitude
which should be noted. One thing is precisely this hope,
this rigor of waiting, the absolute fixation on the return.
Here, in spite of everything that can be said, they are right.
They are the ones who are teaching all the churches a
lesson. We know full well that heretics have always put a
finger on some truth of God that the Church had neglected. We should learn a lesson from their fervor and their
"eschatism," which would be much more useful to our
churches than the pursuit of hermeneutics.

On the other hand, their interpretation of the Bible is
often literalist, always primitive, and sometimes senseless.
This is where hermeneutics becomes necessary once again.
They calculate the time of the return. They assign time
limits to God for his action. They estimate the length of
the stages and fabricate a "philosophy" of history. They
indulge in a fanciful and nonspiritual (contrary to what

they think!) reading of the Bible, and their entire error stems from that.

But why do they act that way, and why are they forever making new starts? It is precisely because they do not have perseverance. They live in that fervor, and in that rigorous waiting—for a while. They give themselves a time limit, one year, three years, of gripping, all-absorbing waiting, then it is all over. One can live a year in such a high degree of tension, but not a whole life. Again, it is possible for a person to remain in a state of exaltation as long as he knows it is going to end on a certain date, but he cannot keep that up on an indefinite basis. It is like a runner in a race who sprints for ten yards because he knows they are the last ten yards. But if the finish line were suddenly removed, if the rules of the race were changed during the running, so that he saw himself in a race in which he did not know the time and place of the finish, he obviously would not sprint. That is why these illuminati have to set a time limit, and have to interpret the Bible in those terms.

Yet their error is rooted in the second and not in the first of these two elements. They are quite right in being fervent, unshakable, exalted, intransigent, focused on one word and one hope. Their mistake is that of reading the Bible in such a way that they enclose themselves within a decisive misunderstanding of God's work, and even of what they are expecting. What they lack is the perseverance to go with their waiting. They lack the fervor of a sustained waiting, which remains ever intense and unshakable through the perseverance brought about by the link with God in his revealed truth, instead of through a dated, perceived, and imminent objective.

That is when hermeneutics becomes indispensable. But it is indispensable within hope, with the waiting as its point of departure. It is indispensable when the entire

Church lives focused on the eschaton, when the *only* thing that counts is the final approach of the Kingdom of God, when the only truth is that there is a heavenly Jerusalem which is coming. With that outlook, in that knowledge and in that faith—Yes! to hermeneutics. Taken by itself, it threatens to freeze faith.

However mistaken their concepts and interpretations may be, the illuminati, like the pietists, have been arousers of the Church, discoverers of a new hope for each generation. They, and not the theologians, are the ones who have set the Church ahead. Joachim of Floris, Münzer,[4] Peter Waldo, and John of Leyden renewed for the Church the decisive tension toward the coming of the Kingdom. Without waiting, revived by these exalted ones, there is no more to Christian life but Church, since there is no hope, only words—words like those I am about to write, words which bear witness but do not give life.

PRAYER

We were saying that hope rests on three things: one psychic, waiting; one spiritual, prayer; and one intellectual, realism. We shall not have a lot to say about prayer.[5] Prayer, very neglected in the Church today, presents no foundation, no usefulness, and no requirement.

On the one hand, man has taken to heart the object lesson that everything happens just as well without invoking God, without entering into a dialogue with him. All goes

[4] What a mistake, very characteristic of our times, without qualification to make of Münzer a social reformer, a political revolutionary, another Spartacus!

[5] On the relation between prayer and hope see J. Ellul, *Prayer and Modern Man* (New York: Seabury Press, 1970).

well without God, as far as the affairs of the world are concerned. So what good does it do to pray, since what we are interested in in any case is the success of the flight to the moon, the election of the president of the United States, victory in the war in Vietnam (never mind the meaning), economic growth and the use of computers for everything (or just as well, the end of hunger, etc.). For all those things there is no need of prayer, which is just a bit of magic assist of ages ago, and unworthy of modern man.

On the other hand, the Christian also is perplexed by the situation noted above. He is afraid of being ridiculous. He yields to the obvious innocuousness of prayer. Moreover, he no longer knows to whom to address his prayer, in view of the fact that he is hearing more and more every day that God is not God, that he is not a person, that he neither hears nor speaks. It is useless to appeal only to Jesus, who died a good while ago in Judea. Of course, he was an example of all truth, but he is closeted in death, and his inexpressible, invisible, and incomprehensible resurrection has not turned his absence into an active presence. So prayer is no longer possible. Anyway, we are attracted by action. There is little attraction in prayer. It is boring.

And yet, we must grasp and understand that without prayer there is no hope, not the slightest. Conversely, the abandonment and loss of interest in prayer is exactly the spiritual proof that we have no hope. The person who claims to be full of hope but fails to lead a life of prayer is a liar. Prayer is the sole "reason" for hope, at the same time that it is its means and expression. Prayer is the referral to God's decision, on which we are counting. Without that referral there can be no hope, because we would have *nothing* to hope for. Prayer is the assurance of the possibility of God's intervention, without which there is no hope. Prayer is the means given by God for the dialogue with him, that is to say, it is the very junction of the future with eternity, where we have seen that our hope is located. In its dialogue it embraces the past presented for pardon, the future defined by the cooperation between the praying person and God, and eternity, which prayer lays hold of through the sighs uttered by the Holy Spirit.

Without such prayer we can piece together a few false hopes to give the appearance of hope, but all that, even when arranged theologically, can only be illusory. That is why it is quite right to recall that hope is based on God's promise constantly fulfilled and renewed. But how can we forget that, throughout the Bible, this promise is linked with the ceaseless outcry of prayer? It is man's prayer which demands the fulfillment, and it is again his prayer which demands its renewal and its ongoing. Without prayer, the promise and its fulfillment are forces just as indifferent and blind as *Moira* (fate) and *Ananke* (necessity).

So without prayer there is no true promise, since there is no one either to receive the promise or to take it seriously. However, just as prayer is prerequisite to the promise (for the promise to become promise!), so it is not the promise which incites man to prayer. Also, since there is no longer any joyous liberty of the person turned toward God, since our general sterility ignores the value of an outpouring, since our rationalism turns our eyes to microscopes and points us to the ground (the moon is another ground, now that we have walked on it), since our efficiency forbids our adding faith to these stammerings, since our gravity prevents our play of free speech toward God . . . where are we to get the meaning, the urgency and the need for prayer today?

Very well, I was led to the conclusion that if we have every reason for not praying, we have just one reason only for praying, namely, God's command. There is no need to look for other explanations or foundations. Prayer today is no longer a spontaneous motion of man toward his creator, nor of a ransomed soul toward his redeemer, nor of the person destined for death and for life toward the one who resurrects him. It can strictly be nothing other than obedience to a requirement which has credence as such, and here there is no need to go into profound analyses and exegesis. Either faith leads me to acknowledge that there is *a* command, and that at the center of that command is an instruction to pray, or else there is no faith.

But if I engage in prayer, then hope is born. If I live hope, I think only of hope in prayer. The two feed on each other. The moment that happens, the question about faith and its content becomes a thing of the past. The act of prayer, a pure obedience without an end in sight, resolves both the problematics of faith and all the impossibilities of human hope.

REALISM

I have attempted to demonstrate elsewhere that realism is the fundamental attitude of the Christian toward the world, and that its intellectual rule is one of the foundations of ethics.[6] We come upon it again here, linked with hope indissolubly. Realism is characteristic of the pessimism of hope in the exact degree we have seen. This hope never consists in thinking that things will work out. Hope

[6] On this question see J. Ellul, "Le Réalisme Chrétien," *Foi et Vie* (1955); *Réalisme et foi chrétienne* (lecture at the University of Amsterdam, 1956); *Prayer and Modern Man* (1970).

can live only in a strict pessimism, but the latter could bring us to a pessimism for which there is no remedy if we do not live by hope.

Once again, hope is not something to counterbalance pessimism and realism, to counteract reality clearly seen, understood, and grasped. Hope finds its substance in realism, and the latter finds its possibility in hope. Without a living hope there is likewise no human capacity to consider the actual situation. Man can never stand reality. He spends his time lying to himself, covering up the real, providing himself with illusions and rationalizations. Marx saw this clearly in his theory of the false conscience and ideology. He could not have seen it, could not have attempted to discern the real and to show it to others, except *with* and *within* a hope. But that hope was deceptive and insufficient to the degree to which it was purely human, to the degree to which it was based on historical analysis, and not on the only possible source of hope. But it must be borne in mind that Marx's thrust was the only acceptable one, and for that reason it was the one which made the closest approach possible to the reality of its time.

Without hope, reality becomes an unbearable mechanism, a continual damnation, a source of fear and apprehension which cannot be appeased. Man can never look situations squarely in the face, yet he is always frustrated and blocked when he fails to do so. The person who fails to look at the real, to accept it even in its most threatening aspects, to see the impasse or the fatality in which he finds himself, can never find a way out of it either, can never surmount the reality nor in any way get beyond it to make history. It is never the positive and comforting doctrines, the philosophies of progress, the historical or metaphysical optimisms, which incite man to become man. The doctrine of the "great Yes" given to the creation, to technology, and to man is a doctrine of stagnation, of systematic opposition to progress and of laissez-faire.

If "primitive" man had obeyed a "great Yes," had obeyed surrounding nature, he would quite simply have disappeared, wiped out by his foolishness. It was by observing the situation in the most realistic way possible: cold, hunger, wild beasts, and all-around hostility, that man formulated the great No. "No! I refuse to accept its being that way. I refuse to accept the universe's being one of cold, hunger, and all the dangers." Then, matured by a still-unnamed hope, man acted and won.

Now we are faced with the same choice. That is why hope is still decisive. In fact, only from the standpoint of that hope we can make a decision. But this decision (political, scientific, technological, economic) only makes sense if it relates to a clear and rigorous view of the real. Without this realism, hope can only fall back into idealism, and it is my belief that idealism, at whatever level, is the worst of all traps, and represents the greatest danger for man. No matter whether it is the idealism of the man in the street, limited to a few simple judgments about happiness and taking refuge in the magazines of the happy life, or whether it is political idealism, believing in formulas and confused over words. (The best example of idealism was Hitlerism. It was actually a great ideal set before mankind. I recall the hundreds of articles written between 1930 and 1936 stating the absolute necessity of setting forth an ideal for youth.) The ideal can only be a lie. Today's ideal is socialism. It entices man once again into discourse without reference to the real, and into action which is quite useless, but alas not harmless.[7]

---

[7] A good example of this idealism without substance, all the more significant because the author lays claim to realism, is the book by Jean Cordat, *Révolution des pauvres et Evangile* (1970). What we have here

Reality needs to be grasped with a minimum of interpretation and considered on its own level. But here it should be emphasized that doctrinal materialism is an idealism. Of course, on the philosophic level the two are in opposition and contradict one another, but on the level of practical behavior materialism functions as an interpretative system out of touch with reality, within which one attempts to give meaning to that reality. One necessarily distorts reality in order to fit it into the system. One cuts it down to make it susceptible of interpretation. That is the great lesson of applied Marxism.

Finally, idealism is equally damnable when it is philosophic. Hope, which feeds on the real, obliges us to reject consideration of the Idea, or of any reality other than that which we can take note of by the means at our disposal (I might call them scientific), of any reality which would be more true than that lived on the level of everyday life. Idealism is a source of man's continual disillusionment. It is his temptation to live something other than himself. Kant and Hegel are Christianity's lie incarnate. They give free play and full vent to the unbridled forces of history—

---

is a synthesis of all the commonplaces about poverty, the third world, colonialism, imperialism, socialism, etc. If I cite this book from among a hundred others of the same stamp, it is because, on the one hand, the author has put forth a great effort at documentation, and he is a Christian of great good will. On the other hand, he presents, to a degree rarely attained, the discord between the accurate observation of a certain number of facts and the frame of reference in which they are placed, as well as the colorplate of interpretation through which they are seen, which is prearranged and strictly inaccurate and which renders the facts completely useless. It is an example of false realism, the realism having been obscured by idealism concerning socialism, neocapitalism, etc. For the unforewarned, the discord is explosive. One emerges from a simple but honest description, only to get into a sort of delirium of verbal explanations and solutions which are pure fiction and dreams.

unbridled, for example, when man, all excited over the development of an idea, fails of course to see that the Prussian State is gobbling up everything, and that this particular incarnation of the idea means nothing but the ultimate bondage of humanity in that age.

Idealism is always misleading about what is happening and going to happen. It was wonderful to set forth an attractive outline of history and its development, but what a fraud, what a swindle, when the only decisive result was the relentless strengthening of the State, the very place where man should have concentrated all his forces to prevent such a thing. Idealism sidetracked him from it. Garlands and decorations give the monster a cheery look, but the monster keeps devouring the very people who camouflaged him, and they are so surprised.

Without realism hope has no reality. It wanders about in the blue sky above, *animula vagula, blandula* . . . , a bit of hope, a charming game, but nothing serious. Hope does not begin to *exist* except in the harshness of an expanding implacable force, in the unanswerable nature of the problems confronting the person, in social oppression and mechanization, in the midst of conflict. Elsewhere, one has no use for hope. One gets along quite well without it. All that is needed is to let things go, to leave man to himself and let nature take its course. Hope is power and action only in the presence of naked reality.

It does no good to tell me that I never lay hold of naked reality, that I can only have a cultural view of things and that pessimism is just as deceptive as optimism, etc. I know that line quite well. I can say this, that a dead man is a dead man. There is a reality there, about which it is useless to quibble, which I meet up with, and which I can do nothing about. It is not a cultural image. Cultural images are interpretations of this reality after the fact. The reality itself is grasped and experienced directly. The moment I begin to examine it, think about it, and interpret it, then yes, I need to be suspicious of cultural images, of color-plates of interpretation, of my psychological optimism or pessimism, of my system of thought, etc. But, for one thing, that in no way changes my experience of the fact, of this raw, given thing which has put me to the acid test. For another thing, it can be counteracted by a certain intellectual rigor and by a critical procedure.

That is why it seems to me that reality is within our grasp, but that it can only be experienced. There can be no sociology or psychology without a personal experience of the fact, which one tries first to grasp and afterward to explain. Hope then acts to keep the interpretation from being a lie, an illusion, a justification. But more than that, it produces the power whereby we are not conquered by this reality, whereby the experience of the death of a person, of a brother, does not bring me to the point of suicide, or of giving up, but becomes, to the contrary, the point of departure for life and hope. Yet this realism cannot be reduced to the purely individual experience of the moment. I only used that concrete example as a reminder of the fact that there is a reality outside our artificial representations. Any genuine and usable realism, the kind which will always remain the necessary condition for hope, has to be defined in its sociological dimension.

Now, for a grasp of the social group and of its history, there are three possible levels. One is the superficial level. Here the emphasis is on happenings, on current events, on personalities. Dubček suddenly appears on the scene, socialism with a human face, the Russians in Prague—it is exciting. One looks for photographs, details, speeches, convinced that this is *very* important, a journey, an army tank, a press conference. Over the past thirty years I have heard it said at least two thousand times (and first on February 6, 1934) that "things will never be the same again." We must not for a moment suppose that this formula, repeated by all the thinkers of May–June, 1968, is new. It was said in connection with Hitlerism in 1933, the war in Ethiopia in 1934–35, the Popular Front in 1936, the war in Spain in 1937. I could go on. Each time, thousands of reporters and intellectuals elaborated on the notion that a decisive turning point had been reached and that everything was radically altered. Actually, practically nothing had been changed in any significant way. Governing groups had undergone modification, speeches changed their themes, uniforms changed color, and slogans had a different content, but with it all there was a rigorous constant: people were killed—with regularity and in great numbers. Had the Popular Front won in Spain, or the communists in Germany in 1933, the number of victims would have been about the same, only not the same individuals.

Again, to concentrate on the spectacular event, to analyze elections and the content of speeches, leads nowhere. Such journalistic acquaintance with the real of current events affords an anecdotal interest. It is undeniably exciting to sit on the balcony of history, but it also represents a distraction from the more profound and decisive reality.

At the opposite extreme, the third level is one of a tremendous abstraction. Here one attempts to comprehend reality in such depth that everything looks like everything else. Among governments and their forms the only thing noted is the phenomenon of power. But it is found that any phenomenon whatsoever of power has the same structures, so one then studies power as such, in any group at all, at any level whatsoever.

But between those two levels there is an intermediate territory. Underneath the events and above the fundamental constants, there are the structures, the movements and the temporary regularities which go to make up the actual history, and which produce an epoch or a regime with its characteristic features. So, beneath the public current events and elections, but above the constant of the phenomenon of power, there is the State, similar under the monarchy and under the republic, similar in a communist or in a capitalist regime. The differences are secondary compared with the phenomenon itself, which is determinative for our epoch.

As an analogy, consider the ocean. On the surface are the waves and the splash brought about by the wind. To be sure, they could be substantial and cause shipwrecks, but those are surface phenomena. In the depths there is a sepulchral stillness. Between the two are the currents, the tides, modifications in the ocean floor, the formation and the shifting of sandbars. My contention is that it is in this in-between that one should apply Christian realism. I have tried elsewhere to show that, from the sociological, political, and economic points of view, it is this in-between which is decisive and the most interesting.

But that is the very territory where we confront the question of hope. We have said that hope takes place when the situation cannot be escaped, and when it leaves nothing to be hoped for. Now, at the level of current events there is no situation without some escape, even if there are local and individual tragedies. It is at that level that things humanly hoped for can play their part (and, of course, for a person facing death without illusion, for example, there is also the great decision of hope, but that is not determinative for the Church and for society). Conversely, hope has no place in the presence of the deepest constants of social or of human life (the fact that people have to eat, or that every society and group has to have power). The reality which hope really confronts, the reality which can bring a person or a society to despair and torpor, the reality which deepens man's sensitivity with its harshness, lies exactly in the in-between. Consequently it is there that realism should be practiced.

DECISIONS

We have been speaking about waiting, prayer, and realism as the three foundations, causes, and expressions of hope. What we have now to realize is that these are three *decisions*. The waiting person is not someone laid to one side like a package, who is waiting because he can think of nothing else to do. Rather, he is a person who has made the decision to wait, and who renews it constantly. He has made a choice from among a number of possible modes of behavior and has selected that one. Prayer, as we have seen, has no other foundation in our day than obedience to the command to pray. That, again, is a decision. The Christian has decided to obey *that*, in contradistinction to a number of others. He has chosen. Realism also is the result of a choice, because most Christians prefer idealism. The latter is more comforting, and it also enjoys more prestige, since it permits of lofty and profound conversation and seems so much better suited to the nobility and to discussions about "Christianity." And when the Christian does turn to realism he prefers either the tremendous depths or the fascination of surface events. Thus the realism which relates to hope is the object of a decision, of a knowledge, and of a setting of limits.

In other words, in all three cases we are basing ourselves on will and choice. Such a decision is capable of being effected at the human level, by the human being.

Of course, to the extent to which there has to be a reason and a motive for making those choices, the person has to be someone acquainted with Scripture, who accepts it as true and is motivated in that direction. But his decision is in no way supplied by a miracle.

Thus hope, that mysterious phenomenon, the most lofty and decisive expression of the Holy Spirit in man today, results from the threefold decision of which we have been speaking. But, like everything in the relationship with God, there is a reciprocal action. If we are capable of making this threefold decision, that is because we are already in hope (perhaps without knowing it, and it will be revealed later on), and if we reject these choices, the hope which has been given dies. Conversely, this triple decision by no means produces hope automatically. Yet it is assuredly given (or revealed, or made obvious) only on condition that we exercise these choices. To take up those options is to live hope already in a series of acts. Hope is always the product, the exceeding work of the Holy Spirit, but our decision appears not only as the lived expression of the hope given to us. It appears also as a challenge flung at the Holy Spirit in order that this hope might be possible. Hope itself is then hoped.

12

Signs and the Incognito

SIGNS?

As we have said repeatedly, hope should be seen, and that immediately makes us think about signs. We have to give people signs of our hope. That was, for quite a while, the usual position stemming from Barthianism. One could only give the world signs of the Kingdom, signs of the Lordship of Jesus Christ. The Church was supposed to be one, or several, of these signs! Actually, that cannot suffice in the final analysis, although it is a course which is just as true as any other, and surely more workable.

First, however, we have to understand that such an ethic of signs really answers to a theology of signs. It is when we consider the revelation and the work, or the person, or the teaching of Jesus Christ as signs that we are led, in consequence, to treat signs as an ethical expression of the truth of God. Can that theological interpretation be maintained? Are signs all that there are? Does the God who reveals himself to us give only signs of what he is, signs to "make us think," or does he indeed reveal himself in his revealable reality? [8] The proclamation of the Name which cannot be pronounced—is that only a sign referring to something else, or is it a *given* reality itself? Is the cross a sign, or is it the actual redemption of all mankind? Is the resurrection a sign, or is it actually and concretely a victory over death? Is the person of Jesus a sign of what ought to be, or of what can be the relationship with other people, or is it actually the presence of God-with-us, Emmanuel? We have to make a choice.

Also, a theology of signs obviously gives rise to an ethic of signs. Here we have to acknowledge that this no longer answers to anything in our society. It is true that in a traditional society, less densely populated, only slightly advanced technologically, and not so complicated politically, a person or a small group could *be* a visible and meaningful sign making people think. Also, they could *give* signs which would be perceptible, though even then with difficulty, as Herostratus demonstrated (yet his sign was not lost, because history preserved it). But in a society like ours, which is complex, overwhelming numerically, advanced scientifically, its eyes popping out with billions of signs coming from everywhere and spread out in all directions, and from millions of signs given by anybody at all for anything at all—in such a society a sign means absolutely nothing. In our day it is not true that a sign makes one think. It is passed off together with all the bric-a-brac from millions of dispatches in a mass discharge. To give

---

[8] I do not, of course, mean that we could grasp the reality in and of itself of God. It is quite obvious that the entire revelation is effected through symbols, and in a cultural context.

signs of faith, of love, and of charity means nothing any more. History has preserved the name of Herostratus, but the name of Hirohito Kagawa, perhaps the most splendid sign to the twentieth century of the love of Christ—who has preserved that? It is part of the necessary realism to see this, and it is part of the diagnosis of the abandonment to know it.

Not only is the sign of Jesus Christ swamped by all the others, but again our society, and man in this Western society, isn't interested in that kind of sign. What people ask for is not an indication of something possible. They want a total fulfillment, the complete solution to a political, economic, pedagogic, psychological problem. Signs look like mockery. To construct a model hospital in which the sick person is treated as a person, is respected as to his will, his dignity and his depths as a person—what interest is there in that, when there is a line of a hundred thousand sick people outside who are not being cared for at all? In that case the sign of Christian love, when it is perceived, is taken as a counterindication. In other words, our society demands total, collective, and definitive solutions, immediate answers. It certainly rejects hope and the orientation toward the Kingdom of God.

But from another angle this total fulfillment does answer to a theology of reality. If Jesus *is* (currently) the Lord (fully so) of the world (the whole world), then Christian action should manifest itself at the level of that present fact and of that totality. Thus we are driven from both sides to get into a total actuality, *not something which signifies*, and to *do*, instead of talking or showing.

Thereafter we are faced with two possibilities. Either Christianity is to be incarnate in global institutions and expressed in a system, in effect embracing politics, economics, etc., and this would be the model for Christendom;

or else Christianity is to blend into the non-Christian movements which are claiming to provide the global solution. Now it is quite clear that in our day people cannot be involved in the path of Christendom, although that ideology has not really been given up. It still lives in the hearts of committed Christians! Nevertheless, if we are to answer to a theology of reality and to the trends of our society at the same time, the other path is the only one left.

But here we must not delude ourselves. It means, for one thing, division, loss of vitality, and dissipation in the current, the superficial, and the ideological, and, for another thing, the renunciation of Christianity itself. It suffices only to consider those who have plunged in that way into our political or social life to discover what amount of delusion (believing that a given reform or revolution will bring about a naturally human, just, and fraternal society), and what a renunciation of the essence of the revelation they can represent. The whole of Christianity is reduced to communicating with and relating to all mankind, to taking part in human struggles for justice and freedom. Confronted by this radical and essential reduction of the revelation and of Scripture, for which only two or three texts can be found in justification, we are obliged to reject equally radically that orientation toward the fusion and diffusion of Christianity and of Christians in the "politico-social movement" of this age.

That orientation, which is the one most current today (involvement in non-Christian social movements at the price of the specific character of Christianity), appears most pernicious from every point of view. It rests not so much on a theology of the world, which serves as an alibi, but on social pressure, on the general overestimation of material issues which places them above everything else so that they become the governing criteria, and on the overestimation of political solutions—all this with a remarkable absence of realism.

THE INCOGNITO

Thus we are quite truly at an impasse. All the traditional forms of the expression of Christianity are eliminated, either for theological reasons or for reasons of necessity. Besides, if we really are in an age of abandonment we should not be too surprised at this. Precisely in this situation there can neither be shown a solution to be brought about here and now by the word of the living God, nor can man contrive any expression of the revelation he has received. There is nothing astonishing about our inability to provide meaning and to come up with answers.

But we cannot leave it at that. We are obliged to say, "And yet there is hope." Now, faced with the world in which we are called upon to live this hope, the latter can only lead us to the incognito. After all, is it not normal that there should be an incognito of Christians toward the world and in the midst of the world, corresponding to the incognito of God, that there should be a silence of the Church toward the world, corresponding to the silence of God? The incognito is perhaps the genuine, serious, and profound form of hope today.

Again, however, we have to understand one another. I certainly cannot fall back on the very attitude I was criticizing above. It is not a matter of mingling in all the world's endeavors, of treating them as fundamental and decisive. It is not a matter of camouflaging Christianity by representing it as a little aside, as an accessory, in any case as something which does not in any way distinguish us from others, in short as a respectable ideology.

Likewise the incognito does not consist in "bearing witness by our works, by service, by our presence," with no *mention* of witness. There is *no* witness through works. There is no witness unless there is union, agreement, and interaction between work and word. The incognito goes much deeper than those little ways of accommodation and adaptation to our society, much deeper than living easily in this world. Nor is the incognito the joyous elimination of the Church, which is charged with all the mistakes and is the creator of obstacles to the encounter with people, false in her theology, necessarily producing a nonworship in her worship (because she is Church), etc. The incognito does not say that, in consequence, the Church has only to vanish into the one thing which counts (in God's eyes, of course, since it counts in our eyes!), namely, into modern society, that she has only to be dissolved in the secular city.

No, the incognito is not the putting to death of the only form given us for living together the love of Jesus Christ. The incognito is both more and less than all those things. For the sake of making it understood, I would like to fall back on an historic experience, that of Israel.

For two thousand years Israel has been the people of the incognito. For three thousand years it has been the people of hope. Without any doubt, Moltmann is right in anchoring his theology of hope in the resurrection, and in interpreting the resurrection in terms of hope by putting it back entirely in the framework of Jewish theology with the impetus of the life of the chosen people. Israel willed it. It sought to be the people of the promise, and that is what Neher emphasizes in connection with his rejection of Christianity. This rejection stems from "the credit which Jewish pertinacity accords to the silence and to the promise." "Not yet," cries the Jew, when faced with Christian messianism. Nothing is consummated in the history of the world, and Abraham is always on a Mount Moriah. The doors remain always open to the infinite energy of the Possible, and the Word has not yet spoken his final word. He may not even have spoken his first word. Taking up the theme of the two Strasbourg statues, the Church triumphant and the Synagogue humbled, he bears witness to the fact she sees with her eyes blindfolded and she hears "as Abraham heard, surrounded by silence, not like Prometheus to overcome or to fail as a philosopher, not like Jesus to die and rise again, but as a Jewish patriarch to *hope*."

Israel is a people centered entirely on hope, living by that alone, a hope always carried through and never actualized, a people accustomed to the silence of God, acquainted with his abandonment, yet living by hope nevertheless. As the one hoping people of the world, it is Israel which provides us with the model for this age. Since being broken as a nation, it has buried itself in the incognito. Outwardly accepting the manners and customs of the peoples in whose midst it is settled, it is nevertheless always different, displaced, unlike, incapable of the sociological or spiritual communion forever set before it.

It is unlike because it has a hope which is incarnate. It lives this hope as a people, in a secret, mysterious, and hidden, yet always rigorous and total way. It is united by the spiritual tie of an absoluteness, always close-knit, steeped in the secret of its festivals, its traditions, its chants, and its prayers, always entirely amiable and forming all possible relationships, yet at the same time completely firm regarding the most serious of all things, the deep well. It strictly conserves the spotless content of the revelation, and thereby maintains unity among its members. Because they have such energy and intelligence, a sign of depth, they have it in them to do great things and to occupy the top positions in every society in which they are found (for it takes exceptional energy and intelligence to live the incognito). Again, from this very fact, the known mystery and the social success appear as strange, incomprehensible, and as presenting a real issue.

That is an example of the incognito. In this age of the abandonment of the world and of the Church, I think that Christians have to direct themselves exactly in that path, and should take that as a model. Now we, Christians and churches, are at the present time in a situation quite similar to that of Israel in the early centuries of the Roman Empire. It is sometimes said that this is the end of the era of Constantine, and that we find ourselves once again in the position of the second century A.D. That is correct with regard to the break between Church and State and with regard to the relation between Christianity and the non-Christian society, but in other respects it is incorrect. There is a difference between a young movement with a great future and an old organization with a great past.

The comparison that should be made is the comparison with Israel. It was an old religion which was accorded its place among all the others. It was the object of misunderstanding, seeming to be known without really being known, politically suspect, strange, and involving rites and symbols no longer understood, trying without success to make proselytes, endowed with a strong organization, in collision with an explosion of new beliefs and religions, the victim of socio-political condemnation at the same time that it was a power. That is really where we are. We, the Church, are like Israel in the first and second centuries. Israel has found the true answer to this situation, an answer which has made it possible for it to come through two thousand years of persecution. It is the incognito and the steadfastness in hope. We today could not hope to find a better response.

But in the Christian realm there is an additional theological motive. If we are to enter into hope, we have to live in the order of the resurrection, and consequently in complete discontinuity between that which is headed for death and that which denies death. It is a discontinuity which we can not possibly rearrange. "Hope, as hope in the resurrection, is the living contradiction of that out of which it proceeds and which is placed under the sign of the cross and of death." But there cannot be a visible, effective contradiction to the past. If there is a rejection of the present (known) reality, that is in the name of something incomplete and unfulfilled, in the name of the expectation of a new action. We Christians, among ourselves and as brothers in the faith, can at the most discern traces, gleams, and indications of this, but these are completely useless, meaningless, and ridiculous to those on the outside, and they can never convince them either of that to which they refer or of the validity of our hope.

All the Christian themes of hope are incapable of being transmitted. In order to be understood, they require signs to be perceived, a spiritual asceticism, a knowledge of the Bible, a substantial high-mindedness which can never be given and can only be the result of long initiation. Because there is hope, there can never be a direct transmission of its object, nor any other possible attitude than that of the incognito. Because there is hope in the *resurrection,* the only attitude is that of those who are dead (and by baptism that is surely what we are!), but also of those who do not display themselves carelessly.

But let us be careful. This incognito is in no way an easement. It is not simply a matter of keeping quiet, of dis-

sembling, of not exposing ourselves. It is not a matter of
becoming assimilated. It is a matter of remaining the firm
and constant bearer of a truth which is no longer uttered.[9]
There is incognito when behind a mask or a pseudonym
there is a *person,* who is a person because he has chosen
to be buried in this incognito, has chosen to hide the serious and the decisive. If there were nothing to hide, if one
were to forget the glorious secret of the hidden God, of
the closed Word, if one were to succumb to not hoping
any longer, then there would be no more incognito. The
person (the Christian) would merely have become his
own mask, the knight who is not.

It is a matter of not for one moment changing this truth
because others no longer believe it, or because it is incapable of being shared with others. There is incognito only
in the unflagging perseverance behind these masks. Hence
it is the creation of a *seeming accommodation,* of an acceptance of everything done in this world. It is a seeming
accommodation only, because one has concluded that all
those things, politics or money, unionism or social action,
technology or art can be done since there is nothing decisive or very serious about them. They are neither the essential nor the living things. But one can arrive at that conclusion only from the standpoint of something assured and
maintained as an essential and living thing.

Is that to say that this is a "backing down," a "hypocrisy," a return to an interiorized, individual faith, and a
giving up of the proclamation of the faith? By no means.
Hope never resigns itself; and the role of the incognito is
never played alone, but together (the chosen people together, in this case the Christians, I scarcely dare say the

[9] This may correspond to Bonhoeffer's famous "discipline of the arcane,"
if indeed I understand correctly what he meant by that. I am not so sure,
when I read the disparity of interpretations put out by his commentators.

Church). The needed incarnation is just this incognito. Likewise, it is never an attitude of discouragement, or resignation (taking refuge in silence because one does not manage to be heard or understood).

In reality, the incognito is not this surrender to the lack of understanding of the Gospel. It is the *refusal to speak*,[10] a refusal based on not throwing pearls before swine, and since God is silent it is important not to be a false prophet acting out a farce by pretending that God is speaking. It is there that hypocrisy is found, not in the dreadfully hard role of the incognito.

Again, let us not fall into another error. It is not a refusal to speak among brothers of the same hope. To the contrary, it is more important than ever to enter together into hope's struggle with God. It is more important than ever to pray together and meditate together on the Scriptures. It is more important than ever without letup to transmit the "good deposit" and thereby (by that alone, to the exclusion of sociological considerations) to build the most hardcore, the most loyal and, just too bad, the most exclusive Christian nucleus.

It is a refusal to speak to those who turn a deaf ear, who do not want to hear, who turn away, thinking to have arrived at a judgment of something they know nothing

[10] One could gain the impression of a certain inconsistency here with what I have said repeatedly above (pp. 127, 146), to the effect that hope should speak, and that we have neither the right to hide it nor to keep quiet about it, using the abandonment as an excuse. In reality, to live hope implies the same paradox as that set forth in Scripture. On the one hand, "Do not throw your pearls before swine" (Matt. 7:6), and on the other hand, "Preach the word, be urgent in season and out of season" (II Tim. 4:2). The incognito presupposes silence and an insistent word at the same time, on condition that this word is not a *flatus vocis*. We have no excuse for not speaking our hope, yet for living our hope we have only the genuineness of the incognito.

about. It is a refusal to answer false and vicious questions, just as Jesus refused to work miracles, or just as he gave answers off to one side of the traps which were set for him. Thus the incognito consists in giving oneself, yet in being other than the person on whose behalf this is done, because, while it is impossible to refuse a certain communion with people, still the abject surrender of the self is completely useless, since the milieu is strictly incapable of comprehending what one is and what one lives.

PRESENCE

Already I hear the cries of those who are infuriated by such scandalous proposals. "But that is a Christian ghetto, the good conscience turned in upon itself, the refusal to be present to the world." Ghetto? Perhaps, but there is little likelihood of a ghetto, given our wide dispersion throughout this society, both physically and intellectually, based on facility of transportation and on profession. It would be more to the point to call it a "third order." Is it a Protestant third order? Surely not. Protestantism and Catholicism both have come to the end of the road as sociological realities. We cannot go back to the sixteenth century to make them live again. No one is interested in that. Those who are out to kill or dissolve the churches at all costs are wasting their time. All they have to do is to let evolution and circumstance take care of it for them. But "Christians"? Yes indeed, and tough ones. So, a Christian third order (careful! not externally constructed with a few good intentions), made up of unrelenting people who have lived their entire lives on the basis of that loyalty.

But then does that not refuse a presence to the world?

I must have changed! I was, I think, one of the first, if not the first, to spread the slogan: "Presence to the modern world." Am I taking it all back by announcing the incognito? I do not think so. It is, rather, that there has been a continual misunderstanding surrounding that presence, through its being interpreted as political action or commitment along all the world's paths. If, twenty years ago, I was focusing my research on communication and revolution, it was because it was (as now) a matter, in the essential sectors of our society, of introducing the unusual, the novel, the incomprehensible, and the radical, which would restore to communication and revolution a new possibility, a new youth and a knowledgeableness, in view of the fact that they were totally shut off, closed in and without any outlet. It is now my opinion that the form of this extra- (or para-) social action is precisely the incognito.

If Christians take seriously the evolution of this society, they have to understand that it is not by commitment to action that they can make any important changes in it, but by the insertion of a completely new and unexpected dimension, the incognito. It is that which is presence to the world, through the shock of refusal, through the gap left vacant, through the resulting chasm, through the unlooked-for break in the conversation. It is the manner of the presence to the modern world which has changed for me, and not its importance nor its necessity.

But is there not a contradiction between what I was writing about hope as creative of history, and the incognito, which is always interpreted as a retreat and an absence of history? Here again we have to go back to the only example of the incognito, that of the Jewish people.

Do we have to ask ourselves whether Israel has been

absent from history? Is it not, rather, Israel which has made far more history in the end than anyone else? It has been done through individuals, but through individuals raised in and issued from the incognito. Who has had more influence on the course of modern history than, for example, Marx or Freud? Are not the Jews accused by some of being the initiators of capitalism, and by others of being responsible for communism? If history is looked at closely, and without the usual Christian prejudice, it turns out to have been forged at least as much by the Jewish incognito as by Christian activism. In the Middle Ages it was the banker-baron combination. For us Christians today it is a matter of finding a comparable from of intervention. That is the great challenge with which we are faced.

To play this role of the incognito requires exceptional forcefulness, not to slump back into lifeless little coteries, into false secrets, into the game which does not cost anything, into lying to oneself, into confidential halfheartedness, into the contented purring of liturgies, into the constant harping on formulas which are never put into practice. The people of Israel experienced all that, lived it, fell into it. But at the same time Israel has also been other than that. It has always been caught back up again to live the true incognito.

This incognito implies a faith which is trenchant, absolute, and undivided. It is there, and only there, that we find the issue of faith. In order to endure in this ambiguous and tense situation, there is needed a rigor of faith far greater than that of setting out to bear witness to it in speeches in the public square or in church. The reason is that this faith is no longer nourished by conversation with others, and in this time of abandonment it is no longer nourished by a Word from God either, so it has to be all the more firm and clear-cut.[11] To the extent to which it rests on hope, it has no need to submit to the evaluation of its content, supportively or not, by what is culturally revealed.

Consequently (if waiting and perseverance are really the essentials) the questioning mania of our times has to be entirely rejected. The continual "And what if . . . ?" "Is it really so . . . ?" can come only from an anxious mind looking for ways of affirmation which escape him because the milieu to which he is appealing says to him that what he is telling it can only be his own say-so. Faith lived in the incognito is one which is located outside the criticism coming from society, from politics, from history, for the very reason that it has itself the vocation to be a source of criticism. It is faith (lived in the incognito) which triggers the issues for the others, which causes everything seemingly established to be placed in doubt, which drives a wedge into the world of false assurances.

At the same time it offers points of reference and of certainty for those who live this incognito together, as well as for those who are quite willing to be called in question, for those who find themselves in confusion, in anguish and uncertainty. For the latter, and without forcing anything, the incognito can be partially lifted and points of reference partially given. Surely the certainties in question

[11] Must I repeat again that when I speak of the certainty and firmness of the faith, I in no way mean by that the proud tranquility of the statue representing the Church at Strasbourg, nor the refusal to hear criticisms and objections (but what are all the accumulated attacks of men, compared with the unrelenting one of God's silence), nor the complacency of achieved results, nor the claim that theology is the science of sciences, nor the idle belief that we have all the answers, either the faith or the revelation, nor . . . , nor. . . . That all seems to me so very simple, so to be taken for granted, so clear, that I am always surprised when someone begins these criticisms all over again, and confuses the certainty of the faith with those feeble attitudes.

can never simply be learned. It is not the recitation of a catechism, nor a mystical outpouring, nor a body of intellectual verities.

What I'm describing here is a way of life which is total and different. It is the way of life of those who walk with an unshakable certitude in the midst of uncertain crowds, and who raise persistent questions in the midst of doctrines and bodies of knowledge which are too assured. Thus the certitudes can only be acquired through a personal relationship. If they are sufficiently solid, they should produce the question to which Peter alludes ("Always be prepared to make a defense to any one who calls you to account for the hope that is in you" [I Pet. 3:15]).

So we have to reject the world's uncertainty and not let ourselves get caught in the mesh of questions, which are only expressions of the weakness of our faith and of our guilt complex at being Christian. To say that "today" there can no longer be a Christian affirmation, but only questions (put to ourselves and to the Church concerning the content of the revelation), is not to be ahead of the times, on a plane with science and at the forefront intellectually. It is to be behind by some four thousand years. It is to put oneself back before Abraham.

Of course, if this incognito demands such firmness, such a rigor of faith (which from now on, under these circumstances, depends on that alone for its sense and value), it implies as well, and at the same time, an almost unbelievable hope. After all, an unheard-of dosage of hope is required for going into the incognito. It takes a lot to bring down the curtain, knowing all the while that the show is not over and that the audience is not really going to leave, since they are struck by the lowering of the curtain right in the middle of the tragedy and the comedy. It is a hope for the sake of holding on to the certainty that our silence (and prayer, of course!) will, *in the end,* be more eloquent than our speeches, our revolutionary proclamations, our involvements, our services, our devices for keeping things livened up, our commitments, and our publicity. It is a hope for keeping alive the certainty that our incognito will come to an end one of these days, because the silence of God will come to an end.

Here, hope has a decisive role to play. It makes us live in the certitude that in one generation, or in ten, after we have lived this incognito and have held onto this hope, God will speak again and his truth will burst upon the world. From that point of view, hope establishes us in a situation of radical distance in relation to the trends of the modern world, which, for one thing, is unable to wait any longer and wants everything right away, and on the other hand wants to know when. Hope, in the incognito, makes us see that the one important thing is to convey hope itself to the succeeding generation, even if there are only one or two at a time to pick it up and bear it.

But it is still hope, hope to keep alive the assurance that out of the depths of our incognito we are influencing the history of the world more radically than by all the outward interventions, and that history is not actually made in decisions of state nor in revolutions, nor in scientific discoveries, but at the heart of a fierce hope, which, in the incognito, does battle for its affirmation. Today, only in the incognito is there a source of history for our times. All the rest is appearance and talk, which comes too late in spite of the agitation.

This incognito, which is a whole lifestyle in itself, also excludes a lifestyle, and it puts an end to searching tendencies. Thus, after the zeal for questioning, it also eliminates the fuss over problems of communication and the obsession to understand everything in terms of the kerygma. To be sure, the standpoint of the kerygma holds an interest for the reading of the Bible. To be sure, in the area of human relations it is not without interest to look for better means of communication. I have never said that the incognito forbade theological reflection (in fact, that is where it should be located), nor that it forbade participation in the works of man. To the contrary, it is because there is that participation that there *can* be an incognito. Otherwise there would be an absence pure and simple.

But we must not be upset over the small return from the communication of the Gospel, nor over the new psychology, nor over the sociological situation of modern man which shuts him away from the Gospel. The latter does not have to be exploded, scattered, wasted, and spread around. It needs to be concentrated, regrouped, intensified, and compacted, as "the lightning is concentrated around Caesar." That is the choice; and if hope is indeed the heart of the Christian life today, that is the orientation.

RIGOR

The incognito makes possible the concentration of the spiritual life. Rigor makes possible the concentration of the intellectual life, polarized on the revelation. It avoids diluting the all or nothing, which is the only expression of our fidelity available to us. Now the excessive concern for communication, for conveying the message, leads to just the opposite. It leads to a spreading thin, to an intellectual incongruity, which under the appearance of profundity produces endless redundancies (beyond anything ever

302 · *Hope in Time of Abandonment*

known at the height of pietism!). The decisive issue is diluted by the successive bursts of excitement over all the social and political problems.

The obsession with communication blots out the substance of the message to be conveyed. We are indeed children of this age and of this world, dominated by a greater concern for form, medium, structure, and speech than for the thing said and for its content. True, it is being explained to us that the form is the foundation, and that there is no other content to speech and to the printed word than the structure, but that is just what we have definitely to reject.

Christ's being put on a cross does not mean that the form of the cross taken by Jesus at that time *is* the message of the cross. If I make use of that example, it is not for nothing. That was the thrust of numerous interpretations, more or less Gnostic in nature: the cross is the plus sign, or its vertical and horizontal arms show the union of the vertical relation with God and the horizontal relation with man, or it has reference to the oldest symbols dating from the age of the cavemen, or it is the well-known symbol of the belly-button of the world, which right away carries us back to pre-Buddhism, etc. These dissertations about the cross as such completely forget that the important thing is that Jesus, known as Son of Man and Son of God, should have been put on a cross. They correspond exactly to the current dissertations on structure and communication. The incognito, to the contrary, which shuts off that kind of fascinating exploration, brings us back to the one focal point.

It could seem strange that I am here combining trends which appear to be opposed to one another: those of kerygmatic research, of anxiety over communication, and of structural analysis, but these, in fact, really represent one and the same tendency, appearances to the contrary. In all three instances the Spoken of God is replaced either by a human proclamation of a message or by a structure (internal or external), that is, by a magnitude or by an activity which is strictly human and horizontal. One ignores the fact that none of that holds the slightest shadow of interest unless it is God who is speaking. The incognito, on the other hand, freed of the anxiety over communication, forces us to face up. Since it is no longer a matter of discoursing about . . . , what sense does it make to receive what I interpret merely as a discourse about . . . ? Can I bet my life on this word, if it is only a word of man?

As long as I play the comedy, as long as I am on the platform of the theater for an audience, as long as I am putting on my act as Christian in front of others, as pastor, theologian, politician, socialist, revolutionary, I can operate on the basis that "God is dead." There are only horizontal relationships. As far as the kerygma is concerned, I do not need to know whether it corresponds to anything. I simply receive it as discourse and transmit it as discourse. It is the presence of others which allows me to play the comedy, to play it to myself—and in the process to avoid the final question. The incognito closes that kind of escape route and forces us to be decisively honest. If this were the only virtue, it would be the primary work of our times.

But then, if that were all one had "to do," what disillusionment, what disdain from the troubled person of our century, what a lack of concern. However, the incognito implies a great deal in terms of works! First of all, the organization itself of this incognito. It is not a case of each returning to his own home and saying, "It is quite simple. We do not need to bother about anything!" It is not a matter of withdrawal, nor of individualized opinion. The incognito is a way of being whole. It implies communion and a community. Consequently, it calls for a revision of all our church life if hope is to be at the center of our life and of our witness, and if hope is to be expressed through the incognito. It calls for a revision of all our activities, our administrations, our liturgies, our teaching procedures, and it calls, perhaps, for the recovery of a certain esoteric quality, whenever (and only *whenever*) it furthers the awareness of the incognito.

Then there is another work, which perhaps is decisive for the course of history. It is an act which is outward and visible, though doubtless it, too, is marked by the incognito. It is the meeting, the link, the marriage with Israel. If it is true that we are in an age of abandonment, and that our calling as a Church is precisely to be born to hope, that means that we have to benefit from the harsh experience of Israel, the bearer of God's promise for all nations yet living in the abandonment, a chosen people, rejected yet still chosen. We have also to understand Paul's parable of the cultivated olive tree and the olive tree grafted onto it. It was not a matter of the root of faith only, but the root of hope as well. Just as, had the Church managed to be truly the Church, she would have been able to bring to Israel the true witness of its salvation in Christ (but that failed, through the fault of the Church), so likewise now we have to bring to Israel the new living hope. This surely does not replace the hope specific to Israel, nor does it rescind it, but it should be a help to it in its long march through the same night and toward the same Kingdom.

All ecumenical endeavors are of real interest. They certainly have a degree of value (oh, how relative), but they represent too much the herding together of decimated, fear-ridden flocks, which are regrouping for defense against the big bad wolf, and who play the hero by piling up excesses which are mistaken for courage and for an advance into the Kingdom. Only one ecumenical enterprise makes any profound sense today, precisely in this today of abandonment. Only one implies the total meaning of Jesus Christ, and that is the communion of Christians with Israel. Only there can hope be witnessed to in its fullness.

All the political endeavors to which Christians are giving themselves can be fascinating, useful, full of meaning, but there is only one *political* endeavor on which world history now depends; that is the union of the Church and Israel. It is not a matter of predicting the future, nor of the fulfillment of past prophecies difficult to interpret. It is indeed a matter of political reality, in the sense that these two communities, of the incarnation and of the Word, must join forces so that, in effect, this Word of God might finally be written (in the sense in which Gabriel Vahanian understands Scripture).[12] That is the juncture in which "sacred history" can emerge and come to life again. It would be a sacred history neither of the Jewish people nor of the Church. It would be written in counterpoint to the technological history of these times.

Now, just as the Old Testament shows us, in effect, a history which is hidden (separate because hidden) in the heart of the events, and one which is more true than the political agitation (in the narrow sense), and in relation to which universal history takes its meaning; just as the

[12] I am not forgetting that Islam also is concerned with the incarnation of the Word, and that it, too, is heir to the revelation in Abraham and Jesus; but I would accept Massignon's interpretation, according to which Muhammad is the "negative prophet," that is, claiming to come *after* Judaism and Christianity and to go beyond them, he actually has introduced nothing new in any sphere. Islam is a restatement of Judaism and of Christianity. Thus Muhammad is a prophet in the sense that he attests the fact that along this route there is nothing more to be added or renewed. Hence Islam does not appear to me to have the same fundamental importance that Judaism and Christianity have for the profound meaning of the history of mankind.

Apocalypse describes the course of history for us as the running of four horses, one of which is white, the Word of God; so today the profound truth of our history can only be given to it by this union of Israel and the Church, the two bearers of hope for mankind, who must henceforth be one in order that all political actions might receive a meaning. What is needed now is that the community of the abandoned, since its hope is indestructible, should be able in its unity to say with Abraham, *"Hineni"* ("Here am I"), with Jesus, "Father, I praise thee," with the first Christians, *"Maranatha."* That is where the beginning and the end of every political act in the modern world is to be found.